The Iron Horse in Indian Country

Published in Cooperation with the
William P. Clements Center for Southwest Studies,
Southern Methodist University

The Iron Horse in Indian Country

Native Americans and Railroads in the US West

ALESSANDRA LA ROCCA LINK

OXFORD
UNIVERSITY PRESS

Oxford University Press is a department of the University of Oxford.
It furthers the University's objective of excellence in research, scholarship,
and education by publishing worldwide. Oxford is a registered trade mark of
Oxford University Press in the UK and in certain other countries.

Published in the United States of America by Oxford University Press
198 Madison Avenue, New York, NY 10016, United States of America.

Library of Congress Cataloging-in-Publication Data
Names: Link, Alessandra La Rocca, author.
Title: The iron horse in Indian Country : Native Americans and railroads in
the US West / Alessandra La Rocca Link.
Other titles: Native Americans and railroads in the US West
Description: New York, NY : Oxford University Press, 2025. |
Includes bibliographical references and index.
Identifiers: LCCN 2025002009 (print) | LCCN 2025002010 (ebook) |
ISBN 9780197674406 (paperback) | ISBN 9780197674390 (hardback) |
ISBN 9780197674420 (epub)
Subjects: LCSH: Indians of North America—West (U.S.)—History—19th century. |
Railroads—West (U.S.)—Political aspects. | Railroads—West
(U.S.)—Social aspects. | Indians of North America—West
(U.S.)—Government relations. | Indians of North America—West
(U.S.)—Land tenure. | Settler colonialism—West (U.S.) | Indians of
North America—West (U.S.)—History—20th century.
Classification: LCC E78.W5 L54 2025 (print) | LCC E78.W5 (ebook) |
DDC 978.004/97—dc23/eng/20250214
LC record available at https://lccn.loc.gov/2025002009
LC ebook record available at https://lccn.loc.gov/2025002010

DOI: 10.1093/9780197674437.001.0001

Printed by Marquis, Canada

To Robbie, my partner in all things

Contents

Acknowledgments

I've long aspired to live by the poet Mary Oliver's maxim that "attention is the beginning of devotion."[1] Our digital age puts attention at a premium unlike ever before, though book-writing remains one great act of sustained attention that I have come to cherish. This work is the result of the attention and care of many wonderful people and supporting institutions. My love of history began as an undergraduate at the College of the Holy Cross, where I studied under the careful guidance of Gwenn Miller. My work on the history of the American West and Native America gained steam at the University of New Mexico, where Cathleen D. Cahill, Margaret Connell-Szasz, and Virginia Scharff greatly expanded my knowledge on these subjects and smoothed out the stilted language I used to convey my emerging ideas about them. Virginia's "Writing Like a Historian" course remains a major touchstone in my development as a writer and thinker, as does my time under the tutelage of Durwood Ball as a copyeditor with the *New Mexico Historical Review*. At the University of Colorado Boulder, I learned from a cohort of incredible scholars, including Virginia Anderson, Freddy González, Kwangmin Kim, Patricia Limerick, and Marcia Yonemoto. The germ for this project was planted during Louis Warren's Athearn Lecture when he described several Lakota Ghost Dancers traveling by train to meet with the Paiute Ghost Dance prophet, Wovoka. Louis then mentioned a cachet of documents in the National Archives that set me on course for research. From there, the project took shape under the careful watch of Thomas Andrews, Elizabeth Fenn, Clint Carroll, Paul Sutter, and Phoebe Young. Thomas Andrews was and remains an invaluable mentor. His attention to the project was unparalleled, and many of the better parts of this book can be traced back to his early edits. Lil Fenn picked up the torch from Virginia and pushed me as a writer: the few places where the prose glows is a result of her handiwork. Thomas and Lil continue to inspire me as both a scholar and a person. There is not enough real estate here to thoroughly account for the many ways I improved under their guidance.

While in graduate school I met several people who supported this book and its author, including Spring Greeney, Caroline Grego, Juliete Larkin-Gilmore, Rebecca de Lorinzini, Patricia Marroquin Norby, Graeme Pente, Brianna Theobald, Lindsey Passenger Wieck, and Rebecca Wingo.

Cameron Blevins, Maurice Crandall, Julia Frankenbach, Justin Gage, and Elliott West provided invaluable feedback on chapters at critical stages in editing. In addition to edits, Justin acted as a second set of eyes in the archives; I am grateful for the sources he passed along. Julia not only offered her editing skills, but also opened up her family home when I needed a place to crash while researching. I am lucky to have spent so much time with her in Colorado and California. Sara Porterfield and I walked each other through the hardest parts of the writing process, and I now cherish the friendship that grew from our shared struggle. Kent Blansett and Elaine Nelson took me under their wing as a young graduate student and have seen me through all of the peaks and valleys in the following years; I cannot thank them enough for their mentorship.

This project stands on the collections at several libraries and archives and the talented people who work in them. Scholarships and awards from the Huntington Library, the University of Colorado Boulder, the Western History Association, and the Newberry Consortium on American Indian Studies made travel to many of these places possible. I benefited in particular from the National Archives, the Library of Congress, the Huntington Library, the Bancroft Library, the Oklahoma History Center, the Gilcrease Center, and the Newberry Library. One major gift to this book came in the form of an American Council of Learned Societies (ACLS) Dissertation Completion Fellowship. I hope the organization reconsiders its decision to end that fellowship program; as a new parent in the final stages of dissertating, the resources and flexibility proved pivotal to getting this book off the ground.

My time as a fellow at Southern Methodist University's Clements Center for Southwest Studies allowed me to take this project from dissertation to book. Andy Graybill, Neil Foley, and Ruth Ann Elmore welcomed my young family to Dallas and helped make my time there exceptionally productive. My cohort of fellows consisted of powerhouse female scholars: Tsianina Lomawaima, Mary Mendoza, and Celeste Menchaca. My manuscript workshop set the project on a new course thanks to their feedback and to the guidance provided by my workshop chairs: Phil Deloria and Ari Kelman. I could not suppress my shock when they agreed to review my manuscript, and their comments sharpened my thinking along several planes, as did the edits offered by Paul Conrad and Ed Countryman. Thanks, too, to Elizabeth Ingelson for the captivating conversations and camaraderie while there.

While at the Clements Center, Patricia LaBounty of the Union Pacific Railroad Museum reached out about organizing an event for the 150th anniversary of completion of the first transcontinental railroad. She sought to bring a diverse group of stakeholders together for frank conversation about the impact of rail expansion on Native peoples. A small and hardscrabble group of committed people made the first iteration of "Railroads in Native America" (RRNA) possible. I stand in awe of what we accomplished in Omaha and later in Ogden, and I look forward to what unfolds in Sacramento in 2026. I consider my work for this initiative and the resources it provides to Native and non-Native publics to be a critical part of my methodology as a non-Native scholar, and I am grateful to Patricia and the RRNA steering committees for giving me opportunities to put my skills to work outside academia.

Returning to my hometown after thirteen years away was at once grounding and deeply disorienting. Several folks helped smooth the transition back, including Katherine Massoth, Debbie McLachlan, Abby Shue, and the incredible women in the now-defunct Podcast Club and newly established Coven Book Club. Elise Franklin has touched this book and my life outside of it considerably; I am lucky to be in her orbit. Mary Maier has been a dear friend since our teens; her immense creative talents encourage me in my own small endeavors. An exquisite writer in her own right, Elizabeth Relish did a fine job of updating the bibliography, and I am thankful for her hard work. Rio Hartwell pulled through with indexing magic on a dime. My wonderful colleagues at Louisville Collegiate School continue to inspire me as a teacher, while also cheering me on as a writer. Watching my students register new ideas and develop as writers themselves makes the long hours spent grading and planning worthwhile. I know many of my students are looking forward to using this book in a less conventional way, say as a doorstop or sleeping aid, while several others have promised to pull it out of their college library. Regardless, their delight in my own research and writing made the final push on revisions more manageable. I am indebted to them.

To give quality attention is largely a matter of time. This book would not be possible without caregivers who devoted their time to my children while I was on "book time." Lisa Cofer La Rocca, my stepmother, spent many hours upstairs with my son while I churned out chapters in my basement office. In Dallas, Veronica Peña poured love on my months-old daughter. The teachers and lovers-on-littles at SMU Childcare Center and Second

Presbyterian Weekday School left a lasting impact on our kids and helped this frazzled working mom navigate new parenthood. Charlotte Link, my mother-in-law and Foster and Elenora's "Honey," devoted so much of her time, delicious food, and creative talents to our family that we will spend the remainder of our days returning her favors.

My family's handprints are on everything I do, and I am forever grateful for them. My mom, Margaret Kaelin, was my first teacher in empathy; I learned how to consider issues from multiple perspectives thanks to her generosity of spirit. My dad, Renato La Rocca, has always encouraged asking "the big questions" and resisting easy answers. My siblings and their families bring the fun, while also putting up with a fair amount of "book talk." The gusto with which they live out their own lives inspires me to keep doing my best work. This book wouldn't be here without Chae La Rocca, my brother with the megawatt smile. The Link family have supported this project from the very start, while also giving me plenty of opportunities to leave it behind and get some much-needed rest in their company. I consider myself lucky to be living close to many of them.

Foster, the sunshine on my shoulders, and Elenora, my lapis-eyed ladybug, have gotten a lot of my attention and devotion in recent years. Being their mom is an utter delight. The ditty I sing to them many nights sums it up best: "loving you, it's my favorite thing to do." This book is dedicated to Robbie, my great love and partner in all things. I've long been convinced that we have our own gravitational force: we were pulled toward each other two decades ago, and our mutual attraction remains steadfast. On more than one occasion I almost walked away from this project. It was Robbie who walked me back, who carried enough faith in my abilities for the both of us. His creative spirit, curious nature, and steely determination drew me to him well before this project took shape, and I remain the most proud of the life we've built together outside of the bounds of this book. Thank you, amore mio.

List of Figures

Introduction

The Needles Hogan

The plume of smoke cutting across the night sky must have drawn the officers to the hogan. Inside the Navajo dwelling of packed earth, wood, and stone, they found three Navajo men gathered around a sacred flame for a peyote ceremony. Jack Woody, Dan Dee Nez, and Leon B. Anderson joined thirty other Indigenous men and women inside the structure. Indigenous laborers from the town of Needles, California, located twenty-seven miles to the east, built the hogan from discarded railroad ties in 1947. Woody, Nez, and Anderson had probably been there before. For them, the sacred site was but one reference point in lives spent on the move. Employees of the Santa Fe Railroad Company, Woody, Nez, and Anderson worked in the railroad yards of Needles during the week and then headed home to Tribal Nations in New Mexico, Utah, and Arizona. This commute was punctuated by visits to the Needles hogan, where they embarked on a different kind of journey.[1]

On that singular April night in 1962, the fire died early, their travel cut short. The ceremony was already well underway when the officers cast aside the blanket at the doorway. Sheriff's detective James E. Willis and four other officers entered the hogan at three in the morning and moved to arrest the participants. The peyotists reminded Willis that they were members of a state-sanctioned religious corporation, the Native American Church (NAC). In an appeal to their First Amendment rights to religious freedom, the peyotists explained that the sacred peyote button—a small, spineless cactus containing psychoactive alkaloids—was inextricably tied to their faith. They also produced their membership cards for Willis's review. It made little difference. Woody, Nez, and Anderson (Figure 0.1) left in handcuffs, charged with violating California's anti-peyote law.[2]

The court case that evolved out of the arrests marked a watershed moment in the legal protection of Indigenous religious freedoms. The American Civil Liberties Union (ACLU) came to the defense of the Navajo peyotists, as did the president of the national NAC, Frank Takes Gun

Figure 0.1 The peyotists and railroad laborers on trial. Front row (from left): Jack Woody, Dan Dee Nez, and Leon B. Anderson; Back row: ACLU lawyers Rufus Johnson and A. L. Wirin. Los Angeles Times Photographic Archive, UCLA Library Special Collections.

(Crow). In their defense, the ACLU lawyers referenced the articles of incorporation filed by the California branch of the NAC. The articles cite the religious use of peyote buttons for sacramental rites. After a San Bernardino court ruled against the peyotists, the defendants appealed first to the Los Angeles District Court of Appeals, where the guilty verdict was upheld, and then to the California Supreme Court. Seven of the eight California Supreme Court Justices concurred with Justice Matthew Tobriner's majority opinion, which declared peyote the "theological heart" of the Native American Church and therefore exempt from the anti-peyote law. "The varying currents of the subcultures that flow into the mainstream of our national life give us depth and beauty," Justice Tobriner observed. "We preserved a greater value than an ancient tradition when we protect the rights of the Indians who honestly practiced an old religion."[3]

Dating back to pre-contact Mesoamerica, peyote buttons stand at the heart's center of Indigenous rituals. An accounting of the material markers of the faith begins with the sacred button, but it swiftly widens to encompass an array of other important objects that entered into ceremonies as they evolved to suit changing times and diverse tribal traditions: an eagle bone whistle, a fan of eagle feathers, a water drum, and—for some—a cross, Bible, and tobacco. During the ceremony, participants infused these objects with meaning and received visions.[4] The peyote button was at once a curative, a teacher, and a guide. It anchored a faith tradition that promoted healing, renewal, and community across tribal borders, species divides, and national boundaries.

For the Needles peyotists another object proved valuable not for its metaphysical qualities but for its practical application: the railroad tie. Ties shielded the peyotists from the elements and marked sacred space. The worn wooden rails that once carried the iron horse, the *béésh nít'i'* (Navajo, "railroad"), separated the sacred from the profane.[5] Peyotists likely found the ties in nearby Needles, the site of tie yards and maintenance facilities established in the late nineteenth century. Despite the waning influence of the locomotive in the automobile age, railroads maintained a steady presence in the men's lives. Woody, Nez, and Anderson earned their wages fastening ties and servicing cars. They traveled on trains to connect with kin and community across the Southwest. And the ties that once carried them home enclosed a space for spiritual journeys.

However ancient peyotism was, Woody, Nez, and Anderson engaged in a version of the ceremony born on iron roads. Migration was at the center of the intertribal religious revival that emerged in the late nineteenth century on the Southern Plains. Peyotists followed what they called "the road," a term steeped in physical and spiritual significance. In ceremony, peyote directed a spiritual passage, its visions revealing the path to god and to a prosperous future. Beyond the ceremony, following "the road" meant eschewing alcohol, protecting one's community, and working hard. Peyotists also took to roads, many of them fastened in iron and wood, to spread the faith.[6] So fundamental was this aspect of their commitment that the faith leaders called themselves "roadmen."

The organizational body behind the Peyote Religion—the NAC—also relied on a legal document that had long sustained iron horses: the corporate charter. First incorporated in Oklahoma in 1918 to protect the sacred use of peyote buttons, the NAC is now the largest intertribal religious organization in North America, boasting over 300,000 members in the United States, Mexico, and Canada. It is a "sacred company," a modern Indian religion that exists to organize its followers and provide legal protection.[7] The aims of the NAC were and are fundamentally different from those of for-profit railroad corporations. In the early decades of the twentieth century, the Native American Church joined other intertribal Indigenous movements that depended on the mobility offered by rail travel to unite and organize Indigenous communities.

The capture, trial, and ultimate triumph of Woody, Nez, and Anderson allow for a reconsideration of several key elements of modern Indigenous world-building. The peyotists' pursuit of tribal and religious sovereignty in the hogan and in California courts relied on a suite of forces more commonly associated with Indigenous dispossession and loss: corporations, railroads, and US law. The peyotists' movements—both self-directed and under force—reveal the Janus-faced nature of mobility (and immobility) in a colonial world. *The Iron Horse in Indian Country* examines how Indigenous actors in the nineteenth and early twentieth centuries encountered these forces of loss and devastation and found novel ways to refashion them to protect, sustain, and grow their communities. The success of these railway workers and the NAC more broadly is tied to earlier efforts of Indigenous activists and leaders who saw opportunities in restructuring the corporate model, in refashioning modes of travel and communication, and in reframing legal arguments in order to protect and project Indigenous futures in a railroaded world.

The choice of the word "futures" is a deliberate one. Two major intertribal movements in the railroad age—the Peyote Religion and the Society of American Indians—imagined, fought for, and articulated Indigenous futures. Danika Medak-Saltzman (Turtle Mountain Chippewa) explains that Indigenous futurisms today provide "opportunities to explore beyond what is and what has been" and engage in "imagining, creating, and manifesting a variety of possibilities that better represent our [Indigenous] understandings of, our place in, and our responsibility to this world and those yet to come."[8] Indigenous futurist scholarship is rooted in contemporary art, science fiction, and political organizing.[9] *The Iron Horse in Indian Country* attempts to read futurism backward in time to consider earlier iterations of Indigenous world imagining and building that relied, in part, on the mobility offered by railroads.

Indians and railroads have a long and fraught relationship that predates the California gathering of peyotists beneath the railroad ties. Discussions and depictions of railroads have long exhibited a proclivity for muddying fact and fiction, making it difficult to distinguish the myth from the history. Even the term "Iron Horse," which first entered American print culture in the 1840s, communicated the mythic qualities Americans assigned to steam locomotives when they arrived stateside from Britain a decade earlier. Half-machine, half-animal, the "Iron Horse," cut loose on American society, set out to remake a nation. A poem on the subject declared in 1840:

> He asks no more than fire and water
> He wears no bridle, no curbing chain
> He brooks no spur, and he needs no rein
> Only set him forth on the open plain
> And he'll be the last horse to weary or loiter[10]

As this poet predicted, railroads ushered in a new industrial order that would transform American society and the allegedly "open" plain of the US West. This book examines the "work" of railroad colonialism, while also taking up the stories of Native actors these myths blot out—actors who resisted, adopted, and adapted colonial technologies and institutions in order to build distinctly Indigenous futures for themselves, to persist in the face of devastating loss.

In the middle decades of the nineteenth century, Euro-Americans cloaked railroad expansion in the lofty language of Manifest Destiny. Politicians, pundits, critics, and the like painted the railroad as a mechanized bearer of Euro-American civilization. Settlers riding atop an iron horse would fulfill this sacred promise to stretch the nation to the Pacific Ocean. "And the Iron Horse, the earth-shaker, the fire-breather," *Putnam's Monthly Magazine* prophesized in 1841, "he too shall build an empire and an epic."[11] Popular nineteenth-century imagery was also critical to railroad mythmaking. Consider Francis Palmer's "Westward the Course of Empire Takes Its Way" (1868) (Figure 0.2). Produced on the eve of the completion of the United States' first transcontinental railroad, this painting captures a nineteenth-century national ethos of railroad-induced "progress." It portrays a locomotive charging through an open field. To the left, industrious Euro-Americans work plows and direct wagons—a sign of

Figure 0.2 Images like Palmer's celebrated the railroad's colonization of the American West. Francis F. Palmer, "Across the Continent: Westward the Course of Empire Takes Its Way," 1868. Currier and Ives, Library of Congress.

future settlements. To the right, the train's exhaust engulfs two Native Americans, obscuring their view and obstructing their path forward. In Palmer's image, the fate of Indigenous people is clear: they are doomed to vanish in the trailing exhaust of the locomotive.

The popular nineteenth-century narrative captured by Palmer and others constituted but one chapter in a longer anthology of stories—stories that have persistently drawn sharp boundaries between Natives and modernity. These stories have obscured Native peoples who sustained old worlds and built new ones for themselves in the face of incredible obstacles.[12] For centuries, non-Native Americans have depicted Indigenous peoples as premodern bit players in a civilizing melodrama that pushed westward in successive tides. By the turn of the twentieth century, the logic ran, "modernizing" nations had pushed Indigenous peoples aside, physically and culturally. Physically, the United States forced Natives—often violently—onto separate tracts of land isolated from centers of commerce. Non-Natives, one scholar explains, considered Indian agencies "savage islands in the midst of civilized seas."[13] In 1862, at the very start of railroad construction in the Trans-Mississippi West, there were upwards of forty Indian reservations in the region. By the 1920s, long after new track construction waned in the West, there were well over 120.[14] Culturally, depictions of the anti-modern Indian in art, literature, scientific discourse, and popular media separated Native Americans from an industrializing nation. As whites grappled with an increasingly mechanized and stratified society, they drew cultural boundaries that excluded Native peoples from modernity, just as they laid down physical boundaries intended to exclude Indians from mainstream life.[15]

This public narrative about Indians and railroads did not conclude with the conquest of the West, but instead was rescripted in the early decades of the twentieth century by railroad corporations keen on inviting tourists to "See America First."[16] They lured travelers with a mythic Indian existence, one they could glimpse on their western railroad journeys. Railroad companies—no longer in the business of overt conquest—took to promoting tourism, once described as "the most colonial of colonial economies."[17] When automobiles began dominating western tourist travel in the 1920s, the Atchison, Topeka, and Santa Fe (ATSF) unveiled *The Chief*. The crown jewel of the ATSF fleet, *The Chief* was a high-speed passenger train with regular service from Chicago to Los Angeles.[18] Three years later the Great Northern Railway followed suit with its own luxury passenger train, *The Empire Builder*, connecting Chicago to the Pacific Northwest. Everything about the imagery in these advertisements and aboard the trains conjured up a primitive Indian past (Figure 0.3).

Taken together, this imagery obscures a more complicated and interconnected history. Historians have long considered the transformations that the railroad and its corporate overlords generated. They have wrestled with, and often confirmed, its status as an icon of the modern world. Many, if not most of the processes central to understanding life in the twentieth and twenty-first centuries—urbanization, suburbanization, nation-building, colonial exploitation, resource extraction, corporatization, and finance capitalism—are connected to the advent of rail travel. As industrial hardware, trains required a fleet of laborers to operate, repair, and build locomotives, in addition to a vast infrastructure of depots, warehouses, and tracks. Railroads gobbled up energy through the bio-fuels of the day—wood and later coal—that caused a boom in resource extraction across the globe. These were costly undertakings that resulted in new, and often profoundly

Figure 0.3 Atchison, Topeka, and Santa Fe Railway Company Advertisement, between 1926 and 1936. ATSF Historical Collection, Kansas State Historical Society.

problematic, financial relationships between private companies, local and national governments, and individuals. Rail infrastructure shaped the organization of space, as grids of privately owned land fanned out along tracks. Train travel also altered understandings of time, initiating a shift from environmental markers (sun up, sun down) of time's passage, to the unceasing tick of the industrial clock. A novel transportation technology, railroads linked peoples and goods into ever-expanding webs of movement and exchange. As a cultural medium, people freighted railroads with meaning. Without a doubt, trains brought profound and far-reaching changes.[19]

In the nineteenth-century North American West, to speak of railroads is to speak of conquest and colonization.[20] The conquest of the West was a bloody, messy business—a business in which railroad corporations had a tangible stake. Railroad administrators sought land for rights-of-way and finance schemes, and they promoted the settlement of Indigenous homelands by emigrants from the eastern states, Canada, and Europe. To achieve these goals, corporate officials allied with federal, territorial, and state governments.[21] The project in the American West was a settler colonial one: the US government developed programs, sharpened and refined legal frameworks, armed soldiers, and grew its administrative state in an effort to dispossess Indigenous peoples of their land base and replace them with a settler population. Railroads, and the corporate backers behind them, were part of the arsenal that the federal government deployed to contain and eliminate Native peoples.[22] The government justified the inordinate amount of federal dollars and land grants handed off to railroad companies by pointing to the role of railroads in conquest and settlement. Senator William Stewart, a US representative from Nevada, put it bluntly in 1869. Native peoples, he said, "can only be permanently conquered by railroads. The locomotive is the sole solution to the Indian question."[23]

This work is partly a study of the integral role that railroads and rail corporations played in the settler colonial project in the West. Stewart's "locomotive" was actually a vast and sweeping apparatus of legal, economic, military, and administrative forces backed by the US government and railroad executives. *The Iron Horse in Indian Country* highlights how, for one, railroad construction required new modes of land definition in the West, the government grant, which resulted in millions of acres of Indigenous territory falling into corporate ownership. The passage of the Pacific Railway Act in 1864 set the stage for this new conception of compulsory land transfer. Lesser known, however, is the legal means of justifying this land seizure and distribution. This work recounts how non-Native Americans justified their corporate plunder by leaning heavily on the Fifth Amendment's claims to government land seizure for public good, more widely known as eminent domain. Following the Pacific Railway Act, treaties, agreements, and court cases between the government and tribes continued to reference eminent-domain-like language. For the US agents and railroad barons, railroading always served the "public" good. And yet this study also charts the rise of the Society of American Indians, an intertribal activist organization that, decades after the Pacific Railway Act, would lobby non-Native Americans to consider a more expansive public good, one that included the rights and sovereignty of Indigenous peoples and tribal nations.

Additionally, the construction and maintenance of rail lines generated new forms of economic organization—the corporation and its attending wage economy. Railroads' need for land and resources ensured that nineteenth-century corporations yoked themselves to the US government, the primary purveyors in Indian land. Settler colonization in the American West was as much a corporate project as a state one. And yet the wage economies that grew alongside rail lines offered opportunities, however limited, for Indigenous workers like Nez, Woody, and Anderson to seek out sustenance for their kin and community. Cheyennes, Lakotas, Apaches, Pueblos, and others used railroad-related work to maintain relationships with places, people, and animals that often carried cultural, political, and spiritual significance. The corporation, meanwhile, would be refashioned by an enterprising Cayuga/Seneca/Wyandot businessman, an Oneida activist, and Native American Church leaders in an effort to bring prosperity, connection, and legal protection in the midst of US colonial rule.

Finally, the railroad logic of colonialism also altered the nature of state power. A highly contested treaty in the late 1860s set the stage for the dissolution of treaty-making between the US government and tribes, and Congress subsequently gained power over Indian affairs. Congress, deep in the pockets of railroad corporations, regularly acted to shore up their private interests. The US government also grew and adopted more administrative capacities in the railroad age, and deployed a new kind of violence in the form of highly mobile military units. By 1900 this apparatus had by all accounts succeeded in populating the region with non-Native Americans. In 1870, at the start of rail construction, there were roughly 2 million non-Indians residing in states lying west of the Missouri River. By 1900 there were 10.4 million (Figure 0.4).[24]

The numbers, however, belie the messy, uneven, and highly contested nature of railroad-backed settler colonization in the American West.[25] As the following chapters reveal, Native and non-Natives alike had shifting priorities and rationales for their decisions that were rooted in distinct cultural, political, and economic contexts. For colonial agents (corporate actors included) the prevailing rules of engagement were often being drawn out as surveyors and construction crews trespassed on Indigenous lands

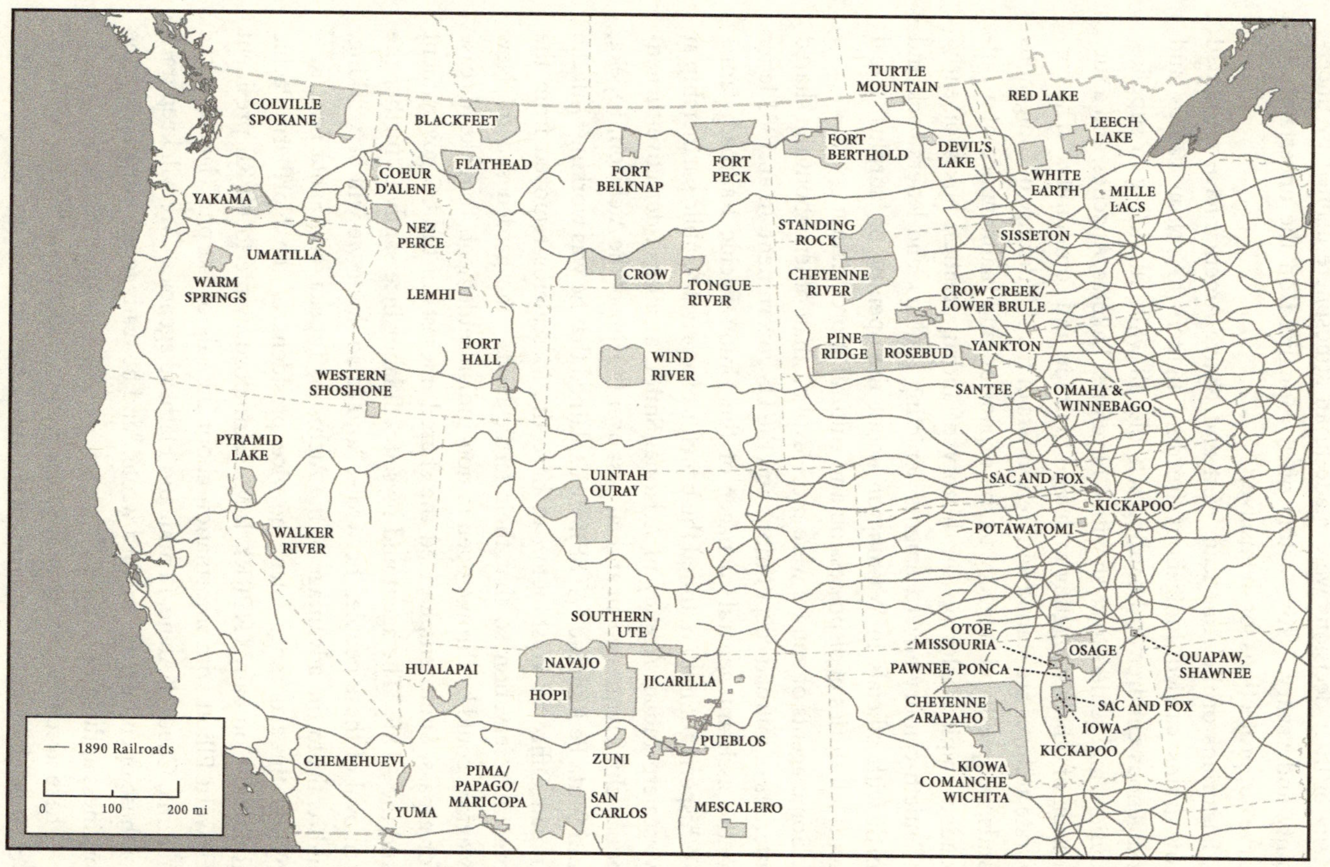

Figure 0.4 Map of Pacific Railway Routes and Indigenous Territories, 1890. Erin Greb Cartography.

and as Indigenous peoples employed old and new strategies for resistance. Many of their decisions were made in an atmosphere defined by uncertainty and vagary. Native actors often capitalized on the uncertainty to carve out protections for themselves.

Historians of the American West and Native America have recounted how trains carried Indigenous freedom fighters to prison camps and Indigenous children to boarding schools, all while funneling in supplies, soldiers, and settlers to clash with Cheyennes, Lakotas, Apaches, and a succession of others struggling to defend their kin and community.[26] The corporate archives are stuffed with reminders of the significance of Indigenous lands, peoples, and imagery to the expansion and maintenance of a railroaded empire. Files on the history of Indian treaties, boxes of early-twentieth-century advertisements depicting Indians, and letters back and forth with officials in Washington about the opening of "surplus" tribal lands tell stories of dispossession and cultural appropriation.

Some agents of empire were more explicit than others about the shared interests of railroad corporations and the US government. In an 1881 letter to the assistant general manager of the Union Pacific Railroad, James "Whispering" Smith outlined the benefits of a private-public partnership at Mescalero Indian Agency in Arizona. Smith, a railroad-detective-turned-police-chief, requested an annual pass over the line of the Atchison, Topeka, and Santa Fe Railroad (ATSF). He explained that he was working with the Indian Office in Washington to have the Mescaleros removed from the present reservation so that their fertile lands, "the garden spot of New Mexico," could be thrown open to non-Indian settlement. To make his case for a pass, Smith emphasized the shared interests of the US government and the ATSF. "The agent and myself will labor incessantly to further the removal of these people," he wrote, "and in so doing we will be working, indirectly, to the advantage of the Atchison, Topeka, and Santa Fe R.R."[27] Nearly three decades later, the vice president of the Northern Pacific Railroad Company (NPRR), J. M. Hannaford, wrote to NPRR president Howard Elliott with information about the sale of "surplus" lands on the Yakima, Coeur d' Alene, Lemhi, and Flathead agencies. "We will keep track of these openings," Hannaford wrote, "and be ready to get our share of the business at the proper time."[28]

These accounts give weight to the notion that railroads were agents of "creative destruction," a term first coined by Austrian economist Joseph Schumpeter in the 1950s to describe how capitalist enterprises continually displaced old modes of relationship in order to institute the new.[29] But this book also examines Indigenous Americans' creative responses to railroad destruction. It recounts the stories of Native peoples who engaged with a colonial technology to protect their kin and communities over nearly three-quarters of a century. What of the Native Americans who rode the "Iron Horse," thwarted its advances, and profited from the increased mobility and access to distant markets it provided? How did Indigenous peoples interact with railroads as travelers, wage earners, and tribal citizens? Contrary to depictions of Indians who "gave way to trains," this book explores the contentious, fraught, and transformative history of Indigenous relationships with locomotives.[30] These historical actors do not blend seamlessly with the image of the anti-modern Indian. Instead, they complicate the stereotypical portrait of the railroad in America. In the railroaded West, the boundaries and definitions of modernity were continually being negotiated and called into question. Native Americans, far from adhering to their scripted roles as segregated anti-modernists, reinvented their cultural mores and material lives in response to railway-induced change. This book is partly an excavation of a hidden history of resistance, an exploration of how Native Americans vandalized rail lines, taxed rail companies, traveled by rail to lobby US presidents, and moved freely on and off Indian agencies—thereby thwarting state efforts at containment and forced assimilation into American society.[31] It is also a story of how diverse, creative, and adaptable peoples capitalized on railway travel to build intertribal relations, earn livings, and maintain their cultures. Out of present dangers, numerous Indigenous actors imagined future possibilities.

* * *

The first four chapters chart the course of railroad colonization in the American West and the ways in which Native peoples acted as integral actors in the building of and resistance to a railroaded region. The final two chapters home in on Native individuals and communities who co-opted and reframed the mobility, the marketplace, and the corporate model that were cornerstones of the rail-powered colonial state to thwart its very advances and project their own visions of the future. Interspersed within these chapters are three interludes that tell the stories of Indigenous interactions with trains. These "Railway Journeys" connect to important motifs presented throughout the larger book; they also attend to the ways the forces covered at a regional level played out in the day-to-day experiences of individuals. Although many of these stories are limited by the colonial archives they emerged from and from my position as a settler historian, they are intended as a corrective to the corrosive and distortive power of American mythmaking.[32]

The railroad first arrived in the West as a rough outline of an idea, one that five groups of surveyors etched on American maps over the course of the early 1850s. Chapter 1 examines the five federally funded surveying parties that fanned out across Indian Country in 1853–1854. Among their ranks were military personnel, artists, and scientists. Americans believed that agents of science could render legible a lesser-known western landscape and settle sectional conflicts over the location of the first transcontinental railroad. These surveyors, however, relied less on western science and more on Indigenous knowledge and goods when mapping their western routes. Mojave and Atsina guides, hospitable Choctaw families, and Hueco water tanks proved crucial to the survival of the survey members and the direction of their route-making projects. To gain access to essential information about the landscape, Lieutenant Amos Weeks Whipple and other surveyors submitted to Indigenous customs of exchange and ceremony. The success of the Pacific Railway Surveys rested not with the ingenuity of a few visitors to Indian Country, but instead with the disposition, knowledge, and technology of Paiutes, Lakotas, Utes, Mojaves, and others.

Chapter 2 shifts to one of the American West's well-worn stories: the construction of the first transcontinental railroad in the 1860s. Long depicted as an epic squaring off between two rival railroad corporations, the Union Pacific and the Central Pacific, this chapter places transcontinental construction within a regional theater of violence and treaty-making and breaking that took place during and after the Civil War. To make sense of Indigenous protests and violence in the West, we must fully account for the ways in which eminent domain—the US Constitutional claim to the taking of private land for "public" good—directed the dispossession of Indigenous lands for railroads. For Native peoples, land seizures in the name of eminent domain translated into dire daily realities. This chapter also addresses scant but suggestive evidence that corporate officials engaged in their own extralegal treaty-making, in which Indigenous negotiators secured free travel along rail lines. These agreements were a harbinger of future concords that involved Native nations, railroad corporations, and the federal government. They also laid the groundwork for a steam-powered Indigenous world in motion.

The influence of railroad corporations on Indian policy became the subject of debate within tribal nations and the United States in the 1870s and 1880s. Chapter 3 explores how Osage negotiations with a rapacious railway corporation impacted Congress's decision to end treaty-making in 1871. Concerned about corporate officials thwarting congressional authority in the settler project of Indigenous land theft, and the subsequent threat to the flow of corporate bribes lining congressmen's pockets, US officials moved to end the treaty-making process after vigorous debate over the Sturges Treaty. This marked a seismic shift in Indian policy-making that placed increased authority in the hands of legislators. Just as railroad construction took hold in the American West, Congress—a group of men deep in the pockets of railroad magnates—took the reins on Indian policy.

Chapter 4 provides a close look at how tribal governments controlled—with varying degrees of success—the course of railroad expansion, first in Indian Territory, then within the broader Trans-Mississippi West. This chapter points to a hidden history of resistance and innovative responses to the marketplace transformations that unfolded alongside railroads. Cherokees, Choctaws, and others sought to shape the course of development on their lands. Tribal governments attempted to charter their own railroad corporations, and when that failed, they opted instead to tax and generate revenue from railroad expansion. Debates in Cherokee and Choctaw Country about how to proceed often created fault lines in tribal communities. Yet many of the negotiations that took place in Indian Territory structured discussions with corporations and federal officials for rights-of-way elsewhere in the West.

The final two chapters turn to the ways in which Indians participated in a railroaded world. By the late nineteenth century, Natives across the West found themselves consigned to smaller land bases possessed of scant and often dwindling resources. Many made a choice to leave for work on railroads or in railroad-related industries. As a result, Indians became wage earners (and, in some cases, wage payers) at a historic moment when the federal government sought to sequester them on isolated plots of land and limit their labors to agriculture. The expansion of railroad lines stimulated a steady business in freighting, which offered many Indians mobility, meaningful relations with horses, and much-needed income. The first Indian-owned railroad company, the Splitlog Railroad, uncovers the Janus-faced nature of individual wealth acquisition within Indigenous communities. Migratory wage work on Southwestern railroads and the rise of Needles,

California, as an intertribal labor center touched on how railroad work—in spite of its poor pay and fluctuating schedule—became one of the many strategies for resistance and economic survival in the reservation era. As freighters building and maintaining wagon roads, and as tracklayers, gang bosses, and business owners, Indigenous peoples made significant contributions to the construction of the modern American West.

The final chapter documents how Indigenous peoples rode the rails to foster intertribal community and map out Indigenous futures in the late nineteenth and early twentieth centuries. Two major intertribal organizations, the Native American Church and the Society of American Indians (SAI), surfaced out of Indigenous rail travel. Its participants created communities across class, tribal, and ideological lines to promote unity and put forth visions for a modern Indigenous future. Their claims to futurity were critical during a historic era marked by demographic decline, the ravages of US assimilation policy, and a settler colonial program bent on the elimination of Indian peoples.[33] The SAI, founded in 1911 by six Indians who had spent much of their lives on the move, became an early incubator for intertribal activism and imagination that was based largely off of Indian reservations and tribal homelands. On reservations, another movement with restorative, imaginative, and unifying qualities emerged: the Peyote Religion. As roadmen took trains to spread the faith across Indian Country, believers found spiritual support for the lifestyle changes that occurred in the reservation era. Their vision for the future took many forms and depended on individual experiences with peyote.

Both the SAI and the Peyote Religion brought calls for repurposing the corporate model for Indigenous needs. In an effort to protect their sacramental use of peyote, Peyotists filed articles of incorporation in several states after 1918. Among early SAI members, Laura Cornelius Kellogg (Oneida) developed her Lolomi Plan of corporate communities that would, in her words, "secure and maintain independence in modern times."[34] The Lolomi Plan, though only briefly realized in a remote corner of Cherokee Country, Oklahoma, "carries the order of protected self government by a means of federal incorporation into industrial communities."[35] Parts of Kellogg's plan would be realized in the Indian New Deal programs of the 1930s, while the expansion of the Peyote Religion could be measured in the growing number of corporate charters filed in US states.[36] Even as tribal communities fought against corporate intrusion into Indian Country—a fight that continues today—they also found unique ways of turning the intrusion to their advantage.

The lives and work of Indigenous men and women like Iratabal (Mojave), Mathias Splitlog (Cayuga/Seneca/Wyandot), Spotted Tail (Lakota), and Sara Winnemucca (Paiute) only scratch the surface of Indigenous experiences with iron horses. In these pages, Native peoples emerge as adaptive and resilient participants in the modernization and technological development of the American West.[37] This history is rife with triumph and tragedy. It is at once a more familiar story of the ravages of settler colonization and corporate overreach, interwoven with unexpected histories of Indigenous resistance, activism, and organization. It ends with a spotlight on the Progressive Era work of Indigenous futurists—men and women, on and off the reservations, who spoke truth to power and dared to lay the groundwork for an Indigenous future within a settler society.

The Iron Horse in Indian Country: Native Americans and Railroads in the US West. Alessandra La Rocca Link, Oxford University Press. © Alessandra La Rocca Link 2025. DOI: 10.1093/9780197674437.003.0001

PART I

ROUTES, 1850–1870

my dreams tilt toward the
west, yet my prayers are drilled deep,
tethered to my home
WEST
Westernized,
west+ward=me
west coast
water(full)

—Esther G. Belin (Navajo),"West," *Of Cartography* (2017)

Such information as might be in their power.

—Lt. Amiel Weeks Whipple, *Reports of Explorations and Surveys…* (1859)

1
Beyond the Grid

The Chemehuevis of the Lower Colorado River orient themselves in space and time through circles. Their sacred origin story begins when Ocean Woman falls from the sky into the sea. Using her skin and the surrounding mud, Ocean Woman creates the western continent. On that continent two women emerge and map out the reaches of Chemehuevi lands, which form a circle running from their sacred Spring Mountains near present-day Las Vegas, then track south across the Mojave Desert. The wide expanse of the Colorado River cuts through the center. Lands in places commonly known today as southern California, western Arizona, and southern Nevada and Utah fall into the Chemehuevi circle.[1] Chemehuevis also measure time in circles; they march to the rhythms of seasonal changes in the landscape Ocean Woman made.[2]

United States Lieutenant Amiel Weeks Whipple charted a path through the Chemehuevi's geographic circle in February 1854. Along the banks of the Colorado River a Chemehuevi leader sketched out a map for Whipple, who was the head of one of five Pacific Railway surveys. Whipple recorded the cartographic knowledge into his notebook (Figure 1.1) as the two men discussed the nearby Colorado River and its tributaries. The Colorado is the map's central feature. Place names and tribes written in the Paiute language adjoin it. It is a map that centers Indigenous knowledge, a map oriented around the life-giving water source that structured life for the Chemehuevi people across thousands of years.[3]

Several years later, a different map reflected the changes unfolding in the Chemehuevi circle and elsewhere across the North American West. In 1867, William J. Keeler, a civil engineer employed by the United States Department of the Interior, completed an elaborate map of US territory west of the Mississippi. "It is a complete railroad map," he explained, "the only one published which shows the whole of the great Pacific Railroad routes and their projections and branches."[4] Intended for use by the Department of the Interior and Office of Indian Affairs, Keeler's map (Figure 1.2) imposed a sense of order on a region still relatively unknown to

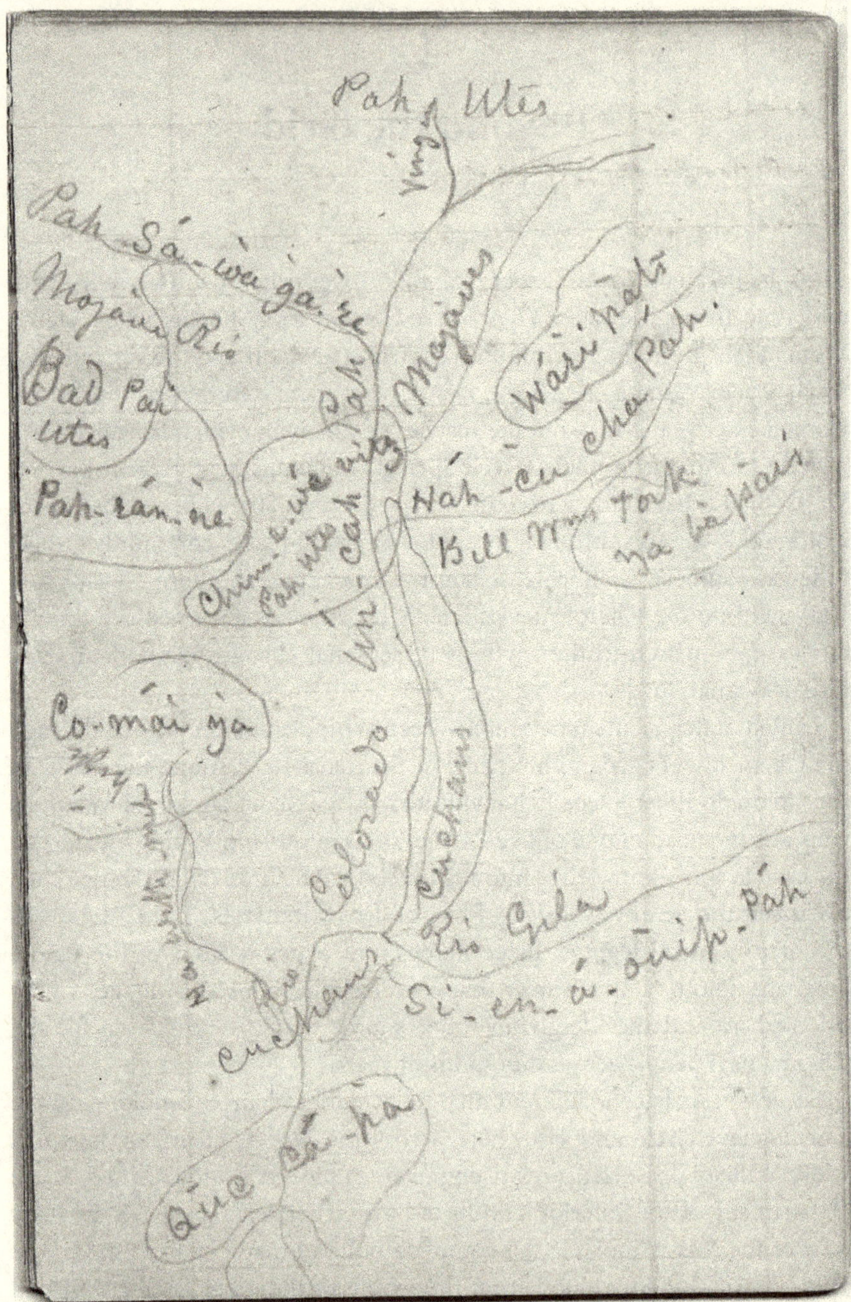

Figure 1.1 Map of Colorado River, from the notebook of Lt. Amiel Weeks Whipple. Amiel Weeks Whipple Collection, Oklahoma Historical Society.

Figure 1.2 W. J. Keeler, *National Map of the Territory of the United States from the Mississippi River to the Pacific Ocean . . .* (Washington, DC: J. F. Gedney, 1867), Christopher C. Augur Papers, Everett D. Graff Collection, folio Graff 2281, Newberry Library, Chicago, Illinois.

Euro-Americans, with large swaths of space only sparsely populated by non-Indians. The eastern and western extremities of the map—along with major metropolitan areas—are cloaked in a grid, indicating lands surveyed by the federal government. Projected railway lines snake across the landscape, intersecting with the angular configurations of western states and territories.[5]

Like many maps made in service of empire, truth waltzed with fiction, estimation, and hearsay in Keeler's cartographic rendering. Published two years before the completion of the first transcontinental railroad, Keeler's map claimed the West for the United States. The bounded nature of Keeler's map, its air of order and organization, speaks to larger colonial imaginings of the American West. In his telling of western expansion, Keeler imagined the gridded blankets along the West Coast and Midwest closing in on the center of the region, the tightening noose of rail lines domesticating a landscape and its original inhabitants. White settlement, resource extraction, and an expanding capitalist marketplace—this was the modern future Keeler and his allies envisioned for the United States. Many American people, still reeling from a bloody civil war, cast their lot with Keeler and dreamed of a conquered West that might unify and enrich the nation.[6] The Chemehuevi circle would be replaced with the squares of US colonial order.

The grid, much like the locomotive, remains a powerful image of modern industrial life. A tool of land acquisition, the grid was born alongside the United States. The US Public Land Survey System (PLSS)—also known as the Rectangular Survey System—emerged after the new country acquired the Northwest Territories from Great Britain following the American Revolution. Before the PLSS, colonists relied on topography to mark ownership. Hills, riverbeds, and tree stands bounded spaces for local inhabitants. The main issue with this strategy was the impermanence of most topographic markers. Rivers shift, trees fall, and hills erode, which meant that boundaries changed according to the whims of nature. Grid plans work in seeming opposition to nature, imposing squares on spaces previously bounded by the curves of a riverbed or the serrations of mountain peaks. Working from two baselines, one running east-west, another north-south, surveyors worked outward, measuring with 66-foot chains.[7] This repetitious, seemingly menial work was central to the project of US territorial expansion. Chains in hand, surveyors in the nineteenth century carved up the American West into squares of assigned value, squares that were promptly handed off to corporations, non-Indian settlers, and local, state, and federal governments.

Beyond its tangible application, the grid also reflects western society's faith in the triumph of rational thought and industrial progress.[8] Keeler's map is but one part of a multipronged process of estrangement of Indigenous peoples from their homelands that would unfold in the American West over the course of the nineteenth century.[9] Here the grid is powerful abstraction, a visual rendering of land ownership centering on turning the earth's surface into commodities for individual or group consumption.[10] Keeler's map plotted property and proprietary claims within a large and rapidly expanding global land market initiated by European colonists. Operating at the intersection of colonialism and capitalism, Keeler's grid marks the United States' understanding of land as property, as something owned with clear, if shifting, economic value. Once measured and registered in US legal codes, the transfer of property would occur alongside the transformation of Indigenous lands into property.[11]

Keeler's map—however emblematic of US colonial designs—belies the confusion, uncertainty, and messy nature of western expansion in general and the Pacific Railway surveys in particular.[12] The image conveys a "knowing" of the Trans-Mississippi West, one that hides the fact that the agents of empire who poured into the region over the course of the nineteenth century entered Indigenous homelands regularly disoriented and yet cognizant of the gaps in their knowledge. In spite of powerful national narratives depicting the region as a largely unpeopled Eden, non-Indian explorers, gold seekers, and early settlers were keenly aware that Indigenous peoples and non-Indian settlers had long made homes in the West. While Keeler's map suggests that Indian Country was increasingly falling into the gridded colonial order—a cartographic narrative that would play out across other maps in the late nineteenth and early twentieth centuries—the history of the Pacific Railway surveys from which Keeler drew his information tells a different story.[13]

It is unlikely that Keeler consulted the Chemehuevi map directly, but he certainly relied on the information Whipple provided—from the Chemehuevi cartographer and from other Indigenous peoples. To compile his map, Keeler pored over the official reports from the five Pacific Railway surveys that traveled through the Trans-Mississippi West from the summer of 1853 to the early months of 1854.[14] After the passage of the Pacific Railway Act in March 1853, Congress ordered Secretary of War Jefferson Davis to undertake what one historian calls "the impossible."[15] Five survey parties—consisting of members of the Army's Corps of Topographical Engineers, soldiers, and a smattering of civilian scientists and artists—set out to survey the West and file reports on potential railway routes. Surveyors also documented relevant geologic, botanic, and ethnographic data. They had one year to complete the task.[16] Isaac A. Stevens, a Massachusetts-born member of the Army Corps of Engineers, led the survey between the 47th and 49th parallels.[17] Captain John Williams Gunnison directed a similar effort along the 38th parallel, through Missouri, Kansas, Colorado, and Utah. Gunnison's life came to an abrupt end in Utah, when a party of Utes killed him. Lieutenant Edward Griffin Beckwith took over, leading the team through Utah and into northern California. Lieutenant Amiel Weeks Whipple headed the survey along the 35th parallel, which included much of Indian Territory, northern Texas, New Mexico, and Arizona. Following closely behind these summer surveys was the party of Lieutenant John Pope. Pope and his men set out to investigate a route across the Llano Estacado, a mesa running from eastern New Mexico into Northwestern Texas, through to Preston, Texas, on the Red River. Lieutenant J. G. Parke, meanwhile, headed east from California along the Gila River to connect his survey with Pope's, together mapping out the 32nd parallel.[18] While Pope, Parke, Gunnison, Beckwith, and Stevens mapped out the width of the West, Lieutenant R. S. Williamson surveyed its length along the California coast in July 1853, in the hopes of locating a passable route for an iron road that would connect California with Washington and Oregon.[19]

Much like Keeler's cartographic rendering of Indian territories, conversations about the Pacific Railway Surveys have marginalized Indigenous peoples. Studies have considered the expedition in relation to events taking place in the East, particularly the effect of these expeditions on the development of US scientific thought and the lead-up to civil war.[20] Taken together, the published survey reports and Keeler's map feed into the widely held belief that the surveys relied on a few enterprising whites who entered an lesser-known landscape and rendered it legible.

Placing the ungridded core of Keeler's map at the center of the narrative instead illuminates the ways colonial imaginings of the region collided with reality. Far from ingenious individuals conquering an unknown land, surveyors appear as men who were deeply reliant on Indigenous knowledge, customs, and goods. These surveyors carried with them the long-standing

Euro-American myth that Native Americans inhabited a pristine wilderness, a place left wild because of their primitive subsistence patterns. Balduin Möllhausen, a German artist accompanying the Whipple survey, wrote in his popular published account of the expedition that "we had before us a primeval wilderness, untouched, unchanged, apparently as it came from the hands of the Creator."[21] To many non-Native peoples, this lack of land use could be attributed to Indians' uncivilized nature. The wilderness construct also served another convenient narrative—that of the unpeopled West, ripe for the taking by enterprising Euro Americans.[22] These narratives provided the conceptional scaffolding for the colonial legal frameworks that justified Indigenous land-taking. In the minds of many nineteenth-century Americans, a chaotic wilderness anxiously awaited modern America's gridded colonial order.

But the western landscape held the markers of Indigenous presence. As Whipple, Pope, Stevens, Beckwith, and others noted, trails, river crossings, half-doused fires, sunken pulleys at watering holes, and stone sketches all served as reminders that they entered Indian Country.[23] These impressions on the western landscape made for a different kind of map—one that charted Indigenous movement, subsistence, and spiritual engagement with their ancestral homelands. Ultimately, the railroad surveys that meandered across the West relied heavily on Indigenous knowledge of the region, employing Native guides, goods, and technologies, submitting to Indigenous customs and rituals, and following markers in the landscape left by Indians. As knowledge keepers and guides, Native peoples played a significant role in structuring the direction—literally and figuratively—of the railway surveys. Not yet aware of the destructive toll the railroad would bring, they helped surveyors carve out the paths that would later be fixed in wood and iron.

Beyond the Grid

Congress funded the Pacific Railway surveys in the 1850s out of a shared commitment to national expansion across the continent. Officials also hoped that the surveyors—a seemingly unbiased group of professionals—could settle fierce sectional disputes over the best location for a transcontinental railroad. Southern politicians unsurprisingly favored routes in the lower half of the region, while Northerners hoped a route along the 42nd parallel would better connect the Upper Midwest and New England markets to expanding commercial networks on the Pacific Coast.[24]

With the exception of Williamson's coastal expedition, these survey parties set out unsure of the final course they would take. Their routes posed both human and nonhuman obstacles. "The country through which they would pass was intersected by bogs, marshes, and deep morasses," Stevens reminded his men before they embarked, "rivers were to be forded and bridged, mountains and valleys to be crossed. The first 180 miles of the journey along the 47th and 49th parallels was [*sic*] reported to be through a continuous marsh, barely practicable, where every man would have to go through mud and water."[25] The forbidding landscape and climate were not the only challenges. "It was necessary," Stevens added, "to give great attention to the Indian tribes, as their friendship was important to be secured, and bore directly upon questions of both the Pacific railroad and the safety of my party."[26]

Stevens's concerns about the human geographies before them was warranted. In addition to environmental obstacles, the Trans-Mississippi West was a world in transition, rocked by violence. Native Nations in the early 1850s faced an onslaught of challenges that varied greatly based on geographic location. In locales rapidly falling within the gridded colonial order—Texas and the Pacific Coast—Comanches, Klamaths, Pomos, and others tried to fend off repeated attacks on their communities. In the center of the region, the arrival of Mormon settlers in the 1840s set off tensions between Shoshones, Utes, and settlers in Utah Territory. By the early 1850s, Mormon settlers under the direction of Brigham Young were preparing for war with the Utes, and skirmishes between Ute bands and Mormons were common.[27] The major power brokers on the Southern and Central Plains, the Comanches, faced a war of extermination by Anglo Texan settlers. A noxious combination of settler violence, drought, disease, and famine sent the Comanche population into decline in the early 1850s, and Comanche leaders, maintaining a tenuous grasp on their expansive trade system, sought alternatives to war.[28] In California, a state-sanctioned genocide was underway following the discovery of gold along the American River in 1848. In 1850, the California State legislature passed a law that allowed for the capture and use of Native peoples as forced workers. California's governor openly supported the formation of compulsory and volunteer militias designed to kill Indigenous peoples in the territory. Fighting broke out across California as a result. The largest massacre in US history took place in California Territory on Clear Lake in 1851, and as surveyors were making their way across the region, upwards of 500 Tolowas were killed in Northern California along the Smith River. These state-sanctioned killings, paired with environmental destruction and disease, led to the rapid decline in the California Indian population in the 1850s and 1860s.[29] North of California, Modocs, Klamaths, and other Pacific Northwest nations were also embroiled in bloody conflicts with newcomers as settlers poured in from the Oregon Trail and encroached on Indigenous lands and resources.[30] As these violent episodes make clear, gridding the land extracted a terribly destructive toll.

Encroachments from settlers and soldiers onto Indigenous lands also exacerbated often tenuous relationships between Native groups. On the Central and Southern Plains, the removal of hundreds of thousands of eastern Natives in the 1830s to eastern Indian Territory set off conflicts with Kiowas and Osages who claimed the lands where eastern refugees sought to rebuild their homes.[31] In the Upper Missouri, dwindling game populations stirred up conflicts among Northern Plains groups over hunting grounds. Dakota, Crow, and Blackfoot peoples held a tight grip on the fur trade and on their respective territories. Their political power and leverage were tied to their trade in furs, and as game populations continued to decline, established sociopolitical orders slipped out of balance. In the early 1850s the Blackfoot engaged in near constant raids on fellow tribes. Declining bison populations forced Assiniboines, Lakotas, and Crees to push onto western tributaries of the Missouri, traditional Blackfoot hunting grounds. These encroachments only exacerbated tensions among Northern Plains communities.[32] In the Southwest, Navajo and Comanche raids on Pueblo communities for livestock and captives persisted in the political confusion following the Mexican-American War. Because of growing tensions and ongoing violence, Native leaders engaged in specific protocols of reception and exchange when engaging with each other. Knowledge of such customs could mean the difference between life and death for newcomers to the region.

The federal government had little influence in the region at this time, but the blueprint of settler expansion was nearly complete. The West of the 1850s was a place where, as one historian claims, "conquest had been announced but not imposed."[33] The federal government had begun to lay the groundwork for the imposition of US rule, beginning with the creation of the Department of the Interior (DOI) in 1851. The DOI's oversight of both the General Land Office and the Department of Indian Affairs made it clear that the two bureaucratic programs were part of a joint expansionist agenda. US officials created the DOI to help efficiently populate newly acquired western territories with Anglo settlers, while simultaneously bringing western lands firmly under state control.[34] The Indian Department, newly relocated from the Department of War, set out to make treaties that would mark territorial boundaries of Native Nations and protect overland travelers. Many of the treaties, without sufficient state resources behind them and without the necessary knowledge of political and social protocols on the ground, were largely ineffective and were routinely broken. One of the largest treaties in the region, at Horse Creek in 1851, included representatives from Crow, Sioux, Arikara, Gros Ventre, Assiniboine, Mandan, and Cheyenne nations. Native responses to the treaty were lukewarm. The treaty stipulated that most of the Great Plains would remain Native lands with the caveat that the United States could build forts and roads through it. Participating tribes were to receive $50,000 in annuities over a fifty-year period to maintain peace between tribal groups and to avoid any injury to overland travelers. Rough boundaries were sketched for tribal territories.[35] With the DOI at the helm, the national push for gridding the region officially began.

It was into this dynamic, complex, and politically charged atmosphere that Pacific Railway Surveys set off in 1853. Beyond ensuring friendly relations with Indigenous inhabitants of the region, Stevens and the other surveyors knew that they depended on Native peoples to guide them through often treacherous physical and sociopolitical landscapes to carve out the paths that railroads would later follow. Indigenous customs, goods, and cartographic knowledge proved crucial to the colonial mapping of the region.

Hosts

On what was likely a hot and sticky July day near Scullyville, in Indian Territory, a gentleman known as Mr. McKinney opened his front door and headed out to the fence that lined his property, his trusty canines bounding beside him. He spotted several men just as they were hopping his fence. McKinney invited them in for dinner, taking them through the carpeted entrance of his estate and introducing them to his wife and children. The three men were lacking in food supplies and anxious of information about the surrounding country. It is likely that they also discussed the purpose of their visit to Choctaw Country: to survey a possible route for a transcontinental railroad. McKinney obliged his guests with what he knew of the Staked Plains to the west and sent them off with full stomachs. The visitors, Lt. Amiel Weeks Whipple and two comrades from his surveying party, were impressed by the "respectable degree of civilization" found at McKinney's residence. McKinney, a Choctaw man, provided Whipple and his men with much-needed sustenance and information about what lay ahead for the survey party west of Scullyville.[36]

Two days later, Whipple returned to the survey camp in Choctaw Country to find that a Choctaw woman stood guard in front of the party's "best cow." A pair of herdsmen explained to Whipple that the woman refused to leave the beast, and she stood beside it with a stick in hand. They were unsure about how to proceed. The herdsmen considered denying the woman's claim to the hoofed beast, but they "dislike[d] to use force," and perhaps most importantly, "they were surrounded by a great number of Choctaws." After a brief meeting with the local Indian agent, the Choctaw woman left with the survey party's prized beast, no doubt a payment for the last few days of service and hospitality that the Choctaws had granted the Whipple party.[37]

These two encounters in Indian Territory point to the webs of exchange and custom that bound railway surveyors over the course of their journey. It is clear from Whipple's account that he and his men were very much guests at the mercy of local Indigenous men and women for resources and much-needed information. Whipple and his men were also uncertain about the nature of the landscape and the best means for traversing this little-known region. Reliant on Indigenous cartographic knowledge and goods, the surveyors submitted often to the requests of Indigenous hosts and delegations. In Indian Country—in Choctaw Country—the surveyors might herald the coming of an indestructible "Iron Horse" and champion the grandness of their "Great Father," but the Choctaw woman still got her cow.

The Pacific Survey parties regularly spotted markers of Indigenous presence before seeing Native people. In the evenings, surveyors reported plumes of smoke from nearby camps and villages. "Indian signal fires streamed high above the mountains on which they were built," Lt. Beckwith wrote while encamped near the Uncompahgre plateau, "doubtless to give motion to their friends on our route of our approach."[38] In another instance,

John Sherburne, a surgeon and geologist assigned to the Whipple expedition, was wary of camping when too many fires were seen in the distance. On March 8, after crossing the Sierra Nevadas with the help of two Mohave leaders who served as guides—Irataba and Cairook—Whipple's party camped near several parties of Paiutes. Cairook and Irataba explained to Whipple's men that the valley Paiutes were friendly, but the mountain Paiutes were known to be hostile to the Mohaves and other visitors. Sherburne looked on with concern at the glowing mountainside that evening. "Last night from camp their fires were seen quite plainly three miles from us," Sherburne wrote, "there being so many unmistakable signs that they were all around us, we concluded to take our turn at standing guard."[39] Billows of smoke reminded Sherburne, Beckwith, and others that they were entering an inhabited land.

On other occasions, tribes sent official and unofficial delegations to meet with the surveyors. Shaved Head, a principal chief of the Comanches, met with the Gunnison party in August 1853 near Fort Atkinson along the Arkansas River. Shortly after arriving, Shaved Head made for Lieutenant Beckwith's tent with "marked gravity." He then took Beckwith's hand, "shaked [*sic*] three times quickly, and then three times slowly and emphatically, raising his hand high and dropping it low." He came, according to one surveyor, to "eat with us in friendship."[40] After leaving Fort Union in the Upper Missouri in early August, the Stevens party were greeted by a war party of nearly a hundred Blackfoot under the charge of White Man's Horse.[41] Stevens was eventually able to convince the war party of the survey's peaceful intentions, and he invited the Blackfoot warriors to accompany them across the Northern Plains to Fort Benton.[42] In the Southwest, two Navajo men rode into Whipple's camp east of the Little Colorado River, only to depart shortly after hearing that Whipple's team had recently been to Zuni pueblo, the site of an ongoing smallpox outbreak.[43] These regular visits made it clear to the surveyors that they were in Indian Country.

During these visits, surveyors regularly submitted to Indigenous rituals and protocols. A month prior to Shave Head's visit with Gunnison, Assiniboine chiefs Big Thunder and Little Thunder invited a few visitors to their sprawling camp along the Souris River near the Upper Missouri. A number of Assiniboine warriors rode out to greet the Stevens surveying party, who arrived at camp after noon on July 27. Stevens noted that the first man in the procession "came toward us with the back of his uplifted hand toward us, as a signal of friendship, and then they shook hands with every member of our party."[44] Around 1,200 Assiniboines occupied the camp, the dwellers dispersed among 150 lodges.[45] Of those 1,200, over 80 community leaders met with the Stevens surveying party in a formal ceremony of reception that featured the distribution of pelts and two buffalo robes. Farther west, a visiting delegation of Gros Ventres made their own demands, asking that none but Stevens's "principal men" visit their camp for a formal ceremony and meeting.[46] On these occasions, Stevens recognized that he had to exchange goods and sit for hours before asking questions or seeking assistance from his hosts. This submission was not unique to Stevens. Lt. Robert Williamson made clear the need to follow Indigenous protocols when his survey team was seeking a guide. A Tygh village welcomed the Williamson survey ahead of crossing the Cascade Range in Oregon. Williamson, desperate for a guide through the mountain pass, solicited the village leader for a guide. "After a long a ceremonious council which Indians always require on great occasions," Williamson reported, "I succeeded in hiring the young man."[47] Submitting to Indigenous customs of exchange was critical to the survival and continued movement of the surveyors, which is why the surveys set out with wagons loaded with goods to exchange with their hosts (Figure 1.3).

Indigenous rituals establishing friendship and reciprocity did not dilute the pointed conversation that often followed. Big Thunder and his comrades, for example, used their ceremony of reception to inquire about what the railroad would bring into their country, and stressed that previous negotiations with leaders in Washington had gone awry. One leader noted the relationship between increasing white settlement and the decline of local game populations. "We know," he explained, "that as they [whites] come, our game goes back. What are we to do?"[48] Another participant made a request for the protection of Assiniboine territories—territories laid out in the 1851 Horse Creek treaty—from the encroachment of Lakotas from the south and east. The Assiniboines placed their grievances about Horse Creek at the feet of Stevens and his men, insisting that the surveyors "relieve us from these troubles."[49] Another leader raised concerns about the prospect of a railroad, which he believed would result in his people being "driven from these plains."[50] Stevens fended off these questions and promised more conversation at a treaty council the following year. The hosts, however, had made their case.

Figure 1.3 John Mix Stanley, *Distribution of Goods to the Assiniboines*, 1860. State Historical Society of Missouri Art Collection.

Not all of the meetings with the surveyors were friendly in nature. In the fall of 1853 a Hueco man entered Whipple's camp on Walnut Creek in the Blackland Prairies of central Texas. He explained to Whipple and his men that their previous Hueco guide had led them astray. On the advice of this new camp visitor, Whipple and his men traveled five miles east, running into a large prairie fire. Whipple, already irked by the unwelcome Hueco guest, hinted that the fire might have been the workings of other local Huecos in order to ensure the party's "destruction." Whipple and his men plodded through the scorched remains with increasing alarm. No suitable forage for their livestock was in sight. Four days later, another conflagration lit up the night sky, increasing Whipple's concerns. Scorched prairies surrounded the Whipple party as it trekked across Hueco lands. While this burning was certainly part of a yearly cycle, the Huecos may have also considered it useful to repel other undesirables, namely Whipple and his men.[51] There is no doubt that fire assisted Indigenous peoples interested in expelling unwanted visitors from their homelands. Walter Scribner Schulyer, a soldier on the Yellowstone expedition some years later, mentioned that the Lakota were rapidly burning off the grass, "trying to harass us."[52]

Farther west, in Paiute Country, the surveyors got embroiled in a broader contest for goods that turned violent. On March 10, 1854, the Whipple party left behind a Mexican herder with three mules and no arms. The next day, when he failed to arrive at camp, three other herders armed themselves to look for him. The search continued until the men stumbled upon the man's moccasins and bloody shirt near a Paiute camp. Whipple suspected that the herder was killed in order to procure the three mules. In retaliation, Sherburne ordered his men to set fire to the Paiute camp, eliminating cooking supplies, food stores, and weapons.[53]

The bloodiest encounter between the railroad surveyors and Indigenous peoples unfolded in Utah Territory in October 1853. Throughout the fall of 1853, Mormon settlers and Utes had been involved in a series of skirmishes. Resistant to expanding Mormon settlement in the early 1850s and Mormon efforts at converting local tribes, Utes raided several Mormon towns.[54] Mormon settlers under the leadership of Brigham Young began organizing militarily and setting up defenses around settlements. Gunnison and his men stepped into this tense atmosphere. On October 26, 1853, a band of Utes rode into the Sevier River bottom and surprised a party of twelve trespassers. Arrows whistled through the air and many found their marks. The Utes killed eight men, including Captain Gunnison, who led the survey between the 38th and 39th parallels. Four others escaped, one stumbling into Lt. Beckwith's camp to share the news. Breathless and "barely able to articulate,...he sank into a seat," Beckwith recalled. The man conveyed "the painful intelligence...that Capt. Gunnison's party had been surprised in their camp in the narrow river bottom." The visitor believed he was the only survivor, though others would be found later.[55] The captain of the party's infantry ordered Beckwith to set out to the site. Firearms in hand, Beckwith and his comrades were prepared for a skirmish that never came. Kanosh, a local Ute leader, met with Beckwith shortly afterward and explained that a young group of warriors had carried out the attack, likely in response to a Mormon emigrant train's attack on members of Kanosh's band earlier that year. It was, Kanosh insisted, not reflective of broader Ute intentions.[56]

Gunnison's death points to webs of violence stretching out across Utah and the broader West in the early 1850s as miners, US officials, and other agents of empire made their way onto Indigenous lands. As newcomers beyond the grid, the surveyors' submission to Indigenous customs and protocols generally ensured safe passage through the region. Peaceful encounters with Indigenous hosts only took the surveyors so far, however. Without critical cartographic and diplomatic knowledge, Whipple, Stevens, Pope, and others could easily succumb to the deadly tolls offered up by the western landscape and by less hospitable hosts. Indigenous guides would prove essential to navigating these tolls.

Guides

In mid-August of 1853, John Bushman, a Delaware guide leading the Whipple party across the Plains, refused to continue the journey west from Ft. Arbuckle, located in the Cross Timbers of Indian Territory. Bushman, intimately familiar with the lands and peoples adjacent to the Cross Timbers, had a few reasons for refusing the party's offer. He nodded first to the increasing levels of violence taking place to the west, as Comanches, Kiowas, and others fought over dwindling buffalo and clashed with relative newcomers to Indian Territory, including Bushman's Delawares, along with Choctaws, Chickasaws, Seminoles, and Cherokees.[57] But Bushman emphasized that the landscape itself posed its own share of challenges, especially in the parched summer months. He was matter of fact with his advice: "maybe you find water, maybe you all die."[58]

Bushman exercised a powerful right of refusal that other Native peoples would utilize in their exchanges with the railroad surveyors, but he also provided Whipple and his party with critical information about their path ahead. The western landscape posed a host of obstacles for the survey parties. Water—both access to it and the unavoidable need to cross it—were significant challenges.[59] Aside from water, the land itself presented considerable difficulties, the most notable of which was geologic in character. Stretching across the wide western expanse, seemingly interminable mountain ranges pierced the sky. In the mid-1850s, US officials were deeply concerned that the Rocky Mountains would prove a permanent geographic barrier to western expansion, thwarting their plans to connect eastern markets to a growing California populace and the Pacific trade world.[60] Since it was the surveyor's chief task to find the most "accessible" route for a railroad, Whipple, Stevens, and others had to explore numerous passes.

Then there were the real and perceived human obstacles. Intruding on Indigenous lands, the surveyors understood that they were at the mercy of local inhabitants. To the east, increasing sectionalist tensions only exacerbated this issue, with Northern and Southern politicians deeply divided over where the future transcontinental line should run. Several politicians hoped that the teams of professionals could resolve the political stalemate. Out of necessity, Whipple and others would turn to Indigenous knowledge to help them ford formidable waterways, summit imposing peaks, draw sustenance from the landscape, and navigate the rituals and protocols necessary to move safely through the West.[61] Several Indigenous guides—known to history as Jim, John, Irataba, Cairook, Vincente, and Powerful Earth—made surveyor movement possible beyond the grid.

Natoyist-Siksina' Culbertson (Figure 1.4), also known as Medicine Snake Woman, was undoubtedly one of the most valuable guides on the Stevens expedition. The sister of Blackfoot leaders Seen from Afar and Little Dog, Medicine Snake Woman married the head trader at Fort Union, Albert Culbertson, in 1840.[62] Unions between Indigenous women and trade company men were common at the time; marriage often brought recognition and respect to Indigenous leaders while also ensuring a particular group's privileged access to trade. By the early 1850s, the Culberstons had been navigating the intricate and complicated intertribal politics of the Missouri

Figure 1.4 John James Audubon, *Natawista Culbertson*, 1843. Image courtesy of John James Audubon State Park and the Kentucky Department of Parks.

River fur trade for over a decade. Ahead of the survey, Stevens was rightly concerned about his party's reception among the Blackfoot, who had been increasingly agitated by the growing numbers of Anglo settlers in their territory on the Northwestern Plains. Desperate to pass safely through Blackfoot Country, Stevens reached out to Albert Culbertson and hired him as a special agent for the journey from Fort Union to Fort Benton. Medicine Snake Woman initially planned to stay behind at Fort Union, but changed her mind due to growing concerns about the risks posed to both the surveyors and her people. Worried that the party and the Blackfoot would misunderstand one another, she felt that she could "explain things" and "soothe" her people, if needed.[63]

A master of the intricate diplomatic turns needed to promote peace and continue commerce in the region, Medicine Snake Woman met with local Indigenous leaders and reassured them about the peaceful nature of the survey party.[64] She and her husband sent tobacco and a message to Blackfoot leaders ahead of the survey's arrival in Fort Benton to invite them to a grand council. She also translated between the leaders and the Stevens party at the meeting, in which Blackfoot leaders agreed to participate in treaty negotiations with government officials the following year.[65] In addition to her translation services, Medicine Snake Woman routinely pitched her tent outside of the sentry line in order to be the first person to receive visitors to camp. Stevens noted that she was "in constant intercourse with the Indians, and inspired them with perfect confidence," and reported back to Washington that she had committed the "highest service" to the expedition.[66] In a region marked by increasing competition over dwindling resources, Medicine Snake Woman's knowledge of the rituals and protocols of exchange between Natives and newcomers ensured the safe passage of the surveyors across the Northern Plains.

The grand council at Fort Benton not only set the stage for a forthcoming treaty in 1855, but also provided the Stevens survey with critical information about the path ahead. West from Fort Benton stood the formidable Rocky Mountain Range, and Stevens was unsure of the best route for both his survey party and a future rail line. Medicine Snake Woman, translating between Stevens and her brother, Little Dog, facilitated the exchange of Blackfoot cartographic information. Little Dog gave a detailed account of Marias Pass in northern Montana to the Stevens surveyors. He explained that the Piikani (one of three nations within the Blackfoot Confederacy) had not used the pass for some time, which meant it was "much grown up with underbrush" and would require "some labor for a train to make its way through."[67] Meanwhile, White Crane, a Kainai guide accompanying Lt. Mullan on the Stevens survey, "was instructed to procure…experienced guides and to examine some good pass of which several were known to exist, leading from the forks of the Missouri to the Bitter Root river [*sic*]."[68] The cartographic knowledge and diplomatic skills of these prominent Blackfoots helped map the route that the rail line would eventually take.

The Blackfoot leaders were not alone in providing indispensable information about mountain crossings. In 1855 Lt. Robert S. Williamson led a second Pacific Railway survey through the Pacific coast, across California and Oregon. The central obstacle in their path was the great Cascade Range. A Tygh guide, Sam An-ax-shat, provided the party with the safest route through the range, which radically diverged from the surveyors' initial plans. Once the party made it through the pass, Sam An-ax-shat came upon Anglo settlers in the midst of ongoing war with Indigenous residents. Sam An-ax-shat returned home in haste, fearing for his life. Williamson later reported that the survey party "owe[d] our lives" to An-ax-shat.[69] Nearly a year earlier, three Ute men, etched in the historical record only as Tom, Shippoh, and Joe, provided Lt. Beckwith with much-needed information about the Humboldt Mountains. Beckwith was interested in a particular pass, but according to the three guides, it was "rocky and not passable in its state…with wagons." Thanks to Ute intelligence, Beckwith saved himself days of reconnaissance and perhaps ensured the well-being of himself and his party.[70]

In addition to potentially deadly mountain crossings, each of the five surveys encountered a treacherous river crossing at some point during their journey, and more often than not Indigenous guides pointed to the best fording areas or assisted in the crossing. John Sherburne recalled how Mohaves not only provided crucial foodstuffs, but also helped the Whipple party cross the mighty Colorado River. The Mohaves directed the men to the best crossing location, a swath of the Colorado running roughly 1,800 feet wide. The Whipple men threw a rope over the sandbar in the middle of the river. With a rubber pontoon the party members successfully transferred three wagonloads. The fourth buckled under the rushing water, sending supplies downstream. A handful of Mohaves dove into the water to retrieve the goods. "The Indians saved us many things," Sherburne recalled, "and done us a great deal of service." Sherburne and the other survey members gave these Mohaves three drowned sheep and three live ones for their assistance.[71]

Access to water was also critical to surveyors across the Plains and the Southwest. Following a Zuni council meeting at which the nation approved of the Whipple survey's objectives, Zuni leaders equipped the surveyors with three hired guides: Jose Marie, Juan Septimo, and Jose Hacha.[72] The guides described the country west of Zuni as "level plain, with springs of permanent water at convenient distances."[73] Zunis call the Little Colorado River to the east of their pueblo the *K'yawinan A'honna* or "red river."[74] *K'yawinan A'honna* was on the western border of Zuni territory, but the guides assured Whipple that they could get word to the Hopis to alert them of the survey's arrival and request guiding services from there. Whipple was especially concerned about the labor involved in cutting a path through to the Little Colorado, given the dense thickets of cedar and juniper along the western edge of New Mexico Territory. In response, Jose Marie, Juan Septimo, and Jose Hacha shared the location of major Zuni, Navajo, and Hopi roads, and "at our request they traced a sketch of the Moqui [*sic* Hopi] country and the route they propose to travel."[75] The men left the survey party in early December after returning with news that Hopi leaders refused to provide a guide.[76] It wasn't until late January on their way to the Colorado River that two Indigenous men Whipple identified as "Yampais" (likely Yavapais) approached the Whipple camp after days of tracking the surveyors. The men assisted the survey in several critical ways. They shared the most convenient route west to the Colorado River and to the Mohave villages that dotted its banks. There was a shorter route, they explained, but given the size of the party and their water intake, it was better to take the longer route along the Bill William's River or *Wenachicava* to the Yavapai. They then offered to lead the party to a nearby watering hole in exchange for a meal and blankets.[77]

Jose Marie, Medicine Snake Woman, Irataba, and other Indigenous guides made movement possible for these newcomers beyond the grid, but cartographic knowledge alone could not ensure the survival and completion of the surveys. Stevens, Whipple, and the rest of the survey teams also relied on Indigenous goods and produce to sustain their parties over long journeys. To procure guides, Stevens, Whipple, and others traded cloth, horses, ammunition, beads, and other valued goods. Beckwith recalled when camped near the Abunkarra River that "Indians came hourly to camp to beg and trade off horses."[78] In Delaware Country, meanwhile, Whipple reported, "many well mounted Indians have been in camp bringing the produce of their fields for trade."[79] While Indigenous communities took the opportunity to incorporate these surveyors into their existing commercial networks, the surveyors also encountered parties on the move, engaged in long-standing intertribal exchanges. Whipple commented that he and his comrades "had no previous idea of the extent of this Indian trade."[80] Intertribal trade networks ensured that Indigenous delegations held the bargaining power when it came to engagements with the survey parties. When exchanges with the surveyors failed, Utes, Blackfoot, and others could always approach other tribes for goods. This meant that for the surveyors, inducements did not always work. Some, like Bushman and the Hopi, refused to guide. Others refused to part with prized livestock. Beckwith recalled after spending time with the Utes that "efforts were made to obtain a guide from among the Indians, but no one could be induced by a display of the trinkets, cloths, paints, and blankets they so much coveted, to accompany us even to Wasatch Pass."[81] Beyond the grid, Native peoples held a powerful right of refusal. Those who did choose to part with prized cartographic information could not have known that the routes these outsiders traced would set the course for an invasion.

White Crane, Little Dog, and other guides not only provided critical information about western landscapes, but also connected the outsiders to supplies from western farms, prairies, and waterways. Guides, along with Indigenous trading delegations, either directed the survey parties to or provided the survey parties with sorely needed foodstuffs. As John Sherburne made plain after Mohave guides brought grass for their stock and fish to the Whipple camp, "without these friendly Indians, 'tis impossible to tell how we could have got along." As he gazed over the spread of food before him in February 1854, Sherburne added: "everything we have on the table, excepting mutton, is got from them. Corn bread, fish, beans, pumpkins, and wheat for coffee all come from them and stores enough will be laid in to last until reaching the settlements."[82] On occasion, Indigenous delegations arrived in survey camps with the explicit purpose of trading their products from western lands, fields, and waterways. With this practice, Kichais, Mohaves, Utes, and others incorporated the survey parties into long-standing networks of exchange and dependence, networks that undoubtedly served their own interests while also ensuring the survival of the foreign surveyors.

Tribal delegations regularly invited the surveyors to purchase horses, furs, and other animal products. Upon their arrival at Ft. Union, Stevens recalled that many of his men purchased Indigenous animal goods to protect themselves against the formidable winters on the Northern Plains. "We were much pleased," Stevens wrote, "and much benefitted by the good offices of the Indian women... who fitted us out with a good assortment of moccasins, gloves, and other guards against the severity of the weather."[83] Additionally, the loss of animals—and the prospect of future losses—meant that Pope, Gunnison, and others were eager to acquire additional four-legged companions. After a large party of Gros Ventres invited Stevens and his men into their camp, Stevens asked to purchase horses from them. "We received," he wrote, "several very good horses in place of six very indifferent mules."[84] Members of the Stevens party parted with their firearms in the hopes of attaining much-needed clothing, food, and horses.[85] It is likely that Eagle Chief and other Gros Ventre then took these arms to trade with their allies in the Blackfoot Confederacy.[86] Protecting horses and other livestock was also integral to the success of these surveys. The untimely demise of a Mexican herder on the Whipple expedition was likely due to the Paiutes' interest in his horse. Irataba and Cairook (Figure 1.5), two Mohave leaders who guided the Whipple survey, were keenly aware that the Paiutes' appetite for livestock contributed to violence in the region. When the surveyors gifted them a pair of mules in thanks for their assistance, Cairook and Irataba refused to take them, knowing that the hoofed beasts would make them a prime target for Paiute thieves.[87]

Carting their own wagons full of goods, the surveyors sought incorporation into long-standing movements of goods, peoples, and beasts across the Trans-Mississippi West.[88] Only by participating in these exchanges and by giving their own share of gifts and goods could the surveyors procure the invaluable guides who charted their path across rocky crevices and formidable waterways. The decision to open up these networks to these visitors and to provide crucial guidance rested largely with the Indigenous inhabitants of the region. Despite Keeler's best efforts to plot out a conquered landscape, Whipple, Stevens, and the other men who provided Keeler with his information were subject to the customs and practices of Indian Country.

The five western survey parties did not end up winning the race for construction of the region's first trunkline, though the routes they charted would lay the groundwork for a railroaded region. In the same year that the US government funded the five railway surveys, an enterprising Army officer conducted his own, privately funded expedition along the 42nd parallel, the ultimate site of the first trunkline road. Peter A. Dey of the Chicago and Rock Island Railroad funded Grenville M. Dodge's survey of a railroad route west of the Missouri River. Dey hoped that Rock Island tracks would

Figure 1.5 Irataba (far left) and Cairook (center), two Mohave leaders who guided the Whipple survey, depicted here by survey artist Heinrich Balduin Möllhausen and John Young. Heinrich Balduin Möllhausen and John Young, *Mojaves*, print, 1861. Amon Carter Museum of American Art, Fort Worth, Texas.

butt up against the Missouri at the most desirable location. Dodge set out with an armed party from Council Bluffs, Iowa, in 1853. When he returned to his camp near Papillion creek in eastern Nebraska, Dodge met a large party of Omahas. He found that his surveying camp was "full of Omaha Indians," and, much to his alarm, "they had every man in the party cooking for him." Fearing that his provisions would soon run out, Dodge ordered his men to collect their arms. The Omahas promptly retreated, in a sour mood. The sight must have shaken Dodge. Here, in the valley of the Platte River, Omahas had entered the most intimate of spaces and put Dodge's men to work. In spite of the grand visions for the American West held by Dodge and other starry-eyed surveyors, his team had submitted to the Indigenous residents of the region.[89]

A closer look at the Indigenous customs, guides, and goods that directed the course of the Pacific Railway surveys forces a reconsideration of Keeler's map and what lay beyond the grid. Far from a primeval wilderness, much of the US West in 1853 was populated by Indigenous communities whose physical presence and markers on the landscape served as regular reminders to Whipple, Stevens, and other surveyors that they had entered Indian Country. Indigenous knowledge of the landscape made Native peoples the best sources for route-making. Their foodstuffs and goods—be it corn or moccasins—were critical to the survival of these visitors on Indigenous homelands. The surveyors realized that to scout future lines, they would have to acquiesce to the customs of various Native groups, bestowing gifts, parting with cows, and breaking bread. The latticework of western railways grew out of this foundational reliance on Indian hospitality, goods, and knowledge. Beyond the grid, Indigenous practices prevailed, and the success of the Pacific Railway Surveys rested not with the ingenuity of a few visitors to Indian Country, but instead with the disposition, knowledge, and technology of Paiutes, Lakotas, Utes, Mohaves, and others.

This Indigenous knowledge-sharing would ultimately wreak havoc on Indigenous communities in the West. Ten years and a bloody civil war later, government and military officials would return to the region and set to work on their colonial, grid-making project. The various mountain passes, river crossings, and trail systems that Indigenous guides had invited the surveyors to map out would, over the course of the remaining century, be tracked out in iron, steel, and wood. What once carried mounted Utes, Paiutes, Assiniboines, and others made way for an industrial interloper.

The Iron Horse in Indian Country: Native Americans and Railroads in the US West. Alessandra La Rocca Link, Oxford University Press. © Alessandra La Rocca Link 2025. DOI: 10.1093/9780197674437.003.0002

2

Gridded in Ink, Iron, and Blood

On January 8, 1863, California governor and Central Pacific (CP) president Leland Stanford, clad in a frock coat and silk hat, heralded the start of construction for the Central Pacific Railroad. "The Pacific Coast will be bound to the Atlantic Coast by iron bonds," he bellowed to the crowd gathered in Sacramento. Iron bonds, he exclaimed, "that shall consolidate and strengthen the ties of nationality, and advance with giant strides the prosperity of State and Country."[1] It was a moment infused with showmanship like many others staged along rail lines across the West.[2] A banner with two hands extending across the country, clasped in the center, hung from a nearby wagon.[3] The image left little room for interpretation: railroads promised to bind a nation torn asunder by civil war.

Across the West and almost a year later, Union Pacific (UP) officials held their own groundbreaking spectacle in Omaha, Nebraska. The UP's master of ceremonies, the aptly named George Francis Train, donned a white suit and spoke in hyperbole. He declared that Union Pacific was "the people's railroad."[4] Train and Stanford realized that the nation was sizing up the companies and their enterprises, and corporate leaders intended to stage a successful public relations campaign. The first trunk line railroad in the American West, they reasoned, would act as a unifying force that ushered in a new era of prosperity for the American public. When it came to railroaders, corporate profit served the public good.

Three years after the UP groundbreaking ceremony, a different sort of sizing up purportedly took place. Spotted Tail (Lakota) and his band descended on a UP construction outfit 100 miles outside Omaha. An interpreter explained to the construction foreman that Spotted Tail wished to watch the men lay track. They also toured the locomotive, studying its form and composition. A UP employee then proposed a race between the Lakota horses and their industrial counterpart, wagering that the iron horse would prevail. According to one account, published decades after the alleged event, Spotted Tail reluctantly took a seat in an engine cab detached from the train of cars. A few Lakota horsemen lined up alongside their leader.

In an instant, the locomotive lurched to a start. The horses leapt ahead of the belching engine, but the locomotive slowly gained on the fatigued beasts, outrunning them after a considerable distance. With a whistle, the iron horse declared its victory.[5]

After sharing lunch, the seemingly friendly interactions between Spotted Tail's party and the construction outfit soured. The Lakotas demanded a tribute for passage from the UP crew, requesting all of the beef and flour that the horsemen could feasibly carry from the UP supplies. When denied payment, Spotted Tail grew angry and, according to one account, "threatened to come over some night with three thousand warriors and clean us out."[6] The locomotive won the speed race, but how this new technology might shift power dynamics and access to resources among Natives and newcomers in the region was still undecided. Spotted Tail and his warriors may have only threatened attack along the railroad line, but in other western locales real acts of violence took place as Native people sought to turn back the gridded colonial order heralded by the Union Pacific and Central Pacific railroads.

Spotted Tail likely demanded provisions from the UP crews because the federal government had consistently failed to provide rations and annuities promised to Lakotas by federal agents that same year.[7] By 1866, Spotted Tail had spent decades engaging in military resistance of US advancement, most recently in response to the massacre of upwards of 175 Cheyennes and Arapahos at Sand Creek by the Colorado US Volunteer Cavalry in November 1864. After the massacre, militant Cheyennes traveled north to the Smoky Hill region in northern Kansas/southern Nebraska, where they met with Spotted Tail and Pawnee Killer's Lakota bands and eight or more lodges of Arapahos. George Bent (Cheyenne), a survivor of the Sand Creek massacre and descendent of a prominent Cheyenne family, recalled the decision to resort to violence that winter. "After Sand Creek," Bent wrote, "in the camp on the head of Smoky Hill while the Indians were all mourning the dead, they made up their minds to send around a war pipe and attack the whites at once."[8] In violation of previous treaties, the intertribal coalition attacked stage lines along the Overland Trail, cutting telegraph wires and seizing mail in and around Julesburg, Colorado, a future UP station.[9] When Spotted Tail met the UP locomotive, however, he was changing course and setting his sights on building diplomatic relations with the United States. A decade after his race on the Central Plains, Spotted Tail would be a seasoned rail traveler, having made several visits to Washington,

DC, to negotiate on behalf of the Brules, one of the seven *oyátes*, or tribes, of the Lakota.[10]

The story of western trunk line construction, mistakenly dubbed the nation's first transcontinental, has generated significant public and scholarly interest. The laying of 1,900 miles of track from Council Bluffs, Iowa, to Sacramento, California, between 1863 and 1869 is often cast as a classic western American epic: two grand, guileful, and greedy corporations race across the West, linking two disparate regions and, many hoped, suturing the nation together following civil war.[11] As newspapers in the East ran articles touting the trunkline's great promise for the nation, Natives in the Green River Basin and Utah Territory documented the arrival of rail lines at rock art sites along the trunkline's path, which followed the 42nd parallel (Figure 2.1).[12] The rock art sites and the media fanfare over construction do not, however, tell the story of dispossession that set the stage for the railroading of the region. Behind construction lay the legal foundation for the expansion of the United States' gridded colonial order. Legal fictions lodged in treaties and in the Pacific Railway Act cast an air of legitimacy over these operations. Yet hard truths remained. Beyond the 100th meridian, UP crews crossed into Cheyenne, Arapahoe, Ute, and Lakota homelands (Figure 2.2). To the west, Central Pacific crews building east from Sacramento would cut through Paiute, Shoshone, Bannock, Nisenan, Miwok, and Washoe territories. The public that Stanford and Train invoked at the start of trunkline construction clearly did not include Spotted Tail and other Native peoples in the region.

How did western Indigenous lands fall into corporate hands? The principles of eminent domain offer a key to the answer. Indigenous dispossession in the railroad age relied heavily on the Fifth Amendment's emphasis on taking for "public" good. Railroad magnates, bound tightly through a corrosive mixture of corruption and policy to US legislators, married their private enterprise to the public charge. The result was a major legislative act—the Pacific Railway Act—and a series of treaties with Native nations that authorized the taking of Indigenous lands for railroads. When treaties broke down, sources suggest corporate leaders took matters into their own hands, forming extralegal arrangements with tribes to ensure safe passage of tracklayers. Corporate arrangements allegedly brokered along the 42nd parallel displayed the degree to which railroad leaders felt confident sidestepping decades of Indian policy for their personal gain. When it came to the "public" good, few strategies were off the table. These corporate

Figure 2.1 Ute depiction of a locomotive on a rock face near the 42nd parallel. Special Collections. J. Willard Marriott Library. University of Utah.

arrangements would be a harbinger for future negotiations between government officials, tribes, and corporate agents, and provisions for free travel on rail lines also set the stage for Indigenous rail travel in the American West.

Indigenous negotiators at these treaty tables often consented to rights-of-way and land cessions because of near-term needs for government annuities and resources. Spotted Tail's demand for goods along the UP track was part of broader Indigenous strategies for survival and subsistence amidst the violence and turmoil of the West in the 1860s. And the West was a decidedly violent place during and after the Civil War, as soldiers flooded

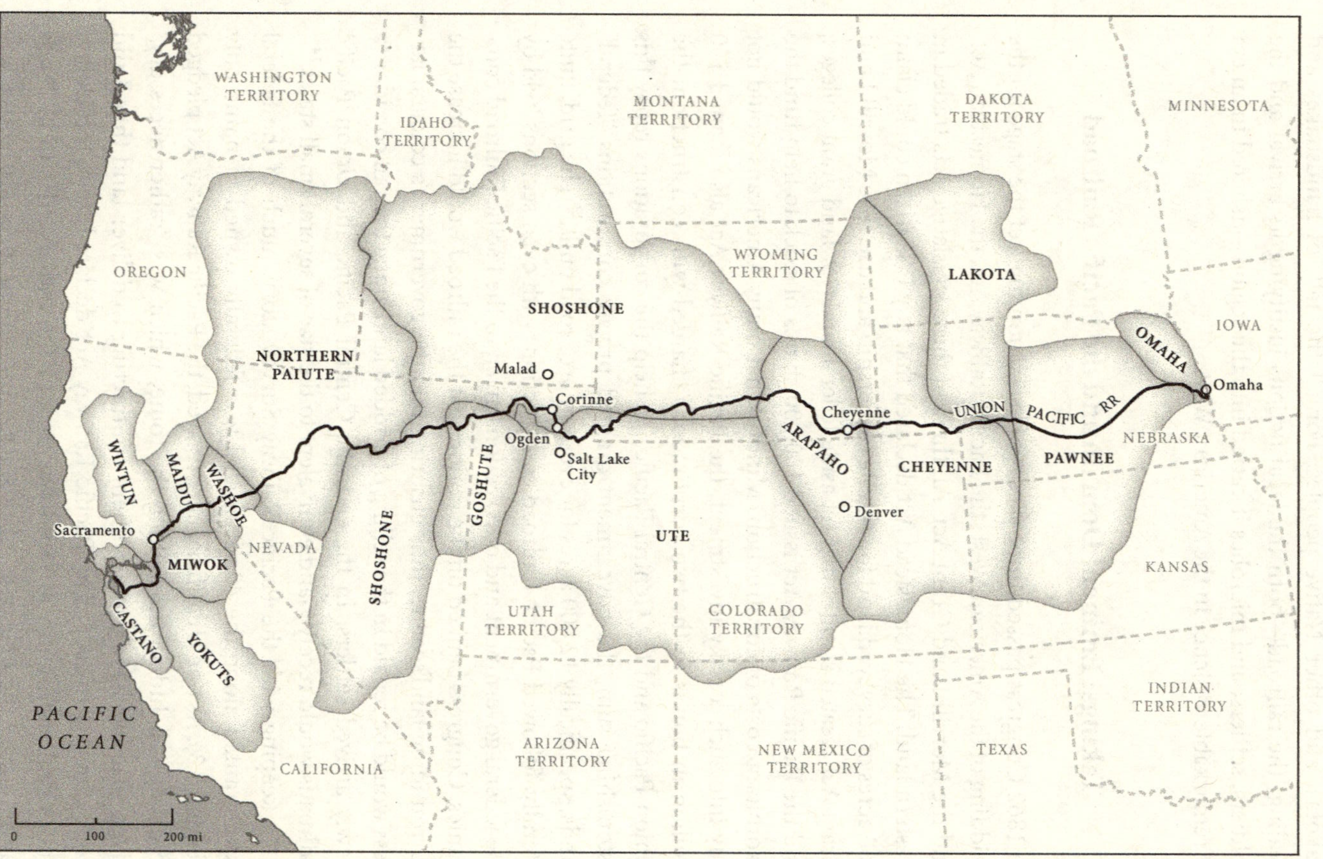

Figure 2.2 The Transcontinental Railroad Route through Indigenous Territories. Erin Greb Cartography.

the region to fight Union or Confederate enemies and later resistant Paiutes, Lakotas, and other Native peoples. For all the talk of handshakes and healing, the railroad—both the legal fictions justifying its arrival and the soldiers, settlers, and microbes it carted into the region—ushered in an era of remarkable violence in the American West.

Takings: Eminent Domain and the Pacific Railroad

In 1862 Congress passed three pieces of legislation that set the stage for the gridding of the American West: the Pacific Railway Act, the Homestead Act, and the Morrill Land Grant Act. All three of these legislative acts traded in western land. The Homestead Act declared that any US citizen could claim 160 acres of surveyed land for private ownership and use. The Morrill Land Grant Act created statutes that set aside federal lands for land grant colleges, and the Pacific Railway Act issued 100,000 shares of stock to help fund the exorbitant costs of construction. Mindful that many Americans would not buy into such a risky investment, the Pacific Railway Act also loaned $50 million in bonds to the two corporations charged with construction: the Union Pacific and the Central Pacific. To help the corporations repay this astonishing sum, the government granted private corporations "federal" lands, specifically 12,800 acres for every mile of road built.[13] The grid, quite literally, followed Pacific Railroad construction, with even sections held by the federal government and odd sections given to the Pacific Railroad companies. Congress banked on the notion that the railroad would increase the surrounding land's value, thus ensuring that the government's colossal largess would be repaid in the selling of gridded land along the rail corridor to newly arrived settlers. In the end, the Central Pacific and Union Pacific railroads would receive land equivalent to the size of several small states.[14]

In keeping with the Pacific Railway Survey story, much of the federal land granted along the 42nd parallel was federally owned in name only (Figure 2.3). As one UP official later relayed, the Pacific Railway Act pledged to extinguish Indian titles along the route, which was "rather necessary," given that "we have a government contracting to deliver land that it did not actually possess."[15] The Pacific Railway Act declared that "the United States shall extinguish as rapidly as may be the Indian titles to all lands falling under the operation of this act and required for said right of way and; grants hereafter made."[16] This language makes clear that acquiring

Figure 2.3 Alfred Hart, *Indian Viewing Railroad from Top of Palisades, 435 miles from Sacramento*, between 1868 and 1869. Library of Congress.

Indigenous lands was a mere administrative formality. Indigenous title would be extinguished—of this there was no question. Embedded in the act was the clear-eyed understanding that Indigenous lands would fund the railroading of the West.[17] Before construction could begin, the US government would have to acquire the lands through treaty and then turn them over to private corporations. This railroad logic of dispossession involved the transference of Native lands into US public domain, then privatizing those same lands for the purposes of rail-line construction and maintenance. This re-privatization process was, according to railroad businessmen, serving the public good.

Seared into the Pacific Railway Act were several foundational fictions: first, that US government had a preordained claim to Indigenous lands. Since the first arrival of Europeans in the Americas, the "doctrine of discovery" animated policy and law creation on behalf of European colonial governments and later the young United States. The doctrine of discovery held that any "unpopulated" lands or lands populated by non-Christians were available to be claimed by Christian Europeans. The doctrine of discovery, in turn, rested on its own fiction: that Indigenous peoples did not use the land "well," meaning they did not use them according to Eurocentric standards.[18]

In 1823 the doctrine of discovery entered the US judicial canon in the US Supreme Court case *Johnson v. M'Intosh*. One of the most consequential rulings in American Indian law, *Johnson v. M'Intosh* gave the federal government a monopoly on land seizures, through either purchase or the elusively defined "just war." This monopoly meant that the United States could ensure low prices for the purchase of lands. The federal government would ultimately pay less than 2 cents per acre for land west of the Mississippi River.[19] *Johnson v. M'Intosh* also declared that Native nations did not hold title to their lands, but merely a "right of occupancy." With *Johnson v. M'Intosh* the US judiciary asserted that Native peoples did not own their land, they only had the right to occupy it and to cede it, and cede it to the federal government only.[20] This case was the first in a trio of Supreme Court cases from John Marshall's court that stripped tribal nations of their sovereignty.[21]

The second fiction that animated the Pacific Railway Act and much of the railway-minded decision-making by corporations and US government officials in the nineteenth century was emphatically repeated by railroad magnates: railroads inherently served the public good. The legal concept of eminent domain—namely the right of a government to expropriate private property for public use—provided the backbone for railroad land seizures across North America in the nineteenth century. As Henry Mills, the leading scholar of eminent domain in the late 1800s, explained, "railroad corporations are *quasi public* corporations dedicated to the public use."[22] Solidified in the Fifth Amendment, also known as the "takings clause," eminent domain sanctioned the taking of private property for public use with just compensation. If a public work served a public good, then the taking was intrinsically justifiable. But when it came to the first western trunkline, its building was in fact a colossal waste of taxpayer capital and resources, and it resulted in a nefarious marriage between corporate barons and US officials that would ultimately erode American democracy.[23]

Native peoples are not considered in this "public." As Cherokee legal scholar Stacy Leeds explains, the US principle of eminent domain meant that "the 'public good' necessitated the taking of land from the Indians so that the land could be redistributed to others who would make better use of the land."[24] Railroads served a public good, and this public good waltzed with the prevailing notion that Indigenous peoples did not properly use their land. Eminent domain explains the preemptive claiming of Indigenous land in the Pacific Railway Act, and it would guide treaty-making in the 1850s and 1860s, particularly in the regular and recurring demands for the federal government's right to build roads or highways through Indigenous lands. Eminent domain was not directly cited in treaties in the 1860s and in subsequent land cessions but, as one legal scholar put it, the treaty-backed expropriation of Indigenous lands "long resembled eminent domain in substance."[25] The foundational principles of eminent domain anchored the Pacific Railway Act and would guide railway-based land cessions and rights-of-way throughout Indian Country in the nineteenth century. A close look at several key treaties affecting lands along the 42nd parallel highlight how eminent domain materialized in policy.

Handshakes of Dispossession: Treaty-Making Along the 42nd Parallel

In 1851, a delegation of Crows arrived at a grand intertribal congregation on Horse Creek in Wyoming. They arrived at the large encampment "in a solemn column, singing their national melody."[26] After several days of dance and deliberation, the Crow signed the Horse Creek Treaty. It was one of many binding agreements between Native nations and government officials over the course of the 1850s. The Crow delegation joined over ten thousand Indigenous peoples gathered along the banks of Horse Creek, thirty-odd miles downriver from Fort Laramie. Leaders from each of the tribes assembled in a grand circle, their kin settled in the fields nearby. This grand circle meeting followed several days of deliberations among the tribes, with dances and gift exchanges cementing long-standing intertribal relations. The document that emerged after the grand council meeting called into question the existing territorial boundaries of the Cheyenne, Lakota, Assiniboine, Arapaho, Crow, Mandan, Hidatsa, and Arikara nations. The treaty was also about making peace between eight nations that often competed for land and resources in the region and promising safe passage for the settlers traveling on the Oregon Trail. An account by John Stands in Timber (Cheyenne) of the meeting emphasized the importance of making amends among former enemies. "There was a lot of excitement from the time it started," Stands in Timber recalled, "because many tribes that had always fought each other were supposed to make friends." "The Indians paid more attention to that part," he added, "than to the council grounds."[27]

Finally, the Horse Creek Treaty recognized the right of the United States to build roads across the Central Plains. Article two of the treaty document made it plain: "the aforesaid nations do hereby recognize the right of the

United States Government to establish roads, military and other outposts, within their territories."[28] The United States was to pay participating tribes a total of $50,000 in annuities per year for five years, along with various gifts.[29] Commissioners D. D. Mitchell and Thomas Fitzpatrick signed the treaty, along with leaders from the eight Central and Northern Plains nations, though Stands in Timber emphasized that the Cheyennes "understood very little of what was signed at the treaty."[30] A similar treaty was made at Fort Atkinson in Kansas a year later in which Comanches, Kiowas, and Apaches agreed to "the right of the United States to lay off and mark out roads or highways—to make reservations of land necessary thereto—to locate depots—and to establish military and other posts within the territories established by the said tribes."[31] Both treaties set up rough territorial boundaries, but their vagueness and insistence on allowing the US government the right of road building and militarization fundamentally called into question Indigenous territoriality on the Plains.

Following the Atkinson Treaty, government officials turned their attention to the East Central Plains, in present-day Kansas and Nebraska. In the wake of the Kansas-Nebraska Act in 1854, Congress authorized Commissioner of Indian Affairs George Manypenny to meet with the Ottoes, Missourias, Omahas, Delawares, Shawnees, Peoria, Weas, and Miaimis. In a whirlwind tour of the Central Plains, Manypenny capitalized on growing concerns about white settlement and dwindling resource supplies in an effort to remove the tribes from some 15 million acres that they held collectively. Many of the tribes would not tolerate wholesale removal, but they ultimately ceded some 14 million acres, settling on small reserves that would be broken up into individual land allotments. Central Plains groups also agreed to allow "all the necessary roads and highways, and railroads, which may be constructed as the country improves."[32]

Farther west, only a portion (some 136 of over 300 distinct tribes) of the California Indians signed a total of eighteen treaties with US officials, setting aside a fraction of the California land base for Indian reserves and allowing Indigenous communities to subsist on nearby lands. As in the Horse Creek and Atkinson treaties, US officials in California recognized that reservation boundaries were porous: use and occupancy of nearby lands was not clearly defined. For California Indians, however, the vagaries would not matter much. In 1852 the Senate threw out the California treaties to keep land under the control of the state and thereby more easily open to private use. By 1864 the Commissioner of Indian Affairs, William P. Dole, proclaimed that the US government did not sign treaties with Indians in California. Just as the Manypenny treaties augured aspects of the future Indian policy of allotment, the California Indians lost their treaty-making status years before the government rejected treaty-making with Native nations in 1871.[33]

As a collection of legal mappings of ownership and place, these early treaties were exceptionally vague. They did, however, share an emphasis on granting US officials the right to build roads through Indian lands. Using the language of eminent domain, roads were seen as public goods that allowed for the direct seizure of land for rights-of-way. Ultimately these documents represented political promises that Natives and non-Natives would break by various means, making much of the land that the UP and CP construction crews entered contested ground. In this atmosphere, Spotted Tail's request for resources from UP tracklayers in exchange for passage is set into sharp relief.

More treaties followed in the 1860s, given that large swaths of land along the 42nd parallel were occupied by Indigenous groups that had not made agreements with US agents. The Superintendent of Indian Affairs in Utah Territory, James D. Doty, organized treaties with Eastern Shoshones at Fort Bridger and Northwestern Shoshones at Box Elder in 1863. Goshutes signed in Tooele Valley in Utah and Western Shoshones signed the Ruby Valley treaty that same year.[34] The same protocol prevailed: all thoroughfares through Indian lands were to be protected and unmolested. "Several routes of travel," one document read, "now or hereafter used by white men shall remain forever free and safe for the use of the government of the United States." Another made specific reference to the Union Pacific and Central Pacific railroad:

> it being understood that provision has been made by the government of the United States for a construction of a railway west from the plains to the Pacific ocean, it is stipulated by the said bands that the said railway or its branches may be located, constructed, and operated, and without molestation by them, through any portion of country claimed or occupied by them.[35]

No land was ceded to the United States, only a right-of-way and rights to survey for minerals, with compensation due the tribes for the loss in food sources from the influx of overland travelers. These treaties contained much of the same language lodged in the earlier Plains treaties, and the principles of eminent domain shine through.

Just as the Fort Laramie and Atkinson treaties broke down shortly after their signing, so too did the United States government quickly neglect its promised payments and annuities in the 1863 treaties on the Great Basin. Shoshones would later file suit against the government for neglect of the treaty stipulations.[36] By the time the UP and CP tracks joined in Promontory, Utah, an Indian Office official was writing to Washington claiming to have no copy of the treaty on hand. Not confident that US and corporate wishes were fulfilled by the handshakes of treaty-making, the United States opted to shore up its claims with the sword. In 1868, the US Army stationed garrisons at Camp Halleck and Ruby to protect Central Pacific crews.[37]

In the latter half of the decade, President Grant authorized a Peace Commission to conclude a series of treaties with other Plains groups.[38] The first major meeting, at Medicine Lodge Creek in 1867, involved representatives of the Cheyennes, Arapahoes, Kiowas, and Comanches. At the meeting, Buffalo Chief (Cheyenne) argued that the land between the South Platte and Arkansas River, just recently bisected by the Union Pacific, was theirs. Senator John B. Henderson, a member of the Peace Commission, responded that the Cheyenne could continue to hunt in that area as long as there was buffalo and provided that the Cheyennes stayed ten miles from any major route. Ultimately, some bands of the Cheyenne signed the treaty, while those under Roman Nose and Medicine Arrow stayed away from the negotiations. No provision about hunting north of the Arkansas near the railroad route made it into the final version of the treaty. A soldier attending the meeting later stated that the Cheyennes "have no idea that they are giving up, or that they have ever given up, the country which they claim as their own, the country north of the Arkansas."[39]

The Medicine Lodge Treaty contained the same kind of vagaries that characterized past treaties and would lead to future violence and Indigenous resistance. To add insult to injury, the promise made at Medicine Lodge was not ratified until 1868 because Congress was busy trying to impeach President Johnson. Congress set aside no money for rations, leaving the communities promised annuities and goods on the brink of starvation. Kiowa leader Lone Wolf would later file suit against the federal government on the grounds that Congress violated the treaty provisions at Medicine Lodge.[40]

Farther north, a local Indian Agent sent Spotted Tail out in August 1867 to recruit his fellow Lakota leaders to meet with federal commissioners at Fort Laramie. He was given a wagon and ponies in exchange for his efforts.[41] Thanks to Spotted Tail, the Peace Commission held another major council with the Lakotas in the spring of 1868. Central to the Fort Laramie Treaty was a request for a right-of-way through Lakota Country for the Bozeman Trail. Lakota leader Red Cloud opposed the clause and spoke out directly against the proposed Bozeman Trail. "Great Father sends us presents and wants new road," he acknowledged, but pointed out that US Army officials had already entered the Powder River before negotiations were complete. "White chief," he concluded, "goes to steal road before Indian say yes or no!"[42] In the end, federal officials promised to remove its posts and military presence along the controversial Bozeman Trail in exchange for further land cessions and a right-of-way for a future railroad.[43]

In July 1868 another official allegedly headed out to negotiate with Native peoples. Grenville M. Dodge, one-time Army officer, private rail surveyor, and chief engineer for the Union Pacific, reported in his autobiography on a meeting with Bannock and Eastern Shoshone leaders at Fort Russell near present-day Cheyenne, Wyoming. According to Dodge—no stranger to hyperbole and outright dishonesty—documents were signed by both tribes, with Washakie of the Shoshone and others agreeing to settle on reservations. Dodge was also assured "protection of the railroad through their country." In exchange, he promised on behalf of the company that Washakie and his peoples "should be carried over our line free, whenever they desired to go." Dodge recalled that it was common to see freight cars filled with Indians traveling along the line.[44]

Dodge was not the only railroad agent bypassing government officials and allegedly making arrangements directly with tribes. In late summer 1867, a CP construction crew of Chinese laborers spotted a party of Paiutes approaching the tracks. The Paiutes opened fire, wounding one grader.[45] The unarmed laborers fled in terror. For the Paiutes, this attack was but one episode in a series of violence erupting north of the 42nd parallel. The Paiute War gripped northeastern Nevada, Oregon, Idaho, and California in the early 1860s.[46] Shortly after the incident, CP's cofounder and construction supervisor, Charles Crocker, allegedly traveled to the Basin to meet with the Paiute leader behind the attack. Calling himself a "big chief," Crocker brokered an agreement with the Paiutes, "with a great big railroad seal to stamp on it." A feast followed the signing.[47]

Little evidence remains of the Crocker meeting besides his own account, though CP founder Collis P. Huntington later recounted the story told by Crocker, adding that the arrangements with CP officials included free travel for the Indians. In these agreements—which they called treaties—Indigenous peoples were, according to Huntington, "given government passes to ride in first-class cars." Railroad operators in the area, he explained, were "to let the Indians ride and treat them well," adding that "we always let the Indians ride when they want to."[48] Free passage clauses would become a point of contention in later years, given that free travel made it easier for individuals to escape the confines of reservations.

In exchange for more goods and free transport, CP officials expected Paiutes to grant the construction crews and locomotives safe passage through their lands. Paiutes also allowed CP crews to take nearby timber for rail ties.[49] The CP crews would not arrive in Paiute lands in Nevada near the Truckee River until 1867, after which Paiutes immediately embraced the opportunity to obtain wage work as teamsters and tracklayers in the Humboldt Basin. Croker noted that Natives labored alongside white and Chinese tracklayers. "At the present time," the *San Francisco Chronicle* reported in 1868, "there are about ten thousand Chinamen, one thousand white men and 'any number' of Indians employed on the road."[50] Paiute women would also visit the construction camps and sell berries and other goods to the workers.[51]

These alleged agreements between railroad officials and Native peoples in the Great Basin, brokered entirely without federal government involvement, were illegal. Since the passage of the Trade and Intercourse Act in 1790, all commerce and diplomacy with Native nations was placed in the hands of the federal government, not private enterprise. While the arrangements Crocker made with Paiutes and others took on an official cast, similar, less formal agreements were made on the Union Pacific lines. W. B. Dodoridge, a telegraph operator for the UP, recalled that agreements with "friendly" Indians along the UP lines allowed them to use the trains for travel. "Without stint," Dodoridge stated, "the Indians availed themselves of the privilege. As a matter of fact, it spoiled them. They spend most of their time, weather permitting, on the train coming and going."[52] Restricted to the tops of train cars or on platforms, rail rides for many Native peoples were, in fact, dangerous journeys.[53]

If the accounts of Crocker, Dodge, and Huntington are accurate, then corporate arrangements were forged alongside or in partnership with nation-to-nation agreements. But the air of consensus and friendliness that may have briefly cloaked these agreements quickly dissipated. The uncertainties woven into the final documents, a chaotic state of affairs in the East following the war, and the growing frustrations of Lakota, Cheyennes, Arapahos, Kiowas, and others at the rapid influx of settlers, dwindling resources, and failures to provide promised annuities ensured that the Peace Commission's efforts at Fort Laramie and Medicine Lodge would break down. Within a year of Medicine Lodge, the Peace Commission abridged the treaty without Indigenous consent, barring Cheyennes, Arapahos, and others from leaving their reservations, and sanctioning the use of force, if necessary, to contain their movements.[54]

Off the Rails: Violence and the Pacific Railroad

In the summer of 1867, months before the grand council at Medicine Lodge, Porcupine, a Cheyenne warrior under the command of Turkey Leg, recalled a recent skirmish with US soldiers along the Arkansas River, south of the Union Pacific line. "The troops had defeated us," he explained, "and taken everything that we had, and had made us poor." To this material devastation, Porcupine added his frank assessment of the group's spirits: "we were feeling angry." Still licking their wounds, Porcupine and his comrades first witnessed a locomotive in motion near Plum Creek, Nebraska. They recalled that "it looked like a white man's pipe when he was smoking."[55] Not long after this encounter, Turkey Leg's band decided to attack the train. "In these wagons that go on the metal road," they concluded, "there must be things that are valuable—perhaps clothing." Red Wolf and Porcupine made the first attempt at derailing the iron beast by tying a large stick to the tracks. At first a human-powered handcar was ditched, later a steam-powered supply train. Only one railroad employee survived. The supply train held calico for the construction crews at the end of track. The Cheyenne party tied bolts of cloth to their horses' tails and celebrated their bounty. "Taking hold of the end of a bolt of calico or silk," George Bent (Cheyenne) recounted, "a young man would mount his pony and gallop widely across the prairie, the bolt of cloth bounding and leaping behind while unrolling in great billowy waves."[56] Others took the coals from the engine and scattered them in the remaining boxcars. As flames engulfed the wreckage, the Cheyennes under Turkey Leg and Spotted Wolf left with their plunder. Another iron horse, filled with US soldiers and Pawnee scouts, rolled up to the derailed cars. They immediately set out after the raiders. Reports stated that a Pawnee captive, Island Woman, was recovered in the ensuing fight.[57]

Porcupine, Turkey Leg, Red Wolf, and the other Cheyennes involved in the attack on the supply train were acutely aware of how their actions fit into a web of violence that gripped their homeland in the wake of US colonial expansion. Indigenous attitudes toward trunkline construction were forged within a colonial context defined by resource depopulation, disease, and dispossession. Over the course of the late 1840s and 1850s hundreds of thousands of settlers streamed into the West, many seeking fortune in the gold mines of California. In the 1860s still more flocked to Colorado gold mines. The influx of settlers would swell once again at the close of the Civil War, just as UP and CP construction crews broke ground.

On the Plains, the rapid decline of bison populations generated nothing less than an economic and ecological catastrophe for tribes dependent on the hoofed beasts for sustenance.[58] In response, Lakotas and Cheyennes adapted, conceding the 42nd parallel and removing north of the line to the Powder River and south between the Platte and Arkansas rivers.[59] Convening with peace commissioners along the North Plate during UP construction, a Lakota leader explained that there was "no objection to this road [the Union Pacific]," but that Lakotas objected to "those on the Powder River and Smoky Hill."[60] As a result, construction on the Southern Branch of the Union Pacific, which cut through prized Smoky Hill hunting grounds, was the site of far more Indian attacks.

The infrequent Indigenous attacks on UP construction lines were largely intended to gain resources and supplies in the face of declining resources and increasing encroachments of surveyors and settlers. Luther Standing Bear (Oglala Lakota), who would later spend considerable time on trains, recalled when his mother assisted in the derailment of a UP train. A returning war party stopped at a rail station for water. The rail agent sent them off without it. "They thought it was strange that white people should run a railroad across their land," Standing Bear explained, "and now would not even let them have a drink of water."[61] When the warriors reported their treatment at the station, a war party was dispatched to attack the line. Standing Bear's mother set out with an axe, following the party back to the tracks. There they tore up a line of rails and cut up the ties for use in their camp. The train crew spotted the Lakota party and set out on a locomotive after the Indians, firing in their direction. Unaware of the mangled track before

Figure 2.4 Theodore Kaufmann, *Westward the Star of Empire, Railway Attacked by Indians*, 1867. St. Louis Mercantile Library and the University of Missouri–St. Louis.

them, the crew kept the locomotive pressing forward, only to crash into the earth and derail. The Lakota party searched the wreckage and procured maple sugar, gingham, and beads. Standing Bear's mother made him a buffalo skin blanket with the beads found there.[62]

The attack at Plum Creek and Standing Bear's account are largely isolated events. For the majority of construction, rail crews remained unharmed. This reality, however, did not stop railroad officials from drumming up the threat of Indian violence and carting in US troops (Figure 2.4). Indeed, Grenville Dodge's UP crews arrived on the Plains armed to the teeth. This was no ordinary construction project. "From the beginning to the completion of the road," Dodge would later claim, "our success depended in a great measure on the cordial and active support of the army."[63] An Army official later reported that there were detachments of troops at every railway station between Fort Kearney in Nebraska and the newly established railroad town of Cheyenne on the Wyoming-Colorado border.[64]

The few direct attacks on the Union Pacific and Central Pacific had more to do with resource depopulation than an out and out rejection of the rail lines. Native nations encountering dwindling bison herds and reeling from disease and displacement looked to railroads to procure needed supplies.

The mules, horses, and oxen that comprised the construction outfit were clear targets for communities struggling to survive.[65] A UP construction boss later reported that one of the subcontractors working along the line lost twenty mules. "They were run off last night," he explained. "I fear the grading will be delayed if we do not have ample protection from the government."[66] UP livestock hauled all of the supplies for construction from established depots to the end of track. Supplies included rail ties, fastenings, fuel for locomotives and trains, and goods for men and animals working on the road. Dodge recalled that the wagon trains transporting these goods were gargantuan. "At one time," Dodge explained, "we were using at least 10,000 animals."[67] With roughly 8,000 to 10,00 laborers working on parts of the iron road at any given time, it was likely that beasts outnumbered human labor along the tracks. Over five hundred teams of men, with over a thousand men responsible for grading alone, worked to lay anywhere from three to ten miles of track a day.[68]

Despite overblown reports of Indian attacks coming from railroad officials like Dodge, Cheyennes, Shoshones, Lakotas, and others who claimed lands along the 42nd parallel largely left crews to their work. On the Plains, Cheyennes, Araphoes, and Lakotas had conceded the lands south of the Platte River and north of the Arkansas. When settlers and later railroad surveyors started to enter the lands north of the Platte and south of the Arkansas, they were often met with violent resistance. On the Great Basin, Shoshones, Utes, and Paiutes largely avoided the tracklayers, focusing their efforts on affairs outside the 42nd parallel. California Indians, meanwhile, directed their attention to resisting a genocidal state and protecting the livelihood of their kin and community. The lack of violence along that route can be attributed to Native people focusing their resistance campaigns and fights of survival elsewhere. As settlers, surveyors, miners, and other outsiders flooded into the region, contests over limited resources, paired with treaty vagaries and inter- and intra-tribal politics, set the stage for violence more broadly. The Great Sioux War (1862–1868), Paiute War (1860), and Black Hawk War (1865–1872) are just a few of the major contests that enveloped the region as tracklayers inched across it.

In May of 1869 the great race between the Central Pacific and Union Pacific came to a close at Promontory Summit, Utah. Andrew J. Russell, hired by the Union Pacific to take photographs along the construction lines, captured an image of the elaborate ceremony staged to commemorate the binding of the American nation. In the image (Figure 2.5), laborers and

Figure 2.5 Andrew J. Russell, *East and West Shaking Hands at Laying Last Rail*, 1869. Oakland Museum of California.

business leaders surround the two locomotives, facing one another at the point where the CP and UP tracks meet. The chief engineers of the Union Pacific and Central Pacific join hands in the center of the photo. Native Americans—whose land the road of steel and wood charged across—are nowhere to be seen. Yet, by the end of May, Indians would figure prominently in an adaptation of Russell's photo. Inspired by Russell's infamous handshake, *Frank Leslie's Illustrated Weekly* published an image of two locomotives, hands extending from their engines, prepared to embrace (Figure 2.6). Men perched atop the train cars cheer. In the foreground, Indian peoples bolt away on horse and foot. "Does Not SUCH a Meeting Make Amends?" the caption read. The query posed by the cartoon refers to amends between the competing railroad companies and recently warring US regions. Native peoples, it seemed, would have to flee the scene.

The handshake remained a powerful metaphor of reunion for a nation still reeling from civil war.[69] And yet, the images celebrating the completion of the first western trunkline railroad failed to consider the countless handshakes among Native peoples, and between Native nations, railroad agents,

Figure 2.6 "Does Not Such a Meeting Make Amends?" *Frank Leslie's Illustrated Newspaper*, May 29, 1869. Library of Congress.

and US officials, that shaped the course of colonization in the West. Numerous treaties, in their making and breaking, paved the way for an iron road through the center of the continent. The breakdown of these treaties set the stage for the eruption of violence not along the lines of the transcontinental, but elsewhere in the region. In the coming decades, the thousands of miles of road would help ignite another set of bloody confrontations known collectively as the Indian Wars.

For US officials, treaty-making emerged as a near-term solution to the "problem" of Indigenous occupancy that the railroad would permanently resolve. The principles of eminent domain lodged in these treaties ensured the taking of Indigenous land for "public" good. As the promises of peace at Little Arkansas, Medicine Lodge, and Fort Laramie dissolved, US Army officials, Indian Office administrators, and legislators settled for biding their time, waiting for the railroads to cart in soldiers and settlers to displace Indian peoples. General William T. Sherman, commanding General of the US Army after the Civil War, made this ambition plain in a letter to Dodge. "I regard this road of yours," Sherman explained, "as the solution of Indian affairs."[70] Senator William Stewart of Nevada echoed Sherman. The same year that the tracks met at Promontory, he states, "They [Indians] can only be conquered by railroads...the locomotive is the sole solution to the Indian question."[71]

In Indian Country, railroads would be met with a host of responses in the coming years as individuals and tribes took to the courts, to arms, and to travel to thwart the US settler colonial program. Take Spotted Tail: four years after his ride in a UP locomotive, he took several trains to Washington, DC. There he shook hands with officials including President Ulysses S. Grant and Commissioner of Indian Affairs Ely S. Parker (Seneca). In his meeting, Spotted Tail aired his grievances "in round terms." The United States had not kept its treaty promises with his people. Annuities had failed to arrive, and whites continued to encroach on Lakota lands in search of buffalo and gold.[72] Spotted Tail, along with Cherokees, Cheyennes, Crows, Pueblos, and other tribes, did not flee the scene. Instead, they found novel ways to protect their interests and effect change in a railroaded world.

The Iron Horse in Indian Country: Native Americans and Railroads in the US West. Alessandra La Rocca Link, Oxford University Press. DOI: 10.1093/9780197674437.003.0003

Railway Journeys

Iron Roads to Washington

In June 1872, an intertribal delegation of southwestern tribes, including O'odhams, Papagos, Hopis, and Apaches, arrived at a train station in Pueblo, Colorado. They marveled at the track that stretched out before them. The delegates inspected the recently laid rails before filing into a railcar. Like so many who first encountered a locomotive, they were awestruck and perhaps fearful. As the train jolted to a start, they crouched on the floor of the passenger car, hands covering their faces. After a few hours on the road, they settled into their seats for the long journey to Washington, DC.[1] In the capital, the delegates visited Congress, discussed new reservation lands with President Ulysses S. Grant, and toured the Armory and Navy Yard. Their eastern sojourn included stops in Philadelphia and New York. The party split on the return home, with one group traveling through California and the other through Colorado before arriving back in the Southwest.[2]

Steam-powered trains shocked and thrilled all those who encountered them for the first time. Yet many US Indian Agents hoped that the Indian experience with railroads, along with their exposure to the industrialized cities of the East, would do more than entertain. Nathan Bishop, a member of the Board of Indian Commissioners, reported in 1872 that "the visits of these Indians to Washington . . . destroy their overestimate [*sic*] of their power as tribes, and impress their minds with permanent convictions of their inferiority to whites in knowledge and power." Bishop concluded that inviting Indian delegations to Washington "has been one of the most effective peace measures which the government has ever adopted."[3] Visits to the heart of empire often included scheduled displays of US military strength, hence the 1872 delegation's visit to the Armory and Navy Yards.[4] The southwestern delegation also witnessed the US carceral program at work, touring Moyamensing Penitentiary in Philadelphia. A White Mountain Apache leader, Miguel, suggested that there might be an innocent inmate present and asked to meet with him. "If there is one I want to speak to him," he explained, "for I was once a prisoner and kept a whole year, in a prison like this, in Santa Fe. I was innocent of any crime."[5] These visits were undoubtedly meant to scare the delegations into submission by threatening violence and imprisonment.

Yet just as the United States was expanding its ability to immobilize large quantities of people, many were on the move. Post–Civil War America was defined by movement. Freed Blacks fled the South after the war; thousands made new homes in Kansas and elsewhere in the West.[6] Euro-Americans flocked westward seeking better economic prospects, while immigrants congregated in the nation's coastal cities. Indigenous peoples, too, continued long-standing migrations and visited new locales, often in passenger and freight cars. The movement of Cherokees, Crows, O'odhams, and others had undeniably political overtones. They defied a colonial program bent on the containment of Indigenous peoples. Native American travel was all the more political when the destination was Washington, DC, the seat of US colonial command. Writing in the early 1870s, Bishop could not predict that the number of Indigenous delegations to Washington would rise over the course of the decade and well into the next. Federal agents, to be sure, invited a fair number of Indigenous visitors to the capital city. But many others traveled without invitations to make their claims and air their grievances.

Miguel and his travel companions traveled freely thanks, in part, to a legal precedent set by another Indigenous delegation. In October 1868, Commissioner of Indian Affairs Nathanial G. Taylor notified Indian agents that Congress had not allocated funds for tribal delegations to Washington, DC, that year. Albert Wiley, the Sac and Fox agent, intended to enforce that policy, using extreme measures if needed. Moses Keokuk, the son of the prominent tribal leader Keokuk, had organized a group of men to visit Washington, DC, and meet with President Andrew Johnson. When Wiley tried to stop the delegation from leaving the reserve, Keokuk responded, "we will go where we please, when we please, independent of the commissioner or anybody else."[7]

Central Superintendent Thomas Murphy instructed Wiley to stop the delegation. Wiley then filed a complaint with the US Marshall, who promptly arrested Keokuk and his peers. In a Topeka court, the judge ruled against the Bureau because no law restricting the movement of Indians existed. The delegation went ahead with its trip to Washington, but not without first filing suit for damages and court costs against Wiley (Figure RJ 1.1).[8] The case eventually made it to the Kansas Supreme Court, which upheld the original verdict. Keokuk's attorney emphasized the basic human right to move freely.

> The defendant in error, although an Indian, a member of his tribe, born out of the limits of any of the States, not a citizen of or owing allegiance to the United States, is still a *man*, a member of a great family of nations, and entitled by the laws of nature, reason and humanity to go when and where he pleases.[9]

Keokuk's attorney stressed the significance of this case for the future of Indigenous mobility. "It involves the rights and liberty of more than a million of men," he exclaimed, "it involved a great constitutional question; an exercise of arbitrary power; a violation of our magna carta; an attempt to destroy the liberty of all of the domestic dependent Indian nations, with whom we are connected by treaty stipulations."[10] The verdict in *Wiley v. Keokuk* ensured that no Indian Agent could legally attempt to detain a peaceful delegation leaving a reservation. With a legal precedent in place, unauthorized and authorized Indigenous delegations continued taking iron roads to the heart of empire.

Many tribal delegations made arrangements through formal and informal channels for an audience with the president. Unauthorized delegations often received financial support from local white patrons, from their tribal funds, or by gathering monies from fellow tribal members. For example, in 1878, Sarah Winnemucca raised funds among the Paiutes for a trip to Washington, DC.[11] Five years later, Lakota leader Red Cloud raised $150 from his Oglala sympathizers for a visit. Fellow Lakota chief Spotted Tail also secured funds from supporters for his travels. When funding could not be provided from their peers, many delegations opted to travel to DC and appeal to Congress for funding after the fact.[12]

Unofficial visits to the capital city continued well into the late nineteenth and early twentieth centuries. In 1886, the Commissioner of Indian Affairs John Atkins issued a notice to agents. "The practice of Indians coming to this City," Atkins wrote, "without first obtaining the authority of this Department . . . must be discontinued."[13] Ten years later, Commissioner C. N. Bliss issued a similar circular. "This practice has become so prevalent," Bliss explained, "that the payment of expenses of

RJ 1.1 Moses Keokuk and his son Charles during an unofficial visit to Washington, DC, in 1868. Library of Congress, LOT 12894.

the delegation bears heavily up on the tribal funds, or is an injustice to the public if paid from government monies."[14]

For tribal communities, Native delegates seemed far more trustworthy than Indian agents when it came to making their case to US officials in DC. Many hoped that face-to-face conversations with the US president and other leaders might influence more favorable policy decisions. The iron roads to Washington provided an occasion to lodge complaints, push for legal clarification, request damages, and stake Indigenous claims in a modernizing world.[15]

The Iron Horse in Indian Country: Native Americans and Railroads in the US West. Alessandra La Rocca Link, Oxford University Press. DOI: 10.1093/9780197674437.003.0004

PART II

REVOLUTION, 1860–1890

Freedom is a precious possession. Restraint a bitter thing.

—Memoir of Edward Day Woodruff (1860)

I don't want any railroad here.

—Satanta (Kiowa), in Stanley, *My Early Travels and Adventures...* (1867)

Make your offer first and we will let you know.

—Red Cloud (Oglala Lakota), Proceedings of a Council at Rosebud Agency (1880)

3

The Twilight of Treaty-Making

> I wish to put it in a paper that the Osage country is a place for white people to come and steal.
>
> —Wah-she-sho-she (Osage)[1]

At the union of tracks, Central Pacific President Leland Stanford hoisted a maul on May 10, 1869, to place a final, golden spike into the West's first major trunk line railroad. Stanford missed his mark, but the force of his hit still tapped the telegraph wire linked to the rail, relaying in a single word the status of the project: "done."[2] The ceremony marked the end of one construction venture, but the sounds of hammers meeting iron, shovels scratching earth, and axes cracking wood would make for a jarring western chorus in the coming years (Figure 3.1). Decades later, Joseph Medicine Crow (Crow) recalled when the first locomotive arrived along the Big Horn River. "Something black, with round legs puffing smoke and pulling a box-like object behind it" cut through his homeland in the Valley of the Chieftains.[3] The iron horse described by Medicine Crow comprised a colossal, ever-shifting herd of horses, snorting steam and folding resources, goods, and peoples into growing networks of commerce and travel. Corporate intrusion into Indian Country quickly seeped into Indigenous homelands, drastically altering the contours of the West.

The railroading of western North America unfolded at an alarming pace, and with the construction crews came a new corporate order. Few companies possessed the kind of wealth or earned the disorienting mix of public awe and ire that railway companies would in the second half of the nineteenth century. In the midst of such profound change, Indians and non-Indians began asking questions: questions about the role of private enterprise in land distribution and settlement regimes; questions about the relationship between government and industry; and questions about what responsibilities corporations had to serve the public good. Railroad corporations' reach was extensive and growing.[4]

Figure 3.1 Northern Pacific Expedition at Camp Cook, 1869. Northern Pacific Railroad Collections, Minnesota Historical Society.

With an insatiable demand for land and resources, railroad barons—with their attending armies of construction workers, lobbyists, and attorneys—found themselves involved in the messy business of US settler colonization. Even as the Indian Office attempted to contain and isolate Indigenous peoples on remote reservations separated from American industrial, social, and cultural life, locomotives chortled alongside or over Indian lands, presenting both opportunities to enter established networks and obstacles to maintaining tribal autonomy. In 1870 Commissioner of Indian Affairs Ely S. Parker (Seneca) felt the tremors of corporate intrusion and warned of its impact. Less than a year after the golden spike sliced through a tie of polished California laurel, Parker acknowledged that efforts to build other trunk lines north and south of the Union Pacific would "of necessity, pass through immense tracts of Indians' country." "The rapid construction of railroads brushing into every section of the country," he added, "is a matter of serious import to Indians generally."[5]

Containment and concentration of Indigenous peoples onto newly formed reservations was central to the land seizures required for both railroad development and expansion of the US settler state. Commissioner of Indian Affairs

George Manypenny, at the conclusion of the Central Plains treaties in the 1850s, reported to his superiors that "there is, in my judgment, but one plan by which [the Indians] can be saved from dire calamities." "That is," he concluded, "to colonize them in suitable locations, limited in extent, and distant as possible from white settlements."[6] The Secretary of the Interior echoed the sentiment nine years later, on the eve of transcontinental construction. "The only plan that holds out any hope," Secretary Jacob Thompson wrote, "is to confine them to small tribal reservations, having well-defined exterior boundaries."[7] In the same year the first transcontinental was completed, the Commissioner of Indian Affairs beseeched President Ulysses S. Grant for funds supporting "the settlement of all the tribes, when practicable, upon tracts of land to be set apart for their use and occupancy."[8] The Secretary of War made it clear that a "double policy" of "peace within their reservations" and "war without...would soon...bring matters to a determination."[9]

The locomotive proved to be the literal engine by which this postwar Indian policy traveled westward. In the wake of the Civil War, railroads transported US soldiers west to violently displace Nez Percés, Navajos, Arapahos, and others from their ancestral homelands and, in many instances, relocate them to plots of land far from their homes.[10] What soldiers could not complete with firearms and cannons, religious reformers executed with Bibles and plows. As construction on the Union Pacific drew to a close, President Grant declared a swift change in US relations with Native nations. His "peace policy" called for the removal of corrupt Indian agents and their replacement with Christian missionaries. Religious reformers traveled across the American West to educate Natives on the art of "civilized" living. Baptists spread out along the Union Pacific line, where "mission stations" appeared overnight to address "numbers of stray bands of Indians along that railroad."[11] In the minds of President Grant and others, the railroad carried these great civilizing forces westward.

The physical containment of Indigenous peoples facilitated by trains is an established part of the history of the nineteenth-century West. Lesser known, however, are two related developments: the impact of railroads, specifically railroad corporations, on the legal and economic containment of Indians in the second half of the nineteenth century; and the impact that railroad expansion had on the reorganization of the US state. After the Civil War, the Indian Office, an administrative arm of the federal state headed by the Commissioner of Indian Affairs and under the direction of the Secretary of the Interior, set policy. Within a few years, however,

Congress would claim increasing control over Indian policy, specifically after the end of the federal treaty-making relationship with tribes in 1871. This chapter examines how a treaty forged in Osage County laid the groundwork for this reorganization in Indian policy-making.

Railroad expansion into Indian Country also hastened the bureaucratization of the Indian Service. Indeed, the administrative power of the federal government grew significantly during the same years that railroads expanded across the region, which created tensions between the legislative and executive branches when it came to Indian policy. By 1885 the commissioner of Indian Affairs was so inundated with paperwork that he requested additional funds to hire an assistant commissioner to help him handle it. "The amount and variety of business detail daily passing through the office," the commissioner complained to the congressmen who exercised the power of the purse in the US system, "is so great as to render a personal examination of any one man of the clerical work connected with its [*sic*] physical impossibility."[12]

Questions about the proper administration of Native peoples, especially Native lands, also created tensions between the government and railroad corporations. For all the talk of railroads as agents of US empire, it is easy to overlook when corporate interests diverged from state interests. In the American West, railroad companies depended on the sale of Indigenous territory and "public" lands for their construction capital. The government viewed railroads as an arm attached to a larger body of settlement schemes in the West, schemes that relied on the mass movement of hundreds of thousands of newcomers to the region. By granting large tracts of land to railroads, government officials risked creating situations where settlers could not afford the prices that corporations demanded for land. The territorial and state governments these settlers formed often protested what they viewed as federal government largesse to corporations. It is not surprising, then, that the relationship between the US government, Euro American settlers, and railway corporations could vary dramatically depending on the circumstances. While all three parties promoted western expansion and the dispossession of Indigenous peoples, their collective appetite for Indigenous homelands and resources occasionally put them at odds.[13] Nowhere were these tensions more apparent than in the Kansas lands of Osage Country, where they led to the dissolution of US government's treaty-making relationship with Native nations in 1871.[14]

Protests came not only from settlers and the territorial governments that represented their interests. The principles of eminent domain continued to animate legal debates about Indigenous land-taking, but the government was still required to provide "just compensation" for seized lands and make some semblance of a claim for the road's public good. The second task was pro forma. The "just compensation" portion, however, required the support and commitment of tribal leaders. The heated negotiations between Osage leaders and state, federal, and corporate officials make clear that land seizures would come at a cost. When possible, Indigenous leaders such as White Hair and Hard Rope worked to carve out future possibilities within present difficulties.

* * *

In February 1866, an Osage headman named White Hair returned to his people's "Diminished Reserve"—a strip of four million acres wedged between Indian Territory and Kansas—and witnessed a disturbing scene. The village he had left along the Verdigris River earlier that winter now housed strangers. Stumps dotted former woodland areas, lodges lay in ruins, and cattle and other livestock roamed the precious grasslands. Instead of their homes, White Hair and his band found new dwellings.[15] After an unsuccessful winter hunt, they realized that all their hopes for cultivating the necessary foodstuffs from their lands were lost. In response, White Hair condemned the invaders and notified the local Indian Agent, George Snow, that the settlers must depart or violence would ensue. Snow forwarded the communication to Washington, but officials there turned a blind eye.[16]

The illegal settlement on White Hair's village was part of the movement of thousands of Euro Americans onto Indigenous homelands in the American West after the Civil War. More than 1,500 squatters tilled soil and erected homes on the Diminished Reserve in 1865 alone. That number swelled to 18,000 just three years later.[17]

In the face of this land rush, the Osages weighed their options. Little Bear, for his part, requested that a tribal delegation travel to Washington, DC, in the fall of 1867 to negotiate for the sale of his people's Diminished Reserve lands. He hoped that in Indian Territory Osages would find respite from Kansas land-grabbers. By late fall, no formal delegation to Washington had been organized. The regional superintendent of Indian Affairs, meanwhile, reported that various non-Indian settlements had already been established on the reserve, and "nothing will keep them off except [if] a military force is constantly stationed there." According to Agent Snow's reports, the Kansas State Attorney General had sent the intruders arms and ammunition.[18] "Something must be done to stop this movement," Snow beseeched his superiors, "their women and children will be driven from their camps before they [members of the still hypothetical Osage delegation] return from Washington."[19] By the spring of 1868, federal troops had arrived to protect Osage lands.[20] They stood as physical reminders that the Osage Diminished Reserve was not subject to pre-emption laws and not public domain grist for the settlers' mill.

The state of Kansas had already been making preparations for rail routes that could connect the Union Pacific, Eastern Division (later Kansas Pacific Railway) depots in Lawrence and Leavenworth to a Gulf of Mexico port city (Figure 3.2). Kansas officials believed that, with service to St. Louis and Galveston, Kansas would be well-poised to ship goods both within the United States and abroad. In 1859 the Leavenworth, Lawrence, and Fort Gibson Railroad company was chartered for this purpose. By 1866 the company, renamed the Lawrence, Leavenworth, and Galveston (LL & G), secured capital support from William Sturges, a Chicago capitalist, and received one-quarter of a 500,000-acre land grant provided to the state for internal improvements.[21] Animating the land grant was the principle of eminent

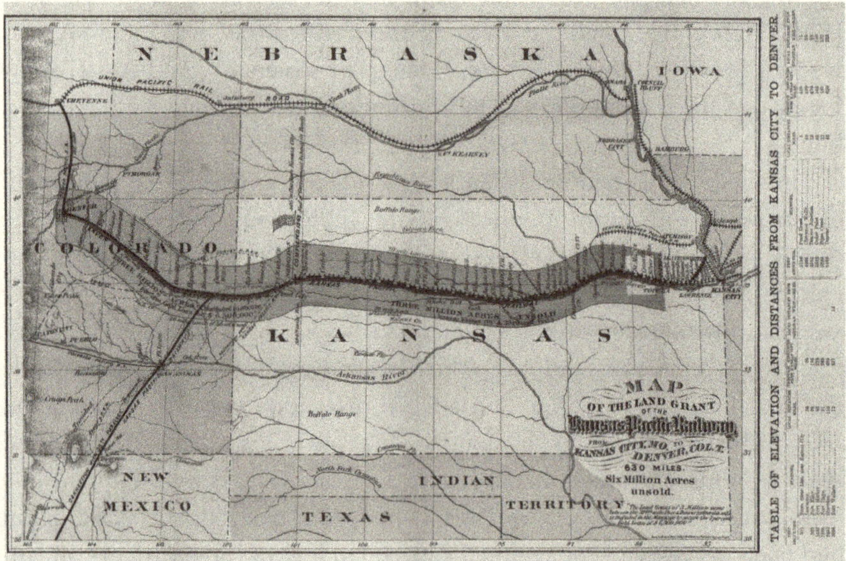

Figure 3.2 This map marks railroad land grants cutting across buffalo rangeland on the Central Plains.

Map of the Land Grant of the Kansas Pacific Railway, from Kansas City, MO, to Denver, CO, 1869. Special Collections and University Archives. Wichita State University Libraries.

domain: land cessions for public good. While the residents of Lawrence and Leavenworth threw their resources into the LL & G, Kansas City capitalists created a rival company, the Missouri River, Fort Scott, and Gulf Railroad, which also sought to connect Kansas to the Gulf.[22]

Kansas officials, land-hungry settlers, and federal agents remained hopeful that the removal of Osages to Indian Territory was imminent, but it was not a simple affair. Agent Snow appealed to the Osages to meet with government officials and make arrangements for their move. White Hair refused initial entreaties by Snow to hold a council on Osage lands. He responded to the request for a meeting by declaring simply that "he had no land to sell." Snow's effort to send a delegation to Washington, DC, also fell through after it became clear that the delegation would have to pay its own way until Congress met to allocate the necessary funds.[23] But the Osage presence in the Diminished Reserve became all the more precarious that spring when Cheyennes and Arapahos initiated raids against Osage villages.[24] War with Cheyennes and Arapahos, paired with an intransigent squatter population, left the Osages in dire straits. By May 1868—one year before the completion of the transcontinental railroad in Promontory, Utah Territory—White Hair and other Osage leaders agreed to Snow's request for a council, which met at the confluence of Drum Creek and the Verdigris River.[25]

Railroad agents from the rival companies joined the deliberations. Charles W. Blair from the Missouri, Fort Scott, and Santa Fe Railroad Company, and William Sturges, president of the LL & G, were active participants in the negotiations. Both company officials requested grants of lands from US government representatives for their companies, which provided transportation south to Indian Territory. Blair's requests made it into the official correspondence and records of the treaty negotiations. Sturges's role in the meeting is lost to history, but his presence there was undoubtedly bound up in the treaty.[26]

On May 27, 1868, Osage leaders—including White Hair—emerged from a series of councils to sign what was later known as the Sturges Treaty.[27] The Osages agreed to sell to the LL & G roughly 8 million acres of their trust and diminished reserve lands for 19 cents an acre, totaling $1,600,000. The terms set out at Drum Creek required the company to deposit $100,000 in cash with the US government in trust for the Osages within three months of ratification. The remaining balance would be paid in annual installments of railroad bonds at five percent interest.[28] According to the final treaty documents, the Osages wanted the railroad to extend into Indian Territory because "it being the only road now in process of construction running directly through the said territory...it will give them in their new home the means of transit and transportation."[29]

The decision to sign the treaty was at odds with the initial sentiments expressed by Osage leaders during earlier council meetings. At these gatherings their concerns were quite clear: former treaty stipulations needed to be upheld before they were willing to sign a new compact, and they deserved reparations for the damage caused by the intruders. Hard Rope made the case succinctly. "In the last six years we have treated away the Neosho country," he complained. "We are here looking for the pay for that land."[30]

What, then, convinced these Indigenous leaders to sign? Some reports say that the Osages revised their stance after a murder during the negotiations at Drum Creek. According to an account written by Father John Schoenmaker, a Jesuit living among the Indians, an Osage party murdered two white settlers at Walnut Creek. The brother of one of the slain men testified before the council. Commissioner of Indian Affairs N. G. Taylor then used the opportunity to threaten the Osages, claiming that they would be imprisoned if they did not sign the treaty. According to another Jesuit account, the alleged murders led to concerns among the Osage that agitated and armed settlers would seek revenge. Osage leaders, fearing settler retaliation, elected to establish a buffer between their new lands in Indian Territory and aggrieved settlers by ensuring that their reserve went to a corporation.[31]

The motives behind the Osage decision to sell lands directly to a corporation remain murky. The role of Sturges in assuring that the Missouri, Fort Scott, and Galveston Railroad Company would not be favored—in spite of offering a higher price and the option for settlers to occupy most of the lands—is unclear. However, the Osages' dealings with Sturges bore markers of past negotiations between Native peoples and Grenville M. Dodge, Isaac Stevens, and other agents of empire who often served both national and corporate interests. Yet on the shores of Drum Creek in 1868, corporate and national interests diverged, inciting a fierce debate in Congress that shaped conversations about the federal government's treaty-making relationship with Indians. Between 1868 and 1871, several critical changes in Indian policy and law took place, the most significant being the decision to abolish treaty-making.

The ink had hardly dried on the Sturges papers when Rep. Sidney Clarke of Kansas and fellow pro-settler leaders in the US House of Representatives condemned it. In June 1868 the House opposed the ratification of the Sturges Treaty and promised to withhold appropriations if the Senate approved it.[32] It became a flashpoint in the ongoing debates about the form and function of the nation's western settlement regime. Clarke led the charge against the treaty, out of concern for "the protection of settlers upon that portion of the ceded lands." Under the current provisions, the settlers, he explained, are "to be dealt with according to the mercy or cupidity of the parties controlling said railway."[33] For Clarke, this act was "one of the most remarkable transactions that has ever occurred in the whole history of this Government."[34] There was speculation that LL & G would enter the land business and, according to Clark, "would readily sell to actual settlers at or more than $1.25 per acre."[35] This prospect, for Clarke and other congressional leaders, would be a gross injustice to Kansas settlers and a violation of the federal government's responsibilities to oversee the dispensation of public lands. Clarke added that another corporation, the Missouri, Fort Scott, and Santa Fe Railway, had made an offer that would have been more lucrative for all parties involved: payment of $2,000,000 instead $1,600,000, with provisions allowing squatters to stay on the land and allocating additional acreage to the state of Kansas for public schools.[36]

What went unsaid in their calls for the protection of slighted settlers was the congressmen's concerns about losing critical funds from railroad corporations. The 1860s marked the beginning of long-standing "friendships" between congressional officials and railroad agents whereby officials managed the politicians through bribery. The Sturges Treaty threatened to undermine this practice. It is no surprise, then, that Congress's rejection of the Sturges affair was swift and unwavering since the treaty promised to cut out the congressional "middleman" and the corporate bribes that powered them.[37]

In an effort to maintain control over western settlement and continue their corporate bribery scheme, Clarke and his comrades homed in on the major legal question attached to the treaty: Did the railway company have a right to receive title to the lands directly from the Osage? The Supreme Court decision in *Johnson v. M'Intosh* (1823) made it clear that the US government owned the exclusive right to acquire Indigenous lands. Before the Civil War, most lands ceded by Native Americans entered the US public domain almost immediately. After the war, the Indian Office began arbitrating the sale of Indian lands to individuals and corporations. Once a sale was made, the Office placed the monies in a trust for tribal use. Yet Congress began to question the authority of the Indian Office to dispense with so much domain.[38]

Congressman William Lawrence from Ohio made the legal case for the Clarke encampment. Lawrence first pointed to the congressional acts establishing Kansas Territory, whereby "settlers were by law invited to occupy these lands and granted the privilege of acquiring titles."[39] Allowing a railroad corporation to oversee the acquisition of titles violated public land laws granting the federal government chief powers over the distribution of public lands. For Lawrence, the question of whether or not the lands were public was clear. Lawrence held that the Osage did not, in fact, hold the title to the lands, but instead possessed merely a "right to occupancy," another key interpretation from the *Johnson v. M'Intosh* decision.[40] The central question of the *M'Intosh* case was whether or not Native Americans could sell their lands to private parties. The Supreme Court unanimously ruled in the negative, with Chief Justice John Marshall outlining the legal reasoning that framed future debates in Congress and in court regarding Indigenous landownership and exchange.[41] According to Marshall, Native Americans "were admitted to be the rightful occupants of the soil, with a legal as well as just claim to retain possession of it, and to use it according to their own discretion."[42] But their rights stopped there. The right to occupancy, in the Court's opinion, did not include the right to dispose of the lands without US federal involvement.

While treaties—presidentially directed and Senate ratified documents—outlined the nature of relations between Native Nations and the federal government, the Commerce Clause of the Constitution stated that Congress retained control and oversight over commercial relations between American citizens and Native peoples.[43] In the Sturges Treaty debates, Lawrence made clear that federal authority to control land transactions rested primarily with Congress, lending his voice to the chorus of government officials who advocated for the end of treaty-making and the growing influence of Congress in Indian affairs.[44]

Rep. Clarke echoed Lawrence in his insistence that railroad companies could not oversee the settlement of Indian lands. The executive branch and Indian Office had mismanaged the treaty process by allowing railroad companies influence on the process of land seizure. The Sturges Treaty, Clarke concluded, "is in violation of the rights of the settlers and of justice to the Indians" and was "unjust to the taxpayers of Kansas, because it places [in] the power of a corporation the means to prevent the speedy settlement of about one sixth of the State." Clarke, along with other Kansas officials, submitted a resolution. "The whole system of permitting or encouraging Indians to cede to private corporations is pernicious," they explained, adding that "in extinguishing Indian titles the government should become the purchaser."[45]

Settlers, Kansas politicians, Clarke, and other members of Congress voiced additional complaints. Some charged that land-hungry settlers coerced the Osage into signing the treaty against their will. Others pointed to the growing sentiment in Congress to stop granting lands to railroad corporations and offer rights-of-way instead.[46] Still other treaty detractors laid out the financial missteps of the treaty, arguing that no tribe in Indian Territory would accept railroad bonds as payment for a new Osage reservation, which is how the Osages intended to pay for new reserve lands to the south.[47]

Local business snafus also ensured that opposition was set against Sturges. In Kansas, public enthusiasm for the LL & G president soured in the midst of the Osage treaty. A dispute between Sturges—a Chicago financier—and local politicians erupted when Lawrence officials refused to grant the LL & G county bonds until the company met several requirements, including obtaining land for a depot in Lawrence and constructing a bridge over the Kansas River. Other locals likely suspected that his interest in the Osage dealings were less about building and supporting the railroad than securing and re-selling Indian lands.[48] Given that several Kansans sat on the LL & G Board of Directors, they were able to ensure that the bonds did not arrive until a deal was agreed to. This local resentment only fueled congressional opposition to Sturges.[49]

The particulars of the Sturges case fanned the flames of public outrage against treaties. "Indian agencies and commissions for making treaties," intoned *Frank Leslie's Illustrated Weekly* in 1869, "have been considered rich 'placers' by greedy corporations and rascally politicians." "The great object now," the weekly concluded, "is to reform our policy."[50] Calls for reform also emanated from the White House, where President Ulysses S. Grant laid out his plan for a "peace policy" with Native Americans. Grant's policy centered on placing religious leaders and organizations in charge of the administration of Indian Affairs and establishing a peace commission that could ensure diplomatic relations in the West and the confinement of Indians on reservations. This utopian vision for a peaceful colonization policy unraveled and violence persisted throughout the 1870s and 1880s.

In February 1869, President Grant, on the advice of Secretary of the Interior Jacob Cox, withdrew the Sturges Treaty from congressional consideration.[51] More than a year passed before a new treaty would be signed and ratified removing the Osages to Indian Territory. At the council meeting determining whether the Osages would accept the new treaty, Osage leaders voiced their complaints bluntly. "The white man has taken our timber and our land," Joseph Paw-ne-no-pa-she (Figure 3.3) stated; "I think we ought to have received something for this."[52] Little Chief joined the chorus, stating that once the Osages settled in Indian Territory they would take measures to protect their territorial independence. "When we go to our new homes," he declared to the Indian Agent, "we intend to make laws... and will call it trespassing to kill our buffalo and other game."[53] "Nothing is more dear than land. Off the land we get our living," Wautanka, from Black Dog's band, concluded: "We can't eat money."[54]

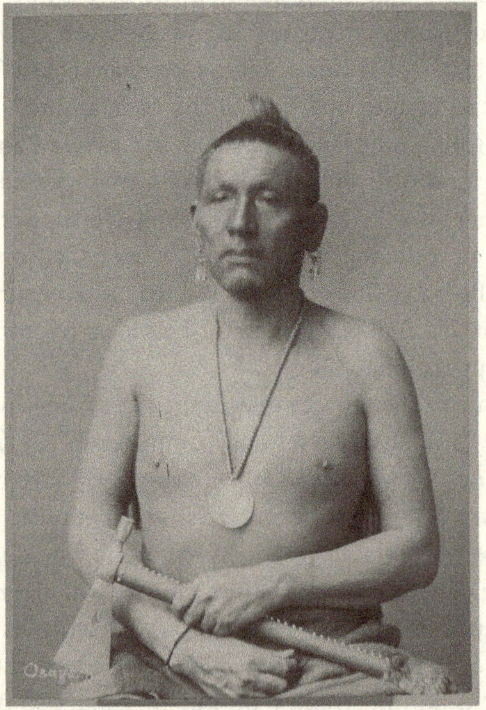

Figure 3.3 Joseph, Not Afraid of the Pawnees, Governor of All His Tribe, 1868. Amon Carter Museum of American Art. Fort Worth, Texas.

In Washington, anger over the Sturges affair drove growing congressional opposition to the executive branch's control of treaty-making. The Board of Indian Commissioners, a body of religious reformers authorized by Congress to work with the Secretary of the Interior to disburse Indian appropriations and direct policy, condemned the treaty-making policy in their first annual report, the same year the Sturges Treaty died in Congress. According to the board, treaty-making "creates the fiction" that Indians have the right to negotiate land claims. The United States promotes "the preposterous idea that they [Indians] are owners in fee of the fabulous tracts of country over which their nomadic habits have led them or their ancestors to roam."[55]

While many scholars have attributed the move away from treaty-making to Reconstruction tensions between President Johnson and Congress, few have considered how ongoing questions about the role of corporations in the settlement project influenced the rejection of treaties and the subsequent ascendency of Congress's role in Indian policy.[56] For several House members, the treaty was the vehicle through which Indian lands could unlawfully skirt public domain legislation. It also threatened the widening web of "friendships" between railroad officials and congressmen. To protect settlers and corporate-Congress corruption, US officials needed to secure congressional control over Indigenous dispossession. When the 1869 Indian Appropriations Bill was brought to the House floor, Representative Clarke again led the charge, this time by adding a provision to dissolve treaty relations with Indians. A measure stating that any agreement or contract made required congressional approval effectively stripped treaty-making authority from the executive branch. In 1871, the Indian Department Appropriation Act included a provision formally abolishing the treaty-making process.[57] It was a decision that reflected congressional concern about losing both control of the settlement project and critical corporate-state partnerships. Representative William Armstrong of Pennsylvania summarized the new status of Indian peoples succinctly in the wake of these decisions: "Our dealings with them will be as mere domestic communities, with whom we may contract, but only with the approval of Congress."[58] Rep. Lawrence, who cut his teeth opposing the treaty process during the Sturges debates, concluded that "hereafter the land policy of Congress cannot be broken up and destroyed by Indian treaties," adding that the bill will protect Native peoples "from spoliation and robbery."[59] But congressmen had been acceding to the "spoliation and robbery" of corporate lobbyists for some time, and the ending of treaty relations with Native nations ensured that the corrupt dealings between railroad companies and elected officials would continue well into the future.

Congressmen interested in limiting executive branch control over Indigenous dispossession used the Sturges Treaty to drum up threats of a corporate takeover of Indian policy. In truth, Indigenous dispossession from both US government and corporate perspectives followed familiar models. The basic model for settler colonial expansion in the United States rests on the Land Ordinance of 1785 and the Northwest Ordinance of 1787. The former produced the grid model of land survey and seizure, while the latter provided a pathway for colonies to become territories and, ultimately, states of the newly formed union. A sizable settler population—60,000 settlers, to be precise—ensured that lands transitioned from dependent colonies administered by Congress to self-governing states. For a state to leave territorial status, it needed settlers and thus land distribution. Railroad colonization followed a strikingly similar model: locomotives required land and settlement to produce necessary capital; the land came through eminent domain-like seizures; that land, too, required Indian containment and concentration. As with the Union Pacific and Central Pacific construction, the colonial model had shifted to add an important twist: land was converted from Indian to public to corporate—a form of private—ownership, though it remained a form of capital until converted to cash through sales to settlers.

The end of treaty-making reflected congressional efforts to ensure control over these twin processes of Indigenous dispossession. Initial tensions between corporate officials, settlers, and government agents in the making and unmaking of the Sturges Treaty soon eased. The Sturges Treaty may have laid bare the problems inherent in parsing out of roles, responsibilities, and rights in the land-grabbing project of postwar expansion, but in other instances all three forces—settlers, corporations, and the federal government—worked in concert to terribly destructive ends.

The Iron Horse in Indian Country: Native Americans and Railroads in the US West. Alessandra La Rocca Link, Oxford University Press. © Alessandra La Rocca Link 2025. DOI: 10.1093/9780197674437.003.0005

4

Negotiating the Rush

> For God's sake, when we bought this country, we did not buy white man [*sic*] with it.
>
> —Principal Chief of the Choctaw Nation, Coleman Cole, *Indian Journal* (1878)

> I am not willing that this Territory shall lie in the way of public improvements.
>
> —Senator Aaron H. Cragin, *The Congressional Globe* (1866)

A year before the dissolution of treaty-making between Native American tribes and the federal government, Cherokee leaders—including Chief Lewis Downing and William P. Adair—laid out a vision for a different kind of railroaded future:

> The Cherokees wish to build and own, but such company of Cherokee citizens as shall be organized under the authority of the Cherokee National Council, the railroad crossing their own lands, meeting and connecting with such as approach their border.... They know that to have the road completed through their country owned by capitalists who are strange to them, who will only look upon their nationality as an encumbrance, and, perhaps, their presence, in any form as a nuisance, would result in the loss of their lands and the desecration of their people.[1]

Downing and Adair penned the petition in response to a punitive 1866 treaty foisted upon the Cherokee Nation following the Civil War that included provisions for north-south and east-west railroads running through Indian Territory. No strangers to US government, settler, and corporate incursions onto their lands, Cherokee leaders acted swiftly to build an alternative model for railroad construction through their lands. When their efforts to take charge of the corporate model failed, they turned to US courts for redress.

Viewed in isolation, the Cherokees' petition could be read as a futile attempt to roll back the great settler-colonial machine that threatened the Indigenous peoples of the West after the Civil War. In the later decades of the nineteenth century, Cherokees and other Indian Territory residents confronted white settlement, corporate encroachment, and federal assimilation policies.[2] For many Indigenous peoples, the funneled chimney piercing eastern horizons represented these three forces bound into a singular, steam-powered juggernaut. The Cherokees, according to one Indian Agent, considered locomotives "the introducers of calamities rather than blessings."[3] And in postwar Indian Territory, calamities they would bring.

With a pro-railroad Congress making major Indian policy decisions, it is no surprise that construction schemes sprouted up with alarming regularity. Indian Territory was free of railway lines during the Civil War, but by 1880 more than 300 routes traversed its plains and woodlands. A rush of building left the region with a total of 1,200 miles of iron paths by the time Indian Territory became Oklahoma Territory in 1890.[4]

The extensive rail network threaded in and out of diverse congregations of Indigenous peoples, many still reeling after forced removal from ancestral homelands and the ravages of the Civil War. The United States removed over sixty-seven tribes to Indian Territory over the course of the nineteenth century.[5] In the 1870s and 1880s, it was here that several iron horses and their corporate lords vied for lands and resources. The central questions about corporate rights and Indigenous sovereignty in Indian Territory reverberated throughout the region. They informed both the claims of corporate and government agents and the efforts of Indigenous communities to negotiate and resist railway expansion across the West. Differing opinions about how to manage railway expansion often fractured Indigenous communities. But the very same challenges also led to intertribal alliances and a multiplicity of resistance efforts that came to characterize important cultural and political activities in the late nineteenth and early twentieth centuries. The petition, then, was one move in a suite of resistance tactics Native communities used to protect their communities in the midst of sweeping and often devastating change.

In the West more broadly, the completion of one transcontinental line prompted Euro-Americans to turn their attention to other transcontinental and branch lines that would stitch disparate parts of the new union together. In 1860, 30,000 miles of railroad track snaked across the United States. By 1890 that number swelled to 160,000 miles, much of it in the

Trans-Mississippi West. To finance construction, the US government handed railroad companies land amounting to the size of small countries. By the 1930s the United States had given corporations over 130 million acres.[6] Within one generation, the Trans-Mississippi West transformed from a land of dirt—and water—ways to a railroaded region, enabling an unprecedented circulation of goods and peoples. Residents of the West had become people of the railroad by the close of the nineteenth century.

One hundred and sixty thousand miles. One hundred and thirty million acres. These figures are so breathtakingly large it is difficult to make sense of the consequences for Indigenous peoples. As laborers beat tie after tie into the earth, Indians across the region mobilized to protect their kin and community from corporate and US rapacity. The trickle had turned into a torrent—one that Native peoples across the West negotiated with varying degrees of success. This chapter explores how Indigenous peoples negotiated these transformations, and maps out the ways in which the United States, allied with railroad corporations, sought to seize Indigenous lands for "public" good.

Railroading Indian Territory

In July 1877, Choctaw Principal Chief Coleman Cole (Figure 4.1) penned a letter to President Grant. The elderly Cole was familiar with the process of negotiating claims with US government agents, having first petitioned the US Court of Claims on behalf of his grandmother, Shumaka, in 1838. Cole argued that his grandmother owned a section of Mississippi land that whites had since occupied. He would go on to take testimony from other Choctaws who resided in Mississippi in the hopes that his people could remain on their ancestral homelands. After the death of his grandmother in 1845, Cole left Mississippi, his hopes dashed.[7]

Soon thereafter the US government ordered all Mississippi Choctaws to Indian Territory and withheld payment for Choctaw Mississippi lands—Cole's included—until the relocation was complete. Not one to idle for long, Cole set to work establishing another court of claims in the foreign lands of Indian Territory. He was instrumental in establishing the institution that held the US government accountable to monies owed the Choctaws from the sale of their lands during and after removal.[8] In this capacity Cole had previously written to Grant, enclosing the Choctaw membership rolls

Figure 4.1 Coleman Cole, Principal Governor, Choctaw Nation, 1874–1878. Oklahoma Native American Photograph Collection. Gilcrease Museum, Tulsa, Oklahoma.

and requesting that soldiers accompany the remaining federal funds owed from the "sale" of their southeastern lands to Choctaws to Indian Territory.[9]

Cole's 1877 letter to the president dealt with an ongoing legal battle between the Choctaw Nation and the Missouri, Kansas, and Texas (MKT) railroad. The railway company, Cole declared, "will not scruple to throw every obstacle they possibly can in our way and deprive our claims if they can of as many of their merits as possible." He took the opportunity to remind the president that the Choctaws' legal arguments were based on "the laws and the treaties."[10] Indeed, Cole dedicated his tenure as principal chief of the Choctaw Nation (1874–1878) to the defense of "the laws and the treaties" that governed Choctaw land ownership and political sovereignty.

Cole was specifically referring to the Reconstruction treaties that structured US relations with the Choctaws and other southern tribes following the Civil War. In 1866 the Five Tribes (Cherokees, Choctaws, Chickasaws, Creeks, and Seminoles) met with a government commission at Fort Smith in

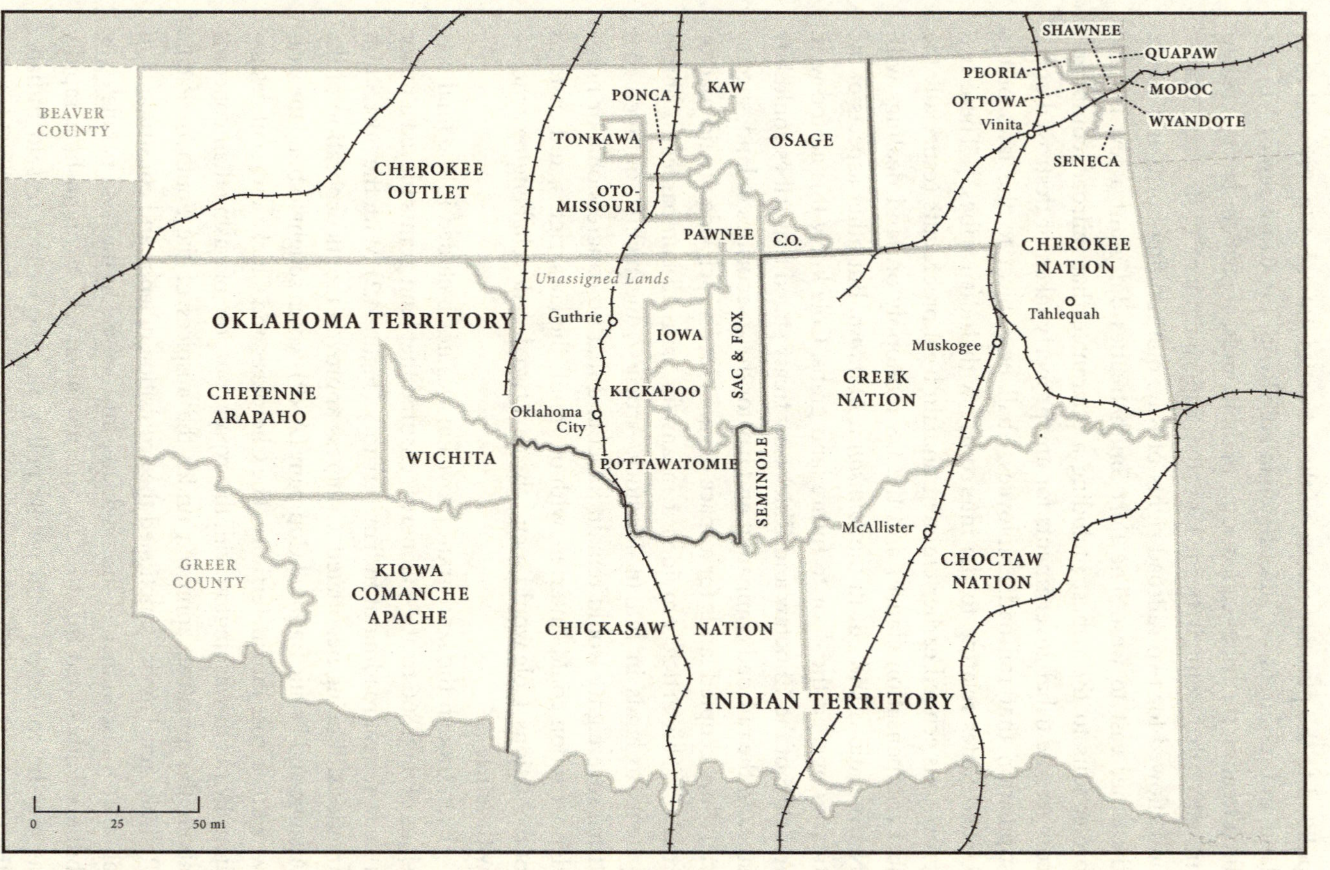

Figure 4.2 Map of railroads through Indian Territory, 1890. Erin Greb Cartography.

northwestern Arkansas to sign treaties of peace. Historians have rightly pointed to the punitive nature of these treaties, intended to strip tribes of land and resources because they had allied with the Confederacy.[11] In the final treaties, the tribes ceded some of their lands, abolished slavery, created an intertribal council headed by the Superintendent of Indian Affairs, and allowed for two railroad rights-of-way: one running north and south, the other east to west. The Fort Smith treaties did grant a few notable protections to the tribes, including a guarantee that railroad companies compensate tribal governments for any property taken or destroyed and a stipulation that railroad employees "shall be subject to the laws of the United States relating to the intercourse with Indian tribes."[12] These two provisions echoed earlier eminent domain legal precedents (especially the just compensation clause) and the US monopoly on land dealings with Native nations laid out in the *Johnson v. M'Intosh*. But other aspects of the treaties opened the door to future land grabs. Cole knew this all too well. Article 6 of the Choctaw and Chickasaw treaty stated that tribes could buy stock in the railroad companies and pay for these securities in land, specifically "unoccupied lands for a space of six miles on each side of said road or roads."[13] This article provided a means for railroad companies to obtain patents to lands in Indian Territory. Article 7, meanwhile, outlined that tribal sovereignty would remain intact and that no congressional or presidential action could "interfere with or annul" the laws, rights, and customs of the nations. Cole would spend the next two decades challenging article 6 with article 7.[14]

Even though the land grant provision was not included in the final versions of the 1866 treaties, Congress ensured that land grants played a major role in the railroading of Indian Territory (Figure 4.2). With the Fort Smith treaties still being negotiated, Congress approved the incorporation of the Atlantic and Pacific Railroad Company (A&P), which sought to build the east-west line across Indian Territory. The Cherokees and Chickasaws sent delegations by rail to Washington with the express purpose of raising their concerns about the initiative, approved under the auspices of the Southern Pacific Railway Act. The bill sanctioned the acquisition of lands and construction of another transcontinental thoroughfare, this one along the 35th parallel. The bill explicitly stated that the US government should "extinguish, as rapidly as may be consistent with public policy and the welfare of said Indians, the Indian title to all lands falling under operation of this act."[15] This is the very same language written into the Pacific Railway Act, the same *de jure* assumption that Indigenous lands were public lands. Rep. James Henry Lane of Kansas shared the delegation's objection to the bill on the House floor while the delegates waited in the nearby Marble Room.[16] The bill passed in spite of their protests. The corporation charged with building the north-south line, meanwhile, first had to win a construction race to the Kansas-Indian Territory border. The winner, the Union Pacific Southern Branch (UPSB)—later the Missouri Kansas and Texas (MKT) after the UPSB fell into receivership—received the right-of-way. A bill passed shortly thereafter provided alternate sections of land throughout Indian Territory for corporate use, "whenever the Indian title shall be extinguished by treaty."[17] In addition to creating a wedge for the A&P and MKT to acquire Indian lands—often through the very heart of their respective domains—Congress also approved a bill allowing other railroad companies to negotiate directly with tribal communities for rights-of-way.[18] The congressional message was clear: Indigenous lands were available to railroad corporations.

Yet the extinguishing of Indian title did not occur as swiftly as MKT, A&P, and US agents had anticipated.[19] The objections voiced by the visiting delegations in 1866 reflected a rising tide of resistance in Indian Territory. The General Council of the Choctaws responded to the passage of the Southern Pacific Railroad Act by sending formal protests to Congress, the US Court of Claims, and, eventually, the Supreme Court.[20]

Rail-powered lobbying in Washington and judicial action were two prongs in a three-pronged strategy of Choctaw resistance. The third involved taking the corporate model into Choctaw hands. The hope was that by controlling the construction and maintenance of rail lines in their homelands, Choctaws could prevent the loss of lands to outsiders and reap the economic gains that railroads might bring. Choctaws moved swiftly and intertribally, creating a joint company with the Chickasaws in 1869. The Choctaw and Chickasaw Railway Company was to be owned and operated by tribal citizens, while the Central Choctaw and Chickasaw Thirty-Fifth Parallel Railway Company permitted non-Native board members. The latter company ensured that an Indian majority remained on the board and granted a capital stock of up to $7 million.[21] Adair and Downing's Cherokee petition followed the precedent set by Choctaws and Chicaksaws here. Their formal proposal ensured US officials that they "have the means to build their roads." They added that, by allowing them to do so, "a nation will, perhaps, be saved." Leaders from all three tribes felt that nothing less than their very livelihoods were at stake when considering the potential of opening up Indian Territory to foreign corporations, settlers, and thus the specter of statehood. "Do the Cherokees ask too much," they proclaimed, "when they ask for existence?"[22] These Indigenous visions for local ownership of transnational communication and transportation networks would be picked up by other western residents—Populists—in the later decades of the nineteenth century.

Indigenous-owned railroad corporations would be realized, however briefly, in Northeast Indian Territory a decade later, but at this point the idea proved short-lived. Commissioner of Indian Affairs Ely S. Parker (Seneca) opposed tribally owned corporations, citing the corrupting influence of market forces on Native peoples.[23] Shortly after the incorporation of the two Choctaw railway companies, the Secretary of the Interior issued a circular halting the survey of railroads in Indian Territory "unless by express authority from the Department."[24] Without the consent of the Indian Office for the survey of these lands, Indigenous-run organizations had little means of acquiring the land and capital necessary to build their own iron roads. Meanwhile foreign railroad corporations, increasingly aware that the tribes would not consent to land grants, resorted to threats.[25]

In spite of the Indian Office's roadblocks, Native peoples persisted in their efforts to contain and control the stampede of iron horses. In western Indian Territory, Lone Wolf's band of Kiowas attacked an A&P survey crew in 1870, shortly after Creeks expelled the same crew from their lands.[26] In September of that same year, the General Council of Indian Territory convened in Okmulgee, Creek Nation. The Council, composed of representatives from the Cherokees, Creeks, Ottawas, Eastern Shawnees, Quapaws, Senecas, Wyandottes, Peorias, Sac and Foxes, and Osages, met in response to an "Oklahoma Bill" introduced in Congress and backed by railway corporations. The bill proposed to open up Indian Territory to white settlement. Though the legislation did not make it to the House floor that year, the tribes acted immediately to protect their interests. In response to the bill, the council drafted a memorial to the president, "protesting against any legislation by Congress impairing the obligation of any treaty provision."[27] To publicize their opposition, the Council published its meeting minutes in pamphlets. Adopting language from the Southern Pacific Act and other congressional bills, the Council took a united stand "against the creation of any government over the Indian Territory other than that of the General Council; and also against the sale or grant of any lands directly or contingent upon the extinguishment of Indian title to any railroad company or corporation now chartered for the purpose of constructing a railroad."[28]

The intertribal council also passed a resolution asking Congress to repeal all of the railroad charters that granted Indian lands to railroads. An intertribal Indian delegation comprising Cherokees, Chickasaws, Creeks, and Choctaws arrived by rail in Washington to deliver the news to Congress. The delegates noted that an estimated 23 million acres of land belonging to Indians could go to railroad corporations "by fair or unfair means," with an estimated value of $230 million.[29] The delegates, including W. P. Adair and Denis Bushyhead of the Cherokee diplomatic corps, reminded Congress that Indian Territory Natives owned their land in fee simple. "They [Congress] cannot," the delegates concluded, "feel...that a free people should have to improve and cultivate their lands...not knowing how soon their country and their homes might be taken from them."[30]

Another powerful appeal on behalf of the retention of Indian title came from William A. Phillips, a tribal attorney for the Cherokee Nation. He met with the Board of Indian Commissioners, a group of individuals established by Congress to oversee and give advice on US Indian policy. The board, unsurprisingly, included an A&P official. In 1871, Phillips reminded the board that the federal government had, in fact, given the Cherokees their Indian Territory lands in fee simple, which meant Cherokees had absolute title to their lands and could dispose of them as they saw fit. If US officials did not understand and act according to this definition of ownership, then, he exclaimed, "anything else is mere violence." Regarding the granting of alternate sections of land along the lines, Phillips made an apt comparison: "it would be just as absurd to grant a railroad company alternate sections for twenty miles wide, on each side of a road from Washington to New York."[31]

In spite of these protests, construction commenced on the MKT and A&P the same year Congress ended treaty-making with Native nations. The connection between the two was not lost on the Creeks. The Creek Agent reported in 1871 that the influx of whites onto Creek lands for the construction of the MKT was a "cause of excitement, and, with many, of apprehension."[32] That excitement and apprehension extended to concern about congressional efforts to "throw open this beautiful country," given that this governing body "has found occasion heretofore to annul treaties."[33]

When it became clear that the tribes could not halt the construction of the A&P and MKT, tribal councils changed strategy and began passing legislation that oversaw the construction and operation of railroads on their property. The Creeks, though compelled to sell up to three miles of lands along the projected rights-of-way through their country, offered the Katy a strip only three feet wide.[34] The MKT, commonly called "the Katy," began construction through eastern Indian Territory in 1871, reaching the Arkansas River at the end of the year. By January 1872 the rails crossed the borders of Muskogee, in Creek Territory. The iron road for the Katy was complete by early 1873.[35] The Atlantic and Pacific did not build past Vinita because of further threats of violence from the western territory tribes and concerns about the financial feasibility of moving freight through Indian Territory.[36]

Land was not the only valuable Indigenous commodity sought by railroad corporations. An Indian Territory agent reported in 1871 that "the first effect of building these roads was to despoil the country along their respective lines of timber, which was already scarce."[37] Choctaws, Chickasaws, and Cherokees responded immediately to the trees chopped down by the A&P and MKT.[38] The MKT, which had entered Indian Territory in June 1870, had already caused enough concern among residents that by September, Indian Agents had requested troops cease timber-cutting operations along construction lines. On December 14, 1870, the Cherokee government passed a tie law ensuring that the local government received benefits for timber siphoned off their lands. Under the law, individuals applied for permits to sell ties to the railroad.[39] It was a means of managing deforestation while also ensuring that tribal governments received dues (5 cents per tie) from profit off communal land holdings. The Choctaw Nation passed a similar bill in 1872, making it illegal to sell timber, rock, and stone coal to railroads without a license. Chief Cole worked with the Council to ensure that construction supplies were channeled through Choctaw institutions that benefited the community.[40]

Yet the legal reach, economic advantages, and environmental protections the tribes sought could extend only so far. Corporations often skirted tribal laws and appealed to the Indian Office and Congress to support their unilateral decision-making in Indian Territory. These efforts to capitalize on jurisdictional uncertainties played out across the region as survey crews entered newly established reservations. Take, for instance, the MKT's inflation of freight and passenger rates through the Indian Territory (12 cents per mile in Indian Territory versus 3 to 4 cents per mile in Kansas and Missouri).[41] In 1876, the Choctaw tribal government retaliated by passing a law taxing MKT 1.5% for the cash valuation of their property along Choctaw lands.[42] Railroad companies blamed their high rates on the lack of land grants they received and on the prevailing assumption that there were insufficient commerce and resources to support a railroad in the territory.[43]

Corporate machinations and excuses did not prevent Indian Territory leaders from articulating their own vision for commercialization that could support tribal sovereignty. Coleman Cole wrote to the Secretary of the Interior in 1876 urging him to authorize tribal taxation of railroad, telegraph, and express companies. Outlining his undeniably modern scheme for commerce in Indian Country, Cole also requested that passenger and freight rates mirror those in the neighboring states. He also called on railway companies to pay for damages to property.[44] In a public protest printed in *The Indian Journal* two years later, Cole could not contain his outrage. In spite of efforts at intra- and intertribal levels to direct the course of railway expansion in Indian Territory, Congress continued to pass pro-railroad legislation and debate the creation of Oklahoma Territory. Again, Cole reminded the public of the US government's responsibility to Native nations. "No use to grumble, no humbug," he declared, "where there is [*sic*] treaties and laws in existence."[45]

Cole represented a broad swath of Choctaws who sought to control the development of their unallotted lands, but other factions, many tied to whites living on tribal lands, disagreed with his policies. With the support of his detractors, the council successfully organized to impeach him during his second term.[46] His successor, Isaac Garvin, continued to levy taxes and legislate against the growing influx of white interlopers settling in Choctaw Country. Gavin prohibited citizens from cutting and shipping hay out of the nation and banned noncitizens from engaging in the stock business. Despite efforts by local whites to challenge the right of the Choctaw Council to tax non-Indians and distribute permits, the US Attorney General sided with Gavin and the Choctaw Council in 1881.[47]

In the late 1870s and early 1880s railroad companies—having finally recovered from a national economic crash in 1873—extended their reach into Indian Territory. Corporate officials believed that a line though Indian Territory could tap growing markets in Texas as well as in the borderlands beyond, but they would have to negotiate with tribal governments and Indian Office officials to secure a right-of-way. Choctaws fractured over whether or not to allow further railway development in their nation. As Choctaws debated their course, Congress dealt a swift blow to Indigenous sovereignty in the territory. With the support of Senator Samuel Bell Maxey of Texas, Congress passed an 1882 measure that granted the Frisco Railway a right-of-way through Choctaw lands without the consent of the tribes.[48]

This 1882 bill confirmed Choctaw fears of congressional overreach in the service of corporate capitalism. With its passage, Congress extended the right of eminent domain over Indian Territory and signed into US law a mechanism by which the federal government could grant Indigenous lands directly to railway corporations. Congress continued to feed corporate greed.

Tribal governments pursued rearguard action in the face of the 1882 legislative calamity. In an effort to restrict congressional decision-making in their new homelands, the Cherokee Council passed a flurry of legislation outlining their dealings with railroad companies over timber, land use, taxes, and rights-of-way. Over Chief Bushyhead's veto, Cherokees passed a law refusing to accept the damage allowances set by Congress and signed a bill that barred the United States from passing right-of-way privileges without their consent.[49] The last bill set the groundwork for the tribe's legal assault on congressional authority in the Cherokee case against the Southern Kansas Railway. The Choctaw and Chickasaw Nations, meanwhile, filed suit against the MKT in the US Court of the Western District of Arkansas.[50]

With their established foundation of social and political institutions and long history of negotiation with the US government, the Five Tribes were better able to effectively tax corporations and submit formal and informal legal protests against corporate expansion in Indian Territory. While the tribes certainly received a modicum of revenue from their levies against railroad corporations, the interests of settlers, railroad corporations, and the US government aligned when it came to the future of Indian Territory. This confluence of interests overwhelmed the Cherokee, Choctaw, and Chickasaw abilities to resist railroad expansion and the territorialization it promised to bring with it.[51] Efforts to repurpose the corporate model for Indigenous benefit, to capitalize on rail travel for political purposes, and to challenge US colonialism in court, however, set the stage of Indigenous activism in the decades to come.

"Danger of a Second Oklahoma"

While the Cherokee, Choctaw, and Chickasaw councils hired attorneys and filed suits, railroad corporations of all sorts sought Indigenous lands across the American West.[52] Corporate agents and surveying parties arrived on reservations in the 1880s eager to make arrangements for railroad rights-of-way. The intrusions of these corporate agents, survey crews, and gangs of laborers into Indian Country underscored the hubris of railroad corporations. Galvanized by the logic of eminent domain, corporate agents were confident that their "public good" enterprises would ensure the continued support of US courts and policymakers. Consent from Native occupants was a mere formality. In many instances, white settlers joined these corporate agents on Indian lands asserting a right of occupancy, one that they had no legal claim to.

In the late summer of 1881, residents of Montana's Flathead Agency caught sight of laborers laying stakes and hauling earth near the border of their reservation. Agent Peter Ronan, unsure whether the railway agents had a right to be there, wrote to the Commissioner of Indian Affairs seeking "instructions, especially pertinent to the situation," given "the danger therefrom that some of the contractors or others may encroach on the lands of the Indians."[53] If the Bitterroot Salish, Kootenai, and Pend d'Orielles agreed to a right-of-way, Ronan asked, would that right also include the ability to locate timber and other construction materials on their lands? Ronan's concerns reveal the legal and political uncertainties around corporate expansion in Indian Country, which corporate officials and US agents of empire used to exploit Indigenous lands and resources.[54]

Throughout the 1880s, Indian Agents looked on as construction crews, corporate agents, and engineers entered tribal lands and staked out land claims for their iron beasts. Agents appealed to leaders in Washington for direction as survey and construction crews descended upon newly established reservations in growing numbers.[55] Months before Ronan's letter, Agent Ben Thomas made an urgent plea to officials in DC for "decided support from the Government to keep the reservation open for the Indians." Thomas had arrived at the newly established Jicarilla Apache reservation in north-central New Mexico to find the Denver and Rio Grande (D&RG) construction crews building across it, and settlers following in their wake.[56] The same crews charged onto Southern Ute lands later that spring without consulting the tribe. Secretary of the Interior S. J. Kirkwood eventually stepped in and demanded that construction stop immediately and that D&RG officials meet with the Utes, whom he portrayed as "alarmed and becoming restless."[57]

Across Indian Country, tribal leaders were indeed alarmed by these wanton intrusions onto their lands. In November 1880, three Lower Brulés, frustrated at the climbing numbers of whites on their lands and ongoing negotiations for a railroad right-of-way, appealed directly to the president of the United States. "We, Iron Nation, Medicine Bull, and Little Pheasant," they wrote, "desire to lay before him our statement concerning certain matters of deep import." Like Choctaw Coleman Cole three years before, these Brulé authors voiced their opposition to corporate and settler invasions. They recounted how the past spring a man arrived in their camp and asked them to sign a paper, "giving, as we understood, the Railroad Company the right to make a survey for a railroad from a point, at or near our agency in a direction towards the Black Hills." The three men went on to explain that a certain Mr. Lawler arrived with the local Indian Agent and attempted to coerce their people into sanctioning the iron road. "This," they proclaimed, "we cannot understand." Iron Nation, Little Pheasant, and Medicine Bull also warned President James A. Garfield that the local agent might have been in the employ of the railroad. "We believe the Agent committed to the interest of the railroad company," they explained, "and likely to overlook the true interests of our tribe." Two men—Baltier Lambert and David Renocountre, an interpreter—signed off as witnesses to the testimony of these three leaders.[58] "We are not satisfied," they concluded, "for an iron road to be built through our country as matters now stand."[59]

Conspiracy, collusion, and corruption clung to railroad corporate agents like a thick cloud of smoke—one that drifted into the halls of Congress, the encampments of treaty councils, and onto Indian reservations. The letter from Iron Nation, Little Pheasant, and Medicine Bull was caught up in the controversy. A later account from Jack Daughtery casts doubt on the validity of the letter. According to this accusation, William J. Smith, the former commissary Sergeant at Fort Hall, Idaho Territory, together with George M. Felt, a local Indian trader, and a *métis* interpreter, "secretly conspired against the peace and welfare of the Lower Brulé." These "false representations" did not reflect Lower Brulé sentiments, but were instead the product of businessmen concerned about losing their trading monopoly with the Brulés as new enterprises unfolded along the proposed railroad route. Felt, Daugherty claimed, held several secret evening councils in late October and early November with the Indians on agency grounds and in his home. The letter from Iron Nation and his allies grew out of those secret conversations. Daughtery argued that the disaffection of Lower Brulé tribal leaders was the result of these "unlawful means."[60] A complex matrix of interests disrupted every decision regarding the direction, location, and construction of iron roads. Depending on the circumstances, the interests of settlers, Indigenous nations, corporations, and state and federal governments could overlap or diverge sharply, influencing the nature of the negotiations across the West.

And yet Indigenous writings and actions bore remarkably similar markers of protest. In June 1880, Little No Heart (Miniconjou) made yet another appeal to the US president. Little No Heart hoped that President Rutherford B. Hayes would attend to his concerns when representatives from the Chicago, Milwaukee, and St. Paul Railroad arrived at the Cheyenne River Agency in Dakota Territory requesting a right-of-way through the Great Sioux Reservation. Like so many other petitions, Little No Heart's letter railed against an iron road. "I would like the Great Father to say," he wrote, "just what rights the white men has on that road." He shared that he and his people were "anxious about this matter, because we look with fear upon any encroachment of the white men upon our reservation."[61] Little No Heart was less concerned about the road itself than the unwelcome settlers it would bring.

A year later, on the banks of Arrow Creek in central Montana, Spotted Horse (Crow) demanded that Northern Pacific Railroad surveyors leave his people's homelands at once, threatening to pull up their survey stakes and burn the grasses collected from Crow Country to sustain the survey party's livestock.[62] The Northern Pacific (NP) Railroad Company, recovered from financial ruin that had halted construction at Bismarck for over a decade, had previously been attacked by an intertribal congregation of Cheyenne, Arapaho, and Lakota led by Sitting Bull (Oglala Lakota).[63] The messages of Spotted Horse and the intertribal anti-railroad coalition were clear: NP surveyors were not welcome.

These isolated resistance efforts did not stop corporate agents from brazenly trespassing on tribal lands without regard to consequences. For example, the Utah and Northern Railway Company built and operated a line for several years on 2,000 acres of Shoshone-Bannock land without the tribes' consent. Adding insult to injury, the railroad made no effort to compensate them.[64] Iron roads also trespassed through Brulé, Crow, Flathead, Jicarilla, and Southern Ute lands. Yet opposition was vocal. Spotted Horse, Little No Heart, and others made their opinions clear, and the council meetings that followed the arrival of construction crews tapped a wellspring of Indigenous opposition to corporate intrusion. In a world in which few materials and exchanges escaped commoditization, Indian consent also came at a cost.

The legal and political path-making for the rails relied on preexisting treaty stipulations, when available. Some preexisting treaties did not contain provisions for railroads, in which case corporate officials sent their requests directly to Congress. In other instances, former treaty arrangements followed eminent domain-type protocols. Echoing the "just compensation" provision of eminent domain policy, treaties stipulated that right-of-way must be granted for railroads 200 feet wide, with the price to be set via negotiations between corporate agents and tribal leaders. In still other cases, treaties allowed railway corporations to proceed through tribal lands so long as the president deemed it necessary for "the public interest." In both cases, just compensation was an afterthought. The land would be seized. Such was the case on Southern Ute lands where President Hayes declared in 1880 that a roughly forty-mile stretch would fall into the hands of the Denver and Rio Grande company because, he stated, "the public interests require the construction of such branches and extensions."[65] In spite of efforts by the local Indian Agent to have D&RG officials meet with the Utes and discuss fair compensation, the company, armed with President Hayes's executive order, ignored the requests and continued building.[66] Only in 1904 did the railroad finally pay for the lands they had invaded nearly a quarter-century earlier.[67]

Corporate agents were often directed by the Indian Office and Congress to meet and procure "consent" from tribal leaders, but by the end of the decade Congress had begun passing right-of-way legislation without Indigenous approval, and compensation stipulations were mere afterthoughts. As scholars explain, by the 1890s the Bureau of Indian Affairs was treating the right-of-way agreement "as a pro forma administrative task of the government, rather than as a process involving the deliberations and consent of the Indian nation involved."[68]

The Indian Office placed right-of-way monies in trust accounts overseen by the government. The US government subsequently disbursed some of these monies to purchase agricultural implements and build reservation infrastructure in support of federal containment and assimilation programs. Even as it endeavored to separate Native peoples from US society and the corruptive influence of corporations, the Indian Office invested Indigenous funds in US banks and even railroad corporations, in essence funding the very corporate behemoths that threatened to unravel Indigenous solidarity and sovereignty.[69]

Yet the councils that convened with local Indigenous communities, railroad agents, and government officials also provided Native leaders with a forum for protest and negotiation. Indians leveraged their platform to negotiate the terms of passage. Take, for example, the deliberations for the Chicago, Milwaukee, and St. Paul Railroad (CMSP), which sought a right-of-way through the Great Sioux Reservation in South Dakota. In early November 1880, a representative of the CMSP arrived on the 25-million-acre Great Sioux Reservation to negotiate a right-of-way, accompanied by US Inspector Robert S. Gardner. In the council proceedings, leaders protested aspects of the proposed deal and listed their demands. Little Pheasant, one of the authors of the letter sent to the president that same month, explained in council that he expected to visit Washington and take the matter up directly with President Hayes before proceeding.[70] Nine days earlier, Red Cloud had made his own series of requests to the CMSP representative. Red Cloud opened the proceedings by asking him to make his best offer for the right-of-way. "All of us here would like to know what we are going to get," Red Cloud explained, since "you could offer a small price and that is the reason we could tell you whether we could take it."[71] If the price was not right, Red Cloud made clear, they would not accept the deal.

When the council convened the next day, Spotted Tail, having gained ten years of experience since his encounter with the Union Pacific locomotive, began negotiating the terms. He requested, first, that fewer laws govern the operation of the railway line. Spotted Tail also addressed concerns about the economic welfare of his people. Long-standing freighting operations from the Missouri River steamboats had provided tribal members with much-needed income. "Look at these young men, they have teams and wagons. I wish you would do something for them. . . . I want you to give them work on your road. I want you to put that on the written contract."[72] The Gardner delegation then moved on to Crow Creek Agency in South Dakota, where leaders demanded 20,000 head of cattle as part of the deal.[73] The requests of Spotted Tail, Red Cloud, and others in the CMSP council mirrored demands at other right-of-way negotiations across the West in the 1880s. While government agents and corporate officials never openly doubted that they would gain access to Indigenous lands, the price for this access was actively negotiated by Indian leaders.

Payment took many forms, but access to rail travel for people and goods was common. The Southern Ute had an unwritten agreement with D&RG

agents that granted them passage on company trains in Colorado. The Walker River Paiutes ensured that the final agreement with the Carson and Colorado Railroad included "the privilege of free transportation of the persons, fish, game & c. of said Indians."[74] The Crow, meanwhile, maintained an informal agreement with Northern Pacific officials to grant free passage on their trains, and Laguna Pueblo oral tradition points to a "handshake agreement" with Atlantic and Pacific Railroad agents affirming that the railroad would keep Pueblos employed on the road when possible, in exchange for a right-of-way and use of a nearby river for water.[75] The governor of Isleta also met with A&P officials and ensured that damages be paid for farmed lands that the construction destroyed.[76] Railroad agents and Laguna leaders met annually to discuss their arrangement in a process they called "Watering the Flower." In addition to employment, A&P (later AT&SF) agents promised free housing for railroad workers and free rail passes for tribal members.[77]

Tribal elders and officials struggled to set the terms by which corporate leaders commoditized their lands and resources. For example, the Tohono O'odham requested that the Arizona Southern Railroad Company fence its entire line in order to protect their livestock from harm. Arizona Southern officers turned to the US government and complained that the request was too costly, but they ultimately fenced the route.[78] Many tribal councils passed laws requiring cattlemen to pay a fine per head of cattle driven through their lands on the way to rail stations.[79] Negotiations for construction supplies and resources—chiefly hay for livestock and timber for ties—took different forms. The Saint Paul, Minneapolis, and Manitoba Railroad Company, for example, negotiated with the Blackfeet for the sale of hay to construction parties at a fixed price.[80] Northern Pacific construction crews paid roughly $2 per thousand feet of timber cut on Salish and Kootenai lands.[81] In an effort to control resource extractions and provide wage labor to tribal citizens, the Salish and Kootenai insisted that Indigenous laborers do the timber cutting.[82]

There were also moments when the right of refusal prevailed. When it came to the CMNP, Iron Nation stated, "We sell you the land for railroad... *and no other*." Iron Nation also reminded government and corporate officials that "should the road ever be given up the land comes back to us."[83] The Puyallup rejected offers by the Puyallup Valley Railway Company to build through their lands. In the same year, the Crow refused access to the Billings, Clarks Fork, and Cooke City Railroad, declaring in council that "they did not want more stakes set in their ground."[84]

When these peaceable means of resistance failed, many resorted to more destructive forms of protest. At Fort Hall in eastern Idaho, Shoshone and Bannocks voiced their concerns about the influx of settlers at Pocatello with the local agent. "Unless something is done to satisfy these Indians," the agent informed his superiors in Washington, "there is great danger of them taking the law into their own hands."[85] In December 1884, the agent at the Flathead Indian Agency reported "mischief" along the Northern Pacific lines. By March, the agent confirmed that the Indians were blocking train travel along the route. Indians at Fort Hall laid ties on the rails near the station of Victor, Idaho. The foreman attempted to drive them off, but he was ultimately sent away at gunpoint. The Indians were later arrested.[86] Two years later, Spokanes visiting Flathead Agency by rail cut several telegraph lines along the Northern Pacific route in Montana.[87]

The protests could not stem the tide of combined corporate and settler interests that flooded Indian Country in the second half of the century. This was most visible in the crowding of settlers onto railroad lands, often resulting in the cession of parts of Indigenous territorial holdings for the creation of station towns. At Fort Hall, for example, whites occupied railroad lands at an alarming rate. The Fort Hall Indian Agent appealed to Washington in 1889 for assistance in removing the trespassers, warning, "there is danger of a second Oklahoma."[88] Squatters had moved into Pocatello, Idaho, hoping to use preemption rights, which were not valid on the right-of-way grounds or on the Fort Hall Agency. In the early 1880s, a similar drama unfolded on the Great Sioux Reservation when white settlers overran the town of Fort Pierre in central South Dakota, migrating there because of the profits to be made on Black Hills wagon roads.[89] At Crow Agency in Montana, meanwhile, reports of stock yards being built at Custer station on the NP line led to concerns that ranchers would use nearby Crow lands for grazing and transport.[90]

As railroads and their corporate overlords gained increasing control of Indian lands, Indians continued to seek avenues to protect their interests and voice their concerns about the intrusions of corporations, settlers, and the US government. The series of railroad agreements made after the end of treaty relations in 1871 point to the defense tactics Native peoples employed against settler colonial regimes and their corporate emissaries. In their efforts to stem the tide of railroad colonialism, Indigenous leaders negotiated for free transportation, higher rates, and Indigenous employment. These early resistance tactics employed by Native peoples unfolded alongside a vibrant and growing community of activists, orators, and public figures who rode iron horses to advocate for their communities.

And yet, their negotiations could not entirely turn back the colonial juggernaut that tore through Indian Country after the Civil War. On American Independence Day in 1884, Congress authorized a right-of-way through Indian Territory for the Southern Kansas Railway (SKR). By 1884 four trunk lines latticed the American West: the Union Pacific-Central Pacific; the Atchison, Topeka and Santa Fe; the Southern Pacific; and the Northern Pacific. Given that some railroad companies were created by congressional law, railroad officials and lawmakers often had close relations, which ensured the speedy passage of rights-of-way acts. Yet the 1884 move by Congress on behalf of the Southern Kansas Railway would not proceed unchecked.[91]

The measures the Cherokee tribal government took to rebuff this imperial overreach followed previously successful resistance tactics. In December 1884, the Cherokee Nation passed a resolution opposing the act and filed a protest with the Secretary of the Interior. In the same session, the tribal council sent instructions to Cherokee delegates in Washington, DC, tasking them with denying any railroad company the right to build a line through Indian Territory.[92] By 1886, the Southern Kansas Railway had submitted a map to the Indian Office for the proposed route, and the US president had appointed referees to help broker adequate compensation for the right-of-way. These referees completed their work by September 1886 and concluded that $93.00 for each mile in compensation and damages was fair. The Interior Department then requested that the SKR deposit those funds into the treasury. In response, Principal Chief Denis W. Bushyhead filed suit in the Circuit Court of Arkansas against the company.[93]

Bushyhead's suit joined other claims and cases pending in US courts regarding damages and compensation owed Indigenous individuals and communities. In Washington, the Northern Pacific Railroad countered several homestead claims made by Colville Indians. The case was settled out of court and the tribe received a mere $2,000 for damages.[94] In 1889, the US judiciary established a court in Muskogee, Indian Territory, which dealt primarily with claims regarding stock killed by the railroad.[95] Filing suit in US courts would continue to animate Indigenous resistance well into the twentieth century.

In response to Bushyhead's action, the SKR filed a demurrer with the Arkansas court, arguing that the Cherokee did not have sufficient grounds to make a case. The US Supreme Court ruled in *Cherokee Nation v. Southern Kansas Railway* (1890) in favor of the railroad company, citing eminent domain and the takings clause of the US Constitution. District Court Judge Issac Parker explained that "the Cherokee Nation is not therefore sovereign," because, he reasoned, the nation cannot exist nested within the sovereign domain of the United States.[96] SKR attorneys made the same claim before the Supreme Court. The appellees stated that the Cherokees' claim was fallacious, because of "an erroneous conception of the nature of sovereignty."[97] The battle for Indigenous lands, then, was intimately bound up in questions of political autonomy and sovereignty. US courts, the Cherokees realized, would not protect Indigenous kin and community going forward. These legal losses made Indian peoples—to use Cherokee author DeWitt Clinton Duncan's term—"outlaws." "Not indeed a criminal," Duncan explained, "but as a man whose rights (if he can be said to have any at all) have no reliable foundation in law."[98] Corporate interests prevailed in Indian Country, as they did across the United States in the late nineteenth century. Chief Bushyhead addressed the Cherokee legislature in 1886 on the subject. "The currents of trade that accumulate from the springs of human industry are as resistless in their course to market as a river is in its flow to the sea," he stated. Adding of railroads, that "everything depends on the way they are regarded and treated, whether their great power will be used for or against—to aid or to injure."[99]

The seeds for Indigenous activism, survival, and intertribal alliance-making would be sown at the turn of the century by harnessing the powers of the railroads to which Bushyhead referred. Those seeking to keep railroads out of Indian Country did not prevail. Railroad expansion dealt a crushing blow to tribal landholdings and to tribal sovereignty. The history of railroads in Indian Country does not end here, however. Shrewd negotiations for free travel on rail lines across Indian Country enabled migrations of men and women off Indian agencies for work, intertribal visits, spiritual revitalization, and activism that became central to maintaining tribal sovereignty and challenging the US colonial order in the Progressive Era.

The Iron Horse in Indian Country: Native Americans and Railroads in the US West. Alessandra La Rocca Link, Oxford University Press. © Alessandra La Rocca Link 2025. DOI: 10.1093/9780197674437.003.0006

Railway Journeys

Heart Work

In the summer of 1875, a respected Klamath leader named Wal-aiks-ski-dat—also known as Dave Hill—enjoyed a filling meal and delivered a public lecture at New York City's prominent Cooper Union (Figure RJ 2.1). In doing so, he joined a growing list of well-known intellectuals and orators who visited the Great Hall, including Abraham Lincoln, Red Cloud (Lakota), Little Raven (Arapaho), and later famed abolitionist Frederick Douglass and suffragist Susan B. Anthony.

Hill had been touring eastern cities with fellow Klamaths and Modocs as part of a lecture company organized by the public reformer and Indian agent Alfred Meacham. The party made stops in Sacramento, St. Louis, Louisville, Lexington, Washington, DC, and Trenton, among other locales. While on tour, the delegation addressed audiences at Alfred Henry Love's Universal Peace Union in Philadelphia and the US Indian Commission in New York City.[1] Hill, for his part, had given a stirring speech at Philadelphia's Independence Hall in March 1875, where he invited eastern Americans to reflect on the costs of their national freedom. He began by acknowledging the storied past of the building, which hosted the drafting of the US Declaration of Independence. "This seems like a sacred place," he stated, "where men ought to think, and not talk."[2] But of the laws created by a nation born in the very room he occupied, Hill could not stay silent.

> I think that the laws that are made are not straight, they are crooked. They leave the Indian out. He has no one to talk for him. Do you think this is what the men up there meant?[3]

He pointed to the portraits of the Founding Fathers hanging on the wall.

> Perhaps they see me now. I am not ashamed to look at them in the eye. . . . I went to see the President, he looks like any other man. . . . I went to tell him

> what my people wanted, but his ear was to[o] small, he could not hear me. I brought all the things in my heart away.
>
> Then I went to see the Commissioner [of Indian Affairs]. He had large ears. He *seemed* to listen to what I had to tell him, but I looked him in the eye. He did not put the things I told him in his heart.[4]

Hill had traveled by rail for weeks to share his heart among foreign peoples. To the crowd gathered in Independence Hall he tried once more to make his case.

Soon after his Cooper Union speech, Hill decided to abandon the lecture circuit and return to his home on the Klamath Reservation. The lecture company was in dire financial straits and it was no longer possible to linger on the East Coast. Hill was ready to leave. The rails that sent him away, he found, would also bring him home.[5]

Hill traveled by rail to Chicago before he ran out of money he had saved from the lecture tour. From there he traveled by foot until he could find work. "Sometimes I had employment in the hay-field, or at chopping wood," he explained, "and in this way would work until I had a few dollars ahead, and then ride a few hours on the cars."[6] And so he worked and traveled until he reached the Union Pacific station in Fremont, Nebraska, where he began taking on a succession of tribal identities in order to claim free travel granted by the alleged agreements between tribes and railway companies. "In this way I managed to get along very well, being first a Sioux, then

RJ 2.1 Cooper Union, New York, 1896. Library of Congress.

a Shoshone, then a Piute [*sic*] , and finally a California Digger," he recalled. He disembarked in Redding, California, and, after three months of travel, returned to his people. "It makes my heart sick," he added, "to think how many times in the last few months I thought I should never see my people again."[7]

Hill would later support false claims that he was kidnapped in New York City, instead of leaving of his own volition. Perhaps the reality that a prominent figure deserted the lecture company cast unwelcome doubts on the entire tour and its leader, Meacham. Meacham then convinced Hill to write a fictionalized account of his abduction in a later publication. The story, like the laws, went crooked. Nevertheless, Hill's heart work stirred eastern American minds and ultimately brought him back to his people and his homeland.[8]

For many Indigenous orators, audiences in American cities offered an opportunity to publicize their plight and protest US Indian policy. In the early 1880s, Sarah Winnemucca (Northern Paiute) traveled across North America to raise funds for a local school and to draw public attention to the needs of her people. The daughter of a well-known Paiute chief, Winnemucca also trekked to various reservations to assess the state of Indigenous peoples. "I can recall half a dozen agencies where I have been," she later wrote, "where teachers with fifty children on the books and five in the school are drawing their pay and scarcely a child can be found who knows a word of English." An advocate of assimilation, Winnemucca crisscrossed the United States and Indian Country in the 1880s to solicit funds and shift public opinion about her community. "My people are utterly destitute," she decried, "numbers of them are famishing in the snow."[9] Indeed, Winnemucca lived on the move in an effort to influence public opinion. She and other Indigenous orators recognized that America's ongoing fascination with Indians offered an opportunity to spread awareness about the ravages of the reservation and allotment system. Winnemucca made several speaking appearances, "eloquently recounting the wrongs of her people," as one newspaper put it.[10] For Winnemucca and Hill, heart work took shape on railways across North America in the late nineteenth and early twentieth centuries.

The Iron Horse in Indian Country: Native Americans and Railroads in the US West. Alessandra La Rocca Link, Oxford University Press. © Alessandra La Rocca Link 2025. DOI: 10.1093/9780197674437.003.0007

PART III

WORK AND NETWORK, 1880–1930

Let me be a free man—free to travel, free to stop, free to work, free to trade where I choose, free to choose my own teachers, free to follow the religion of my fathers, free to think and talk and act for myself.

—Chief Joseph (Nez Percé), *North American Review* (1879)

It seems to me that the great thing this morning that we should take away is that definition of our position in the future.

—Laura Cornelius Kellogg (Oneida), *Proceedings of the Annual Conference on the Society of American Indians* (1912)

5
Indians at Work

In May 1893, a throng of spectators idled on the shores of South Pond. A glassy blue expanse poured between two bleached buildings, South Pond was but one feature among the sights, sounds, and artifices designed for the World's Columbian Exposition. This celebration of the United States' industrial acumen and God-given exceptionalism unfurled on the shores of Lake Michigan to mark the hundredth anniversary of Columbus's arrival in the Americas. The scenes on the pond's shores ostensibly reflected life before Columbus's *Santa Maria* anchored near a Caribbean island. "Here may be found the native Indians," a World's Fair guidebook explained, "who have made their temporary home in the Exposition, living in the exact way their forefathers lived."[1] Along the water Indians worked: they fished, built their homes, and prepared food. They also engaged in a new kind of labor by earning wages while performing before non-Indian audiences. According to the fair designers, the traditional work of these performers offered a contrast to the modern technology, science, art, and industry celebrated elsewhere at the fair. "The Indian," the guidebook concluded, "is intended as a back ground [*sic*] to the Exposition, bringing out by comparison with greater force the advances made during the past four centuries."[2]

A short walk away, at the Anthropological Building, sightseers observed Indian work of a decidedly different variety. Indian labor by US colonial design was on display at the Carlisle Indian Industrial School exhibit (Figure 5.1). The crown jewel of the US Indian boarding-school system, the Carlisle mission was simple. Fair visitors could find it stitched on the banner floating above the display: "into civilization and citizenship." The exhibit showcased the industrial trades acquired by Native American children separated, often by force, from their families and carted by rail to Carlisle, Pennsylvania. Photographs mounted along the wall depicted the students' physical transformations. Steel axes, hammers, and other tools of industry filled a glass case in the center. Students in uniform standing nearby intended to call to mind a different kind of Indian—one engaged in the civilizing mission, on the road to citizenship. In a matter

Figure 5.1 The Carlisle Indian Industrial School exhibit at the World's Columbian Exposition, 1893. Archives and Special Collections, Dickinson College, Carlisle, Pennsylvania.

of minutes, a fair visitor could marvel at an Indian past and contemplate the industrial Indian future—a future in which Lakota, Cherokee, Mojave, and other Indigenous children would no longer be Indian, but American.

Non-Native Americans were the architects of this fictitious narrative, one that pitted the vanishing practices of pre-modern peoples against the industrial, modern, assimilated future designed for their children. The work of threading fishing lines and tanning hides would be replaced with carpentry and household service. Railroad corporations, for their part, would build a profitable tourist industry by circulating imagery of the pre-modern. Corporate advertisements suggested that only on adventures by rail to the far-flung corners of the United States could eager Americans glimpse these ancient forms of living and working.

At colonial boarding schools like Carlisle, the past carried little of value. Supervisors and colonial officials believed the new work Indigenous students engaged in would make Americans out of them. On midnight, October 1, 1893, Carlisle students filed into ten train coaches headed to the World's Fair. The Carlisle student band performed on several occasions during the group's six-day tour of Chicago. They received discounted rates for their travel on the Pennsylvania railroad and paid for their tickets with their summer labor earnings. The kinds of jobs Carlisle students undertook reflected US colonial visions for Native labor in the industrial age. Adhering to prevailing gender norms, agents in Carlisle's summer Outing Program placed female students in domestic service positions, while boys worked odd jobs in factories, towns, and railroad yards.[3] A Carlisle school administrator praised the outing programs, intended "above all" to cultivate "the consciousness of ability to make a living in any civilized community; of not being a dependent, but a valued member of society, and a factor in the labor market."[4] Through the vector of labor, Indians would transition from wards of the government to independent citizens.

Indians had their own reasons for turning to wage work and production in the Gilded Age and Progressive Era. Ten years before the World's Fair, a Paiute prophet in Nevada promoted a religion and dance that celebrated work. He encouraged his followers to "work all the time and not lie down in idleness."[5] Wovoka's Ghost Dance followers took up work, as did countless nonbelievers. Native men and women, often laboring under exploitive conditions, labored on railroads and in railroad-related industries to protect the interests of kin and community. In the Southwest, Fred Kaye (Navajo), a tracklayer for the Atichson Topkea and Santa Fe Railroad, recalled that in his line of work he didn't have to cut his hair. In addition to being able to control his appearance, Kaye reported that he returned to the reservation "with a bundle." He gave half of his earnings to his aging parents and took his mother out to purchase dresses.[6] On the Central Plains, Mathias Splitlog was also consumed with work. A Cayuga adopted and elected chief of the Seneca in the 1890s, Splitlog used his own funds from his business ventures to travel to Washington, DC. In 1896, thanks in part to Splitlog's efforts, the Senecas received a payout of $372.00 per capita from the US government.[7] Both Kaye and Splitlog found that work with railroads provided material protections for their kin and, in the case of Splitlog, for their tribal community.

Employment with railroad companies or in industries connected to the railroad also provided Indigenous men and women with opportunities to leave the confines of the reservation. In the American Southwest, many laborers worked on lines and in hub towns beginning in the 1890s. During this time, Navajos, Apaches, Mojaves, and others found work on their own, often frustrating local Indian Agents who sought to keep close tabs on their wards. The farmer in charge of the Navajo extension in Tolchado, Arizona, complained in 1903 of the "demoralizing" practice of Indians leaving the reservation for railroad work, citing the increased exposure of railroad laborers and their families to the twin evils of liquor and gambling. They also alleged that many of the women who accompanied these men resorted to prostitution.[8] Beginning in the 1890s, Mojave and Chemehuevi men and their families migrated to Needles, California, finding employment in the factories and on track gangs for the Atlantic and Pacific and ATSF railroads. In 1928 researchers under the direction of the Secretary of the Interior visited the Indigenous residents of Needles. Their final report claimed that the Needles laborers regularly and openly criticized US government policy and were often "bitter in their criticism of the field employees of the Indian Service." Mojave and Chemehuevi workers added that they left the reservation because of "difficulties with government employees or because of government policies which were to them objectionable."[9] For these railroad laborers, work was an avenue to escape reservation surveillance and colonial assimilation programs.

As section hands, irrigation workers, and road builders, industrial Indian laborers helped build the West's modern infrastructure. Just as Indigenous guides proved critical in directing the paths of railroads in the West, so too would many Crows, Navajos, Mojaves, Cherokees, Lakotas, and others contribute to the industrialization and construction of the West through their work with, on, or near railroads. "Indians are an increasing factor in the constructive development of the West," the Commissioner of Indian Affairs opined in 1925, "where they are employed not only as day laborers in cotton fields, mines, and on railroad, irrigation, and other construction projects, but are filling responsible posts in business and professional lines."[10]

The enduring myth of Indigenous peoples as anti-modern remnants of the "Old West" has often silenced the stories of Native men and women working in the industrial "New West." This chapter explores the myriad ways in which Indians engaged with the railroad and the market revolution it introduced to their peoples.[11] It begins with the expansion of Indian freighting from the Central and Northern Plains to Native communities across the region in the 1880s and 1890s. Expanding rail lines ultimately choked out freighting opportunities in the West, but the work afforded wagon masters a modicum of independence and mobility at a time when Indians were subjected to physical containment and cultural assimilation.

Freighting died out just as an enterprising Indigenous resident of Northeast Indian Territory sought to refashion the corporate model to build an industrial center run by Native peoples. Finally, the chapter examines the work of Indigenous railroad laborers in the Southwest and the ways in which railroad work both undermined and upheld Indigenous customs and survival strategies in a changing world. Taken together, these three studies of Indian work point to the diversity, adaptability, and ingenuity of Indians in the railroad age.

Yoked to the Wagon

Throughout Indian Country, where iron tracks ended, wagon roads began. Initially, private, non-Indian contractors hauled supplies along these roads. But by the middle of the 1870s it was becoming increasingly clear that these non-Indian wagon masters exploited the Indian Office's lack of oversight, frequently charging for more miles than they actually freighted, stealing the supplies they carried, and refusing to make journeys to reservations in inclement weather.[12] Natives contained on reservations were subject to the whims of these private contractors. Freighters' decisions to take from their wagon loads or their refusal to travel resulted in Indigenous communities either receiving or going without crucial resources. Rations and annuities usually shipped in August or September, after Congress approved Indian Department appropriations in July. For many reservations in remote parts of the West, these early fall shipments were the sole source of sustenance for the winter months.[13]

The villainy of private contractors was made public during the US government's investigation of "Indian rings" in the Dakotas in the mid-1870s. The ensuing reports reference men like D. J. McCann, a freighter who charged the Indian Office for hauling goods to Red Cloud Agency. McCann claimed he carried his load 212 miles from the Missouri River depot to the Agency, but the government investigators later found that the distance was only 145 miles. Appalled by the vast sums of government monies lost in the schemes of "Indian rings" involving men like McCann, the Office turned to a ready supply of available labor: reservation Indians.[14]

In 1875 the Indian Office began purchasing wagons and harnesses for Indian freighters, beginning with Kiowa and Comanche and Cheyenne and Arapaho agencies in Indian Territory. US government agents provided the wagons and harnesses on credit, and the teamsters supplied their own horses. Cheyenne and Arapaho freighters traveled 165 miles from the nearest railroad station in Kansas. The Indian teamsters had the option of receiving $1.50 per 100 pounds hauled or accepting a credit of $1.75 per 100 pounds to invest in their freighting implements. In 1878 alone, Cheyennes and Arapahos carted 300,000 pounds of goods to their Indian Territory agency. By 1880 they hauled over 1 million pounds annually.[15]

Soon after, Indian teamsters were carrying cargo to reservations across the West. Two factors—US legislation passed in 1877 giving Indian freighters exclusive rights to transporting Indian Office goods, and the requests of Indigenous leaders for wagons and freighting opportunities—stimulated the expansion of Indian teaming.[16] "So popular has this branch of industry become," wrote the Commissioner in 1880, "that the demands of these Indians for freighting are largely in excess of the quantity of government freight required to be transported."[17] Freighting was monopolized by Indigenous teamsters at Devil's Lake in Wisconsin, Sisseton Agency in South Dakota, Fort Hall in Idaho Territory, across Kansas and Indian Territory, Uintah Agency in Utah Territory, Warm Springs and Siletz agencies in Oregon, and at Western Shoshone in Nevada.[18] Indian wagon masters freighted for the Indian Office, for agency traders, for US military posts, and for emerging settler towns. "The success of the enterprise," intoned the Commissioner in 1880, "has made it a permanent feature in the policy of Indian civilization."

While the Indian Office may have considered wagon-bound Indians a sign of the success of their civilizing mission, Indians had their own reasons for taking to freighting. In the Dakotas the enterprise took off in part because two Lakota leaders, Spotted Tail (Brulé) and Red Cloud (Oglala), negotiated regularly with US agents to secure necessary implements and work. Acutely aware that established Lakota practices of migratory hunting would cease on reservations, they considered carefully the kinds of labor regimes that reservation occupants could engage in to support themselves. In 1879 Spotted Tail and Red Cloud negotiated with government agents for the acquisition of horses, cattle, wagons, and harnesses in exchange for relinquishing hunting rights in Nebraska.[19] The adoption of freighting was important enough to Lakotas that a winter count depicts the adoption of freighting in 1878–1879 (Figure 5.2).[20] In a petition authored by Red Cloud, Man Afraid of His Horses, and nineteen other Lakotas in 1879, the Lakota men asked first and foremost for wagons and harnesses.

Figure 5.2 Excerpt of a Lakota winter count showing adoption of freighting practices. Winter Count of the Wajaje Lakota, 1758–1759 to 1885–1886. Museum of Native American History, Bentonville, Arkansas.

White freighters, enraged by the loss of business, ended up burning a 240-square-mile radius of grassland on the Lakota agencies in response to the Lakota acquisition of Indian Office freighting contracts.[21]

Luther Standing Bear (Oglala) recalled the early adoption of wagons among his people. His father made plans to open a reservation store and bought a wagon with four *pete-wa-quin* ("packing buffalo," or oxen). Standing Bear remembered that Spotted Tail owned a four-mule team with a wagon to carry his goods, while he traveled comfortably in a top buggy drawn by white horses.[22] The Indian Office distributed wagons to many other reservation Lakotas at Black Pole, a steamboat depot on the Missouri River. Standing Bear recalled camping there with several others while waiting for wheeled transports of their own to arrive. "I was very anxious for my father's name to be called," Standing Bear said, "because I wanted one of those beautifully colored wagons."[23] By 1889, the Dakotas were covered in wagons run by Lakota and Dakota freighters. At Cheyenne River Agency, teamsters carried more than 900,000 pounds of freight, earning $4,000 in pay. The Lower Yanktonai carted more than 500,000 pounds of freight, earning $1,304 in pay. Lakotas and their pony teams carried one million pounds to Pine Ridge Agency that same year; freighters at Rosebud Agency carted over two million.[24] Scenes like the one witnessed by Standing Bear fanned out beyond the Northern Plains too. By 1883, roughly 15,000 Indian freighters were hauling 12.6 million pounds of freight for government and private contractors.[25] The transition to freighting in the broader West was gaining momentum.

What drew Indigenous men and some women to freighting? For one, the cash they earned provided a modicum of economic security that freed many families from relying solely on uneven and irregular ration distributions. Second, freighting provided Indians with an opportunity to maintain their long-standing relationships with horses and mules. Third, since freighting required that men leave the reservation, it gave Natives freedom from the surveillance of the Indian Agent. Some agents required that Indian Office officials accompany the freighting parties, but more often freighters left on their own, sometimes for days or weeks at a time, traversing former homelands.[26] It seems likely that many Indian freighters took advantage of their freedom and mobility to continue habits that were under assault in the reservation era, including the maintenance of long-standing relationships with horses and the visiting of sacred sites. Tribal leaders like Spotted Tail and Red Cloud openly supported the use of Indian freighters who had a personal stake in ensuring that reservation goods arrived intact and on time (Figure 5.3).[27] Indian Office reports repeatedly praise the reliability and timeliness of Indian freighters, a reflection of their desire to ensure that their communities received much-needed foodstuffs and supplies.

Indigenous freighting also shored up communication networks, as mail arrived more regularly thanks to Indian wagon masters.[28] At Pine Ridge Agency, for example, the Indian Agent confiscated a letter held by a Lakota freighter written by a performer in London with Buffalo Bill's Wild West show.[29] The letter, written in Lakota, enclosed money for the recipient, and discussed the purchase of a rifle. The reasons for why the agent withheld the letter are unclear, but it is unsurprising that a colonial agent would be monitoring written communication entering and leaving the reservation. Yet freighters were eager to keep information their efforts to share and receiving crucial information. Their travels connected Indigenous communities and Indian Agents to US officials in Washington and to relations beyond the reservation borders.

The sale of reservation products carted by freighters, paired with the arrival of annuities and rations by wagon, placed Indian teamsters at the very heart of the reservation economy. Most government-contracted

Figure 5.3 Chief Kicking Bear, Young Man Afraid, and Standing Bear, in front of a wagon at Pine Ridge Agency, 1891. Chief Kicking Bear, Young Man Afraid, Chief of all Sioux's [*sic*], Standing Bear. Northwest Photographic Company, January 30, 1891, no. X-31367. Western History and Genealogy, Denver Public Library Digital Collections.

freighters did not receive payment for their trip out, but were paid instead by per hundred weights (cwt) per 100 miles on their return. Many Indian wagon masters brought goods from the reservation on their trips off reservation, such as timber, rugs, and hides. A trader in 1882 reported purchasing $11,0000 in hides at Cheyenne River.[30] After the decimation of the buffalo population on the Central and Northern Plains, teamsters gathered buffalo bones and sold $10,000 worth to traders in what must have been an emotional experience.[31] "Each bone gathered," historian Jeffrey Ostler writes, "was a bitter reminder of all that had been lost."[32] Freighters also carted produce cultivated on the reservation. The subsistence of Crows, Cheyennes, Lakotas, Navajos, Hopis, Klamaths, and others depended on the wagons, teamsters, and beasts that connected Indigenous communities to markets and brought supplies to Indian Country.

Pay varied widely, depending on the distance traveled, the difficulty of the trek, and the rates set by the Indian Agent. Rates could range from 40 or 50 cents to a dollar of more per 100 pounds hauled.[33] Indians at Pine Ridge petitioned in 1902 for a rate of $3.50 per day for freighters, regardless of weight carried.[34] That was in response to demands by the Indian Agent to reduce expenditures to 25 cents per 100 pounds instead of the 50 cents previously allowed.[35] Even though Indian teamsters could not set their wages, freighting earnings went a long way, and many enjoyed their work. Utes, for instance, hauling from Price Station on the Central Pacific Railroad to Ouray and Unitah, had a "special liking for this work."[36] At Rosebud, the agent reported that freighting "is not confined to the young men, but many of the older ones, among whom chief and head men are prominent."[37] Families would also split freighting responsibilities. Those who did not have more than two horses for freighting hitched their ponies to a cart with two horses from another family. The families then split the proceeds from the trip.[38] The monies these freighters earned went to buy clothing, furniture, farming implements, and other necessities.

The benefits of freighting were not only material. Teamsters relied on two to four horses to pull loads, thus continuing long-standing human-animal relationships that held significant cultural value for many Native peoples. Freighting kept horses on reservations at a time when colonial agents sought to rid Indian Country of an animal that they believed contributed to their militant and migratory natures. The agent at Cheyenne River Agency in South Dakota, for example, noted that the seizure of Lakota horses and arms "deprived them of the means to go to war and checked their migratory disposition."[39] But in the Dakotas, despite the confiscation of ponies in 1876, the horse populations rose over the course of the 1880s.[40] Many of the horses were smaller in stature and not bred for carting the weights (1,200–2,500 pounds per wagon) demanded of freighters. US Indian Agents held the right to sell or dispose of livestock owned by Indians, and many sought to replace the Indian herds with large draft horses, such as Percherons.[41]

Freighters carted coffee, flour, construction materials, and other reservation and camp provisions hundreds of miles. They also carried human cargo, transporting Indian Office employees to railroad depots and Indian children to stations en route to off-reservation boarding schools.[42] Indian teamsters also participated in more ambitious colonial removal programs, with wagons hauling entire communities from one confined location to another. In the late 1870s, the Indian Office hired Modoc freighters to cart Nez Percés from Baxter Springs, Kansas, to Quapaw Agency in Indian Territory. When the Nez Percés were forced from the Quapaw reservation and onto the Ponca, teamsters from the tribe carted their kin on wagons.[43]

While wagons often worked with train cars to transport and confine Indigenous populations, Indian teamsters also harnessed their horses and wagons against the colonial order. In 1885, the Indian Agent at the Kiowa, Comanche, and Wichita Agency requested that Indian freighters be directed to another location to pick up reservation goods. The agent reported that at the current location, freighters picked up runaways from the Chilocco Indian School.[44] In Warm Springs, Oregon, Indian freighters volunteered to cart supplies to a boarding school so they could visit their children, which was normally forbidden. In these instances, freighters used the mobility offered by freighting to check-in on and support Indigenous youth living away from their community.[45]

In an effort to keep transportation networks between railroad and steamboat terminuses and reservations intact, Indians also worked tirelessly to build and improve wagon roads across the West. In 1884, more than 100 wagons and drivers set out from Pine Ridge Agency to cut a road to the newly formed Black Hills mining town of Rapid City. Widening an old Indian trail, the teamsters worked with picks and shovels to carve out a new road, one that would carry Indian freighters from the railroad terminus in Valentine, Nebraska, to a flour-delivery point in the mining town.[46] In the Southwest, Helen Sekaquaptewa recalled how Hopi teamsters cleared and maintained the roads for freighting government supplies and goods for the Lorenzo Hubell Trading Post at Oraibi.[47] Many of these roads morphed into branch railway lines and later automobile roads throughout the West. Indigenous laborers thus directed and constructed paths for movement through their homelands as they had for centuries.[48]

As railroad short lines expanded in the late 1880s and 1890s, freighting operations declined. Shorter distances to the agency translated into smaller payouts for teamsters, who turned to work from private contractors when available. Those who could not find more freighting work resorted to other economic strategies for survival. Even so, the brief emergence of Indigenous freighting across the American West reveals how Indians adapted to the market transformations unleashed by railroads in ways that sought to protect tribal interests. Freighting helped money and government annuities flow into communities and Indigenous goods to flow out. It sustained and expanded communication networks among and across tribes, while also granting physical mobility and work with horses that carried cultural and spiritual value. As freighting business dwindled, an entrepreneur in the Central Plains mapped out a different vision for Indigenous prosperity and protection in a railroaded region.

An Indian Railroad

In October 1889 another small western town celebrated the railroad's arrival. In Splitlog City, Missouri, residents excitedly crowded along the newly laid iron road. Perhaps prosperity and opportunity would ride in on the back of the coming iron horse, its tracks a lifeline to distant markets that might invigorate this remote corner of the Middle West. Others watched with trepidation, seeing the same track as a gash upon the landscape, one that brought voracious speculators who would drain the region of its resources. The railroad company's principal owner, Mathias Splitlog (Seneca-Cayuga/Wyandot), was "beaming with pride" as he watched the first steam locomotive rumble through the town. "A glorious vision swam before the chieftain's gaze," a newspaper later recalled. It entailed "a great mining and industrial empire, linked with all corners of the world; American traffic, freight, tourists, flowing through his prosperous towns on his railroad."[49] Maybe this is indeed what Splitlog envisioned. "I go on," Splitlog promised at the ceremony; "I make Cayuga and Splitlog biggest towns in the Ozarks!"[50]

Few markers remain of that dream. In Cayuga, Oklahoma, an empty limestone church rises from a hilltop overlooking Grand River Lake. Down the hillside, an old factory lies in disrepair.[51] In Strawberry Hill—formerly Splitlog Hill—Kansas City, a new coffee shop nods to the neighborhood's former resident.[52] Splitlog's descendants care for an inherited padlock. "The keyhole is concealed," his grandson recalled, "and can only be found by a secret spring."[53]

A padlock—a fitting bequest from Splitlog. He long nurtured a love for machinery and technology, apprenticing with a carpenter and a locksmith as a younger man and developing an intricate irrigation system in Cayuga years later. For decades, Splitlog committed himself to unlocking a region and its people—both Indian and non-Indian—to what he considered the wealth and opportunity that came with marketplace access, the commodification of natural resources, and manufacturing. A product and proponent of Gilded Age industrialization, Splitlog broke into an occupation that largely locked out non-whites: industrial entrepreneurship.

As the first Indigenous railroad owner, Splitlog's story is unique. But Splitlog emerged from a long line of Indians who embraced the ethos of profit-making and private property accumulation central to the Euro-American capitalist ethos. He came of age in a region awash in get-rich-quick schemes. As railroads opened reservations to capitalist marketplaces and as US Indian Office officials attacked tribal land ownership and cultures, many Indians turned to economic individualism. Splitlog allied with this "progressive" faction of reservation Indians, believing that Indian-owned industry and business would help communities in the reservation and allotment periods. Many beneficiaries of private landholding and economic individualism on Indian reservations were able to accrue wealth and savings. With money came political influence, and Splitlog's life reflects that. But for other Indigenous residents of the Ozark region and elsewhere, unlocking the resources of their reservation lands involved sacrifices that severely threatened tribal sovereignty and undermined long-standing cultural and spiritual values.[54]

As a Cayuga of the Iroquois Confederacy that had once fanned across the US-Canada border, Splitlog was born a border crosser.[55] Known as the "millionaire Indian," he was born in New York or in Ontario, Canada, in 1812.[56] At a young age, Splitlog moved with his family to live among the Wyandottes in Sandusky, Ohio. There he secured an apprenticeship with a carpenter and millwright, kindling a lifelong interest in machinery and engineering. From the knowledge gained as an apprentice, Splitlog built a steamboat and trafficked fish and other goods along the St. Clair River north of Lake Superior. According to newspaper accounts and family records, US authorities confiscated Splitlog's boat under allegations of smuggling. On the shores of Lake Superior he made a name for himself as a man on the move: a transporter of goods, peoples, and products.

Over the course of his life, Splitlog migrated (by force and by will) to new lands and into new tribal communities. In Ohio, he married Eliza Barnett, the daughter of a prominent Wyandotte chief, and was adopted into the Wyandotte tribe. The US government forced Splitlog, his family, and several other Midwestern tribes from their homes in Ohio, initiating a march to Kansas, where new reservation plots awaited.[57] Their reservation soon caught the covetous gaze of white settlers, and in 1855, as part of the Manypenny treaties, Wyandottes forfeited their title to lands in Kansas. A treaty-specific allotment program, the agreement forced Wyandottes to select plots of land on or near their former reservation and to accept US citizenship. Splitlog and a handful of other Wyandottes refused citizenship, though Splitlog was somehow able to receive a patent to lands in Kansas.[58]

Splitlog profited handsomely from the allotment and privatization of Wyandotte lands through the leasing and sale of the lands he held in patent, though his decision to refuse citizenship and relocate to Indian Territory suggests that he did not approve of the second major component of US allotment policy: the dissolution of tribal governments.[59] He arrived in Indian Territory in 1874 at the request of "friends," and soon thereafter Seneca chief George Spicer adopted him into the tribe for a fee of $500.[60] The Wyandottes and Senecas had a friendship dating back to Ohio, where the Wyandottes had given a band of Senecas that had defected from the Iroquois Confederacy 40,000 acres.[61] Splitlog, now a tribal member, selected a parcel of land along the confluence of the Grand and Cowskin rivers, on the 51,000-acre Seneca reservation.[62] Given that all Seneca tribal members shared the reservation, Splitlog did not own his land outright, though by making improvements to it he was granted a right of occupancy.[63]

By the late 1870s and early 1880s, Splitlog was using his profits from his Kansas lands to build a regional industrial center. He called his new home Cayuga Springs, and it became a prominent economic hub in Northeastern Indian Territory. By the early 1870s, it was a remarkably cosmopolitan place and home to eight different tribes: Maimis, Shawnees, Quapaws, Peorias, Modocs, Iowas, Wyandottes, and Seneca-Cayugas. This small region housed Indigenous peoples from the Southern Plains, the Great Lakes, and northern California, who spoke languages from four distinct language stocks. Despite their cultural and linguistic diversity, these tribes shared the trauma of forced removal. Like Splitlog, many experienced removal twice. Their small populations also made them especially vulnerable to federal government assimilation programs and the whims of white settlers flooding in from Kansas, Missouri, and Arkansas.[64] Northeastern Indian Territory tribes did not have the numbers, the existing institutions, or the land base that their Five Tribes neighbors boasted to combat pressure from the US government and land-hungry settlers. However, beginning in the late nineteenth century these diverse tribes cultivated cross-cultural institutional and economic alliances born of their shared experiences.[65] By 1898 the Indian Agent wrote that "although there are in this agency eight distinct tribes, there seems to be the most friendly feeling between them," adding that "they intermingle and intermarry to a great extent and from appearances one would think there is but one tribe."[66]

Among these eight tribes mingled thousands of whites who leased land through formal and informal labor contracts with tribal citizens and by illegally squatting.[67] Seven of the Northeastern Indian Territory tribes (the Quapaws were excluded initially) underwent allotment of their lands in 1887, but allottees were allowed to lease their lands to white laborers for up to three years at a time. In 1895 the Indian Office, under pressure from the Indians, nullified all labor contracts with whites and required leasees to submit requests for leases through the Indian Department.[68] Efforts to control the influx of whites into Northeastern Indian Territory, however, would not successfully cease the loss of the Indigenous land base. By 1905 Indian title had been extinguished for 34,000 acres in the region.[69]

Mathias Splitlog, a Seneca-Cayuga and Wyandotte tribal citizen, was a product of this region and imagined an industrial center in its heart. In the winter of 1886, Splitlog formed the Splitlog Land and Mining Company, eager to profit from the promise of gold in the area. Eastern capitalists had shared rumors with Splitlog about a gold vein running from Missouri directly into Cayuga. The Splitlog Company laid out plans for a town, Splitlog City, that would cater to the mines Splitlog purchased. Splitlog City, Missouri, boasted a mill, a blacksmith, a post office, and the opulent Occidental Hotel. Tourists, businessmen, and laborers milled about the hotel, "a scene of backwoods refinement and gay living," with rumored double walls where Splitlog stored his riches.[70]

In March 1887, just two months after Congress passed the Dawes Allotment Act, Splitlog and a handful of other investors incorporated the Kansas City, Fort Smith, and Southern Railroad Company—known as the Splitlog Railroad. As the Indian Office set to work breaking up tribal landholdings into individual allotments, Splitlog imagined an industrial Indigenous future in Northeastern Indian Territory. The town of Neosho, Missouri, had already guaranteed the payment of $40,000 to bring the Splitlog line through that city from Joplin. The railroad would continue south through Goodman, then west to Splitlog City and on to Cayuga Springs in Indian Territory before heading south through Arkansas to the Gulf of Mexico.[71] By connecting his mining center to Cayuga Springs,

Splitlog believed railroads could bring wealth to an intertribal community reeling from removal and desperate for new subsistence patterns.

The dream was never realized. Like so many Gilded Age corporations, the company fell into dire financial straits within two years of incorporation. The Splitlog City mines held no gold, and a lawsuit with another investor drained Splitlog of his resources. Nearly bankrupt, he called off construction of the line to Cayuga. Allegations surfaced that some $80,000 of Splitlog's stock went missing.[72] By 1892 the tracks to Splitlog City had fallen into disrepair from disuse, and non-Indian investors bought up Splitlog's shares and extended the railroad south from Neosho to Arkansas, bypassing Indian Territory.[73] The Splitlog Railroad went under like so many railroads in the late nineteenth century. Yet Splitlog—as an Indian entrepreneur—was especially vulnerable to financial failure because he was an outsider to the mainstream business community. As a noncitizen, Splitlog did not receive the backing and bailouts from Congress, practices that many nineteenth-century companies had come to rely on. To do business across borders was to enter a foreign economic and legal regime that offered few, if any, protections and often sided with the competition. Splitlog learned that firsthand on the shores of Lake Superior and again in the wooded plains of Northeastern Indian Territory.

Splitlog's labors were like those of other Indian Territory capitalists—most famous among them Cherokee Elias Boudinot—who sought personal fortune in the commercialization and railroading of their community's lands. In 1867 Boudinot had introduced his own railroad bill in the US Congress. "My plan," he wrote to Stand Watie (Cherokee) from Washington, "is to allow the Indians to build their own road and own it."[74] Boudinot swiftly lost respect among fellow Cherokees because his actions revealed an opportunist who promoted foreign corporate interests more than a tribal citizen concerned with Cherokee sovereignty. He was a clerk on the congressional committee on land claims and a lobbyist for railroads in the 1860s and 1870s, which gave him inside knowledge that he often used to speculate in land. He openly advocated for territorialization, which the Cherokee Nation and other Indian Territory nations bitterly opposed. Apart from his railroad schemes, Boudinot had built a chewing tobacco factory with the Southern Cherokee chief Stand Watie after the Civil War. The factory sat on the eastern edge of the Cherokee Nation, near Maysville, Arkansas. Like Splitlog, Boudinot envisioned a transnational commercial system, preparing his products for sale to eager consumers in the American South.[75] Boudinot also used the Cherokee white labor permit system to hire non-Cherokees to hold and develop lands on a plot where it was believed that the Missouri Kansas and Texas (MKT) and St. Louis and San Francisco Railroad would intersect. Officials for both lines moved the intersection outside of Vinita, and Boudinot lost his bet on the town.[76] Splitlog's economic exploits were less patently self-serving, though it is clear that he profited handsomely from land speculation and the extraction of timber and produce from his community's lands.

Silas Armstrong (Wyandotte) ultimately succeeded in building the transportation center in Northeastern Indian Territory that Splitlog envisioned. Another Indian Territory entrepreneur and tribal leader, Armstrong created the Wyandotte Association in 1895. Along with fellow Wyandotte A. J. Mudeater, the company was incorporated with $50,000 to build the city of Wyandotte. With the support of a white attorney and secretary, they applied through the Indian Office for a permit to lease a strip of land along the St. Louis and San Francisco Railway (known as the "Frisco" line) and next to the Seneca Boarding School. Within a year, banks and businesses cropped up in the town the entrepreneurs had established. Wyandotte would become the critical shipping point Splitlog had envisioned for Cayuga Springs less than a decade earlier. "It furnished a market for the produce and stock raised by Indians and whites," the Quapaw Agent reported in 1896, "which heretofore they were compelled to convey over bad roads to markets in the State of Missouri and Kansas."[77]

The rise of wealthy Indian Territory entrepreneurs like Splitlog, Armstrong, Boudinot, and others would become set examples for Indian reformers keen on opening up Indian Territory to allotment. The Five Tribes were initially excluded from the Dawes Allotment Act. When it came to the Cherokee, Choctaw, Chickasaws, Creeks, and Seminoles, pro-allotment whites argued that it was communal landholding that created huge wealth disparities among Indigenous populations. Rezin McAdam painted a damning portrait of Indian Territory in the November 1893 issue of *Harper's Monthly*, one colored by his pro-allotment sentiments. "Monopoly of land under the so-called community system of tenure, together with the corruption of the tribal governments and their utter inefficacy," he wrote, "has brought about the decadence of the Five Nations."[78] He called for the incorporation of Indian Territory into Oklahoma. Another newspaper called a Creek cattle conglomerate the "Jay Gould of the Nation."[79] Debates over the growing economic chasms between tribal governments was fodder for pro-allotment Americans.

In reality, the commercialization of Indigenous reservations generated wealth disparities and fissures within the tribal community both before and after allotment. Splitlog's story is no exception. In 1890 Splitlog, at age seventy-eight, was elected chief of the Senecas and held a feast to mark the occasion. He provided 1,500 loaves of bread and prepared three cows for the event. But the celebrations were short-lived. The Seneca-Cayuga later split into two rival political factions, each with its own chief, until the later part of the decade.[80] Some Shawnees and Senecas openly criticized Splitlog's adoption into the tribe, calling him a "white" Indian.[81] Splitlog would spend the remainder of his old age traveling by rail back and forth from Seneca Country to Washington, DC, advocating for his people. While chief, he successfully secured the payment of $372.00 per capita for Seneca tribal members from outstanding treaty obligations. He died of tuberculosis while in the US capital in January 1897, a year before Congress passed the Curtis Act, which forced allotment on the remaining tribes in Indian Territory and dissolved their tribal governments.[82]

Over the course of the 1880s and 1890s, small townships across the West cropped up, eager to siphon from the treasures carried by trains. Splitlog City and Cayuga Springs joined this groundswell of construction, built on the promises of gold and an iron horse. These Ozark towns were unique because they reflected an Indigenous vision of prosperity, part of an Indigenous world that linked US markets to natural resources and manufactured goods on reservations. Splitlog's vision failed, but he joined a growing cohort of individuals who sought to refashion the corporate model to support themselves and, to an extent, their broader communities. In the coming decades an intertribal religious movement would successfully embrace a form of corporatization to protect their movement. Meanwhile, Native railroad laborers were busy constructing and maintaining the roads and railcars that made these visions possible.

Roundhouse, Road, and Home

On a blistering August day, tracklayers united two iron paths in Needles, California. The main line of the Atchison, Topeka, and Santa Fe (ATSF) running west from Isleta, New Mexico, joined with a Southern Pacific track in August 1883. Needles lay along the Colorado River just across the California-Arizona border. Some thirty years earlier, Lt. Amiel Weeks Whipple's survey party had crossed the Colorado just north of Needles, at Bill William's Fork. The union of rails at Needles was a perfunctory arrangement between two corporations, but the town it spawned became an important outpost for tribal communities in the Southwest.[83] Chinese, white, Mexican, and Native railroad workers and their families called Needles home in the coming decades. The Mojaves and Chemehuevis established a permanent neighborhood in the town, which sat on their ancestral homelands along the Colorado. Many Mojaves migrated back and forth from the Colorado River and Fort Mojave reservations nearby, piecing together livings from wage labor and farming. By 1890 over 600 Mojaves resided off their established reservation at Needles, where, according to the agent, "they retain all their old-time superstition and barbarous customs."[84]

Mojave migrations between Needles and their reservations mirrored earlier community movements, prompted by the seasonal shifts of the Colorado River. For the Mojave—the *pipa aha macav* or "people by the river"—the Colorado was the magnetic center of their migrations, pulling tribal members back to its shores year after year. Every spring the *aha homee* or "high waters" deposited sediment and organic debris along the river's banks where Mojaves and other Colorado River residents returned to plant vegetables. After the planting, Mojaves left for months at a time, traveling for trade, subsistence, and spiritual purposes before returning to harvest their crops.[85] To rely too much on overflow from the Colorado was to put lives at risk, making movement for trade central to maintaining an existence in the region. Needles flourished as a stopping point along this route well into the early twentieth century.

Work loading ice into boxcars or repairing engines at the roundhouses of Needles was just one way in which Southwest Indians engaged with the expanding market and wage economies that trains carried into the region. Across the Southwest, railroads carted Navajo blankets to far-flung outlets for sale, and, by the early twentieth century, they brought Euro-American tourists into the region to purchase Pueblo, Hopi, and Navajo pottery and jewelry.[86] Navajo silversmiths, for their part, forged silver jewelry atop severed railroad ties.[87] Navajos in New Mexico also leased lands along the tracks from the ATSF for farming and grazing.[88] Mine cropped up across the region that depended on the labor of Indians and Mexicans who unearthed coal from their homelands to fuel the iron beasts. Trees were felled for ties. And on railroad lines across California, Arizona, New Mexico, and southern Colorado, Pimas, Yumas, Navajos, Tohono O'odhams, Mojaves, Hualapais, and Chemeheuvis found work as tracklayers, gang bosses, timber cutters, boilermakers, and section hands.[89]

Especially on southwestern reservations that were not suitable for farm-centered colonial assimilation and allotment programs, Indians frequently sought wage work off reservations to supplement their reservation-based production of wool, beef, and consumer goods. The Indian Agent at the Torres Reservation in California noted in 1893 that the tribe members "subsist mostly by work performed for the railroad company, in cutting wood for shipment to Los Angeles."[90] Cahuillas at Augustine and Cabazon reservations also toiled on the Southern Pacific lines, citing the poor quality of the reservation land for farming.[91] Hualapai women, meanwhile, took the train into Kingman, Arizona, where they sold baskets at the railroad stop or earned wages as domestic workers.[92]

By 1900, Indian Office officials sought to control the growing tide of off-reservation laborers. Some Indian Agents and local traders negotiated work contracts with corporate officials.[93] The Navajo Agent reported that he worked with the ATSF to employ over 320 Navajo men in 1899 and more than 400 in 1900 to grade road beds.[94] Five years later, the Indian Office established the Southwestern Indian Employment Bureau, headed by Charles Dagenett (Peoria). Dagenett's primary responsibility was to plan and manage the recruitment of wage labor for Indians in the Southwest. He provided annual reports listing the locations of Indian laborers pursuing commercial agriculture, mining, and railroad work. By working through the Indian Office, Dagenett believed he negotiated better wages for Indian laborers. He worked with corporations to create formal employment contracts and employee protections that didn't exist in informal contracts with individual workers. For example, in 1911, Dagenett entered into a contract with the ATSF for the employment of Indian labor on railroad lines west of Albuquerque. The Indians would be involved in ballasting the road for the second line of the ATSF. The contract laid out the terms of employment: the laborers were to work 10-hour days at a rate of $1.50 per day, with 50 cents withheld per month for hospital fees. The provision for medical care costs points to the dangers inherent in track work. If employees labored for a minimum of 30 days, their transportation, along with the transportation of their families, was included. The company promised to furnish fuel and water for communities that congregated along the line.[95]

Tom Ration (Navajo) recalled working along that second ATSF line. Initially, he cut cedar trees for ties. It was a two-man job, each using a handsaw. "Back and forth," he recalled, "that is a hard life."[96] He cut back the cedars between Thoreau and Crownpoint, New Mexico, noting that they "used to be thick, just like a forest." His father was a section leader for laborers and also worked the lumber mill for the railroad. After the cedar industry dried up, Ration took up work on the second line of the ATSF, living in camps along the road from North Chavez, to Winslow, Arizona. His work supported his family on the reservation.[97]

Though Indigenous laborers earned cash from railroad work, the pay was poor. Railroad companies regularly exploited their laborers, and government officials did little to advocate for them. Colonial agents discouraged union activity.[98] The Agency farmer at Pima mentioned in 1906 that he had "many calls from railroad contractors, for Papago [Tohono O'odham] labor," but that many in the community were not interested because of the "bad treatment which they had received in the past from their employers."[99] The previous summer more than fifty Tohono O'odham left for Los Angeles, where they worked for a railroad contractor. The laborers reported that they had been treated and paid well, but not given their return fare back to the reservation. Many then spent most of their earnings or walked home. Contracts like the one Dagenett negotiated offset some of these problems, but pay remained low and seasonal for most. Dagenett noted that just a few years earlier a Los Angeles general manager for the Santa Fe elected to lower rates to $1.00 per day because of the influx of immigrant labor from Mexico, which made this work even less appealing to Southwest Indians.[100]

Indigenous laborers could find work through other, nongovernment connections and were not dependent on the Indian Service to secure wage labor. The Needles community of Indigenous laborers is a prime example of this practice. It developed beyond the oversight of the Indian Office, much to the distress of local officials. The Mojave population alone grew from 669 in 1890 to well over 1,300 in 1899.[101] "Here are about 1,300 Indians without government control and direction," the nearby Colorado River Agent lamented. "The government does nothing for them," he added, "they earn from $50,000 to $100,000 per year working for the railroad company, mostly at track work."

Though his earnings estimates are grossly inflated, the Indian Agent continued on to decry the spending habits of the Mojaves at Needles, claiming that they used their wages to purchase liquor or "tawdry clothing." Or, he went on, "[they] burn it up at their funerals, or divide it with the hobo white element among them."[102] That same year, 200 Mojave kin from the reservation left to visit with relatives at Needles. It would remain an important Mojave gathering place well into the 1920s.[103]

As a critical labor center, Needles also became an important intertribal hub. As people from tribes across the Southwest converged on Needles, they found new ways to organize and socialize. In 1923, a group of Mojave Needles residents formed the Mojave Indian Welfare Committee (MIWC) to make preparations for an annual pow-wow. They sent invitations to their Mojave kin and to Chemehuevis at the Colorado River and Fort Mojave Agencies, the former some sixty-three miles south of Needles, the latter just across the Colorado in Arizona. The MIWC also invited Tohono O'odhams, Pimas, Hualapais, and Yumas to the ceremonies. The committee contacted the nearby Fort Mojave Indian Agent, Leo Crane, seeking stores of flour, coffee, and sugar for their visitors. Crane did not mask his displeasure about the gathering when he replied, denying the MIWC request and urging the Needles Indian community to cancel it. "The Commissioner [of Indian Affairs] does not feel that Indians benefit themselves by leaving home, range, and farm interests to gather for meetings of this character," he wrote.[104] Crane saw firsthand how off-reservation work gave Pimas, Mojaves, and others opportunities to escape the watchful eye of the colonial government.

Needles was also bound up in national contests between labor and capital. A year before the spring powwow, its railroad workers joined with those across the country to strike after the Railroad Labor Board agreed to another cut in wages. On July 12, armed company guards shot through a fence in Needles, killing George Moreno, a Mexican striker.[105] Newspapers also decried the plight of railroad passengers stranded in the town.[106] Corporate guards and the National Guard suppressed the nationwide strike by mid-August, but the Needles labor communities were still on edge. A bombing in nearby San Bernardino in mid-August prompted Santa Fe Railroad workmen to walk off the job again.[107] Mojaves splintered along pro- and anti-strike lines, and the situation remained fraught until the US attorney general issued an injunction in October against striking and other union activities, which effectively killed the national movement and union activity in the Needles area.

Depictions of striking Mojave workers contrasted sharply with the corporate imagery that railroad corporations constructed to sell the Southwest to travelers. The most prominent Southwestern railroad corporation, the ATSF, marketed the primitive and pre-industrial. In 1926 the company began running the *Chief*, a passenger train connecting Chicago to Los Angeles. The crown jewel of the ATSF, this line invoked images of pre-industrial Indians to invite modern travelers to consume a pre-modern past. The *Mojave*, one of the sleeper cars of the *Chief*, passed through Needles regularly. Even before starting this line, the ATSF and another large Southwestern corporation, the Fred Harvey Company, worked together to fashion an image of the primitive, the "Santa Fe Indian," a stoic, feathered warrior juxtaposed with the power and luxury of the railroad cars and various hotels, curios, and tourist destinations constructed for the eastern tourist.[108]

Indeed, many Indian workers made do by performing roles as pre-modern characters for the nascent tourism industry. In 1914 a group of Blackfeet Indians traveled across the country promoting travel to Glacier National Park. Before their departure, the performers wrote to a Great Northern official seeking an increase in pay to $3.00 a day and groceries for their families while they were away.[109] In Chicago that year, Two Guns White Calf (Blackfeet) rose before an audience and spoke in his native tongue. He said he had "come a long way on [the] iron horse to see white brothers" and invited the audience to come to Glacier where he and his people would "build council fires, smoke pipe of peace, [and] give dances."[110] His message was one of unity—unity in the service of a National Park and the railroad (Great Northern) that served it. The Blackfeet also made stops to lure potential travelers in Washington, DC, Atlanta, and New York. In New York, White Calf tested out the latest in modern transportation technology when he boarded a plane at Dobb's Ferry.[111] These Indigenous performers, an increasingly common presence at railroad stops across the West in the early decades of the twentieth century, obscured their own participation in the modern market economy that fanned out along the tracks. They may have displayed anti-modern indigeneity to willing white consumers, but their status as wage-earners placed them firmly within the modern marketplace. Not only did Indians build and maintain the tracks crossed by the *Chief*, but those same tracks also carried carloads of rugs, hides, and jewelry manufactured by Indigenous women and men to markets across the US.

Railroad-related hiring took hold in other parts of the West as well. At Fort Hall, in northeastern Idaho, Shoshone-Bannocks worked on the

Oregon Short Line.[112] Crow laborers were hired to build 110 miles of railroad in Montana and Wyoming, including the grading and laying of ties.[113] At Standing Rock in North Dakota, a number of Lakota and Blackfeet worked with their teams on a railroad extension near the reservation. Around fifty men and their freight teams were employed, earning $3.25 a day.[114] At Pine Ridge in South Dakota, Lakotas helped build branch lines for the Chicago and Northwestern and the Chicago Milwaukee and St. Paul railroads in 1906. One railroad contractor cited his preference for Lakota workers because "they are good men."[115] An agent working beside the Denver and Rio Grande extension in southwestern Colorado reported that "the earnings are not wasted, but in every instance go to the support of their families."[116] For these laborers, migration for subsistence was nothing new, though the nature of work and subsistence they migrated for changed drastically. For example, Tom Black (Mojave) found refuge from the horrors of government boarding schools in railroad work. For Fred Brown (Navajo), work on the railroads earned him a modicum of economic independence in an unsettling economic time. "I liked my railroad job," he recalled, having worked on various tracks over twenty years. In Manuelito, New Mexico, he oversaw a section party, "and it was in my home country."[117] In 1909 a band of Ute fled their reservation in Utah and subsisted primarily by working on the Burlington Railroad in South Dakota, their families moving with them along the tracks.[118] These examples offer a glimpse into the ways Indians participated in the industrialization of the American West through railroad construction and maintenance.

Blindsided by allotment and confronting government-backed assimilation efforts, many Indigenous families felt they had little choice but to move to earn a living in the railroad age. Indigenous workers gathered where short-lines cropped up in the 1880s, 1890s, and 1900s. They migrated along railroad lines and incorporated their seasonal labor with other wage work in mines or on commercial farms, supplementing their income by selling manufactured items or agricultural goods. Though they found novel ways to incorporate track work and the selling of wares into their survival strategies, Native peoples often labored under exploitive conditions. Both the US government and corporations held racialized ideas about the abilities of Indigenous laborers. Railroad barons, bent on expending as little capital as possible, ensured that these men had little room to negotiate for higher wages. It is no wonder, then, that many Mojaves struck alongside their railroad brethren in Needles and that Splitlog and others might try to wrest control over the railroad enterprise from outsiders. Still others used the right of refusal, leaving section gangs to return to their reservations to find other ways of earning a living.[119]

The experience of actual Indigenous wage earners, producers, and entrepreneurs associated with railroad and railroad-related industries has been lost amid the plethora of advertisements that celebrate western spaces and mythic Indians. The anti-modern Indian for tourist consumption satisfied the appetites of a colonial, Euro-American society, but Indians across the United States also turned railroad networks to their advantage, mobilizing goods, ideas, and people in the service of spiritual and political revolution.

The Iron Horse in Indian Country: Native Americans and Railroads in the US West. Alessandra La Rocca Link, Oxford University Press. © Alessandra La Rocca Link 2025. DOI: 10.1093/9780197674437.003.0008

6

Mobilizing for Indigenous Futures

The same year the iron tracks joined in Promontory, Utah, a Northern Paiute prophet imagined a different kind of train. Wodziwob, the earliest known Ghost Dance leader, dreamed of an iron horse emerging from the South, carrying Indian dead. The ancestors' return would mark the most significant transformation in human history to date: the disappearance of whites.[1] Wodziwob's train served a decidedly different purpose than the one charging across the center of the continent in 1869. It would end non-Native existence, bring back Indigenous ancestors, and set the stage for an Indian future. Wodziwob's millenarian prophecy did not come to fruition, but his vision and the visions of a later Ghost Dance prophet, Wovoka, compelled hundreds of followers to take to trains and spread the word of tribal and intertribal unity and renewal.

Both union and rebirth were sorely needed in Indian Country. In the wake of the violence of dispossession and removal, white settlers crossed over newly formed reservation borders, clamoring for Indigenous lands. Within reservation boundaries the long arm of the federal government choked traditional Indigenous livelihoods, practices, and customs, unsettling the social, cultural, and spiritual cosmologies and local ecologies that structured tribal life. The Ghost Dance was to restore what had been damaged, push back non-Native intruders, and carve out a place for Indigenous peoples in a modern, industrial world.

Prophesizing and propagating Native futures was a radical act at the turn of the century. Following the Civil War, Indigenous populations continued their rapid decline even as the cultural currency of the "vanishing" Indian saturated American life. These same decades witnessed the rise of American anthropology, a discipline devoted to the collection and preservation of Indigenous cultural material and knowledge considered doomed to disappear as Natives died off or assimilated into American society.[2] White Americans clamored to view Edward Curtis's Indian photographs, which presented Indian peoples as forlorn remnants of a bygone era.[3] Speaking to a reporter in 1906, a founding member of the Indian civil rights organization, the Society of

American Indians, put it bluntly when it came to white society's captivation with Indian disappearance. "They don't know us," Laura Cornelius Kellogg (Oneida) explained, "they don't know what it means to be killed alive."[4] Wodziwob's and Wovoka's teachings sparked fear among white Americans because they countered the settler colonial logic of elimination.[5] Their teachings diverged radically from Euro-American belief systems and colonial practices. On December 29, 1890, US soldiers sought to silence their teachings and suppress the movement when they killed over 250 Lakota Ghost Dancers at Wounded Knee, South Dakota.

But the Ghost Dance did not end with the massacre of Lakotas at the hands of the US 7th Cavalry in December 1890, nor would it be the only large intertribal movement that articulated Indigenous futures at the turn of the century.[6] This chapter explores the ways in which Indigenous migrations during this period contributed to two intertribal movements that sparked cultural and spiritual revitalization and political mobilization in the early decades of the twentieth century: the Peyote Religion and the Society of American Indians. It aims to reconsider the ways in which these movements imagined and acted on behalf of Indigenous futures in the midst of crisis. Just as US colonial agents sought to snuff out Indigenous presents and futures, Society of American Indian activists and peyotists built and imagined diverse, expansive, and plural Indigenous worlds. Audra Mitchell and Aadita Chaudhury write that BIPOC (Black, Indigenous, People of Color) futurisms "embrace lively practices of mobility and hybridity" in order to imagine "*multiple* futures."[7] Reading these practices backward, we can see the ways in which SAI activists and peyotists embraced both mobility and hybridity to create movements that encompassed a broad range of ideas and diverse tribal traditions. Though widely different in orientation—one movement centered on spirituality, the other on social and political organization—they both displayed an ability to manage sweeping change while simultaneously preserving Indigenous cultures and traditions and projecting them forward.

The two organizations took root in disparate locations, but both relied on networks of exchange and movement powered by railroads. The modern Peyote Religion was born in the late nineteenth century in Indian Territory and was carried to other tribes by traveling roadmen. The Society of American Indians (SAI) was an intertribal organization that emerged outside the reservations. It was founded in 1911 in Columbus, Ohio, with a headquarters in Washington, DC. The Peyote Religion promoted the individual spiritual migrations of the ceremony participants, and members adhered to principles of sobriety, hard work, and prosperity. SAI activists, meanwhile, focused on stripping the Indian Office of its expansive and unchecked powers, educating white America about Indigenous issues, advocating for Indigenous citizenship, and promoting legal cases and federal policies that could support the organization's mission of racial uplift. The SAI, according to its members, would be "the means by which many of his [the Indian's] vexing problems may be solved."[8]

These movements converged in the halls of US Congress in 1918, where members of each organization debated "the peyote question." It was a bitter debate, and the acerbic exchanges between popular anthropologist and peyote supporter James Mooney and SAI activist and ardent anti-peyotist Zitkála-Šá, also known as Gertrude Bonnin (Yankton Dakota), took center stage. For anti-peyotists, the cactus button ingested by the faith's followers was an intoxicant that spelled destruction for Indian peoples and hindered Indian assimilation into American society. "While bullet and bomb are destroying the white man on the battlefields of the world," *Washington Times* reported in the throes of World War I, "the American Indian is called upon to fight an enemy [peyote] which is rapidly undermining his race."[9] For those who followed the peyote road, the button brought life, not destruction. In the wake of the confrontation, peyotists turned to corporatization to protect their peyote use, and their membership grew rapidly in the following decades. The SAI, whose membership fractured on the peyote issue, did not survive the public scuffle.

Both organizations envisioned an Indigenous future by harnessing the communication and information revolutions of the railroad age. Not only did peyotists use physical trains to spread an Indigenous religion, but they would also rely on a modern legal document—the corporate charter—to protect their religious freedom. In an era defined by the rise of institutional organizing, Indigenous peyotists discovered that incorporating could protect their spiritual community.[10] A group of intertribal Oklahoma peyotists filed a nonprofit corporate charter in 1918, creating the Native American Church of Oklahoma.[11] Peyotists in other states followed suit, using incorporation as a means of extending crucial First Amendment rights to their use of peyote in sacred ceremonies.[12]

The SAI's growing communication network, born on steam and steel, set the stage for Progressive Era political activism. SAI members utilized an expansive mail system that dispersed information across Indian Country and the United States to organize and promote their cause. The physical mobility of SAI members was also central to SAI organizing. Among the SAI ranks who traveled to promote the cause was Laura Corneilious Kellogg (Oneida), who imagined the ways in which corporatization could protect Indigenous communities and promote prosperity. Her Lolomi Plan recast the reservation as an industrial cooperative that would buttress tribal independence.[13] Other members, including Thomas Sloan, Arthur Parker, and Carlos Montezuma, challenged the existing corporate and colonial order through their highly mobile and intertribal activism. As a carrier of ideas, information, goods, and people, the railroad undergirded expanding intertribal spiritual, cultural, and political relations in Indian Country.[14]

Taken together, these migrations undermined a colonial program bent on the confinement of Native peoples. In 1899, the Board of Indian Commissioners' annual report assailed Indians on the move. "When they should be at work upon their farms," the report claimed, "they go in large bodies to visit other tribes, spending their rent money in railroad fare."[15] These movements cemented an intertribal Indian identity that became increasingly important as more and more Indigenous men and women found themselves making extended sojourns away from tribal nations. Indians on the move created political, spiritual, and cultural networks that would sustain aspects of old tribal communities and nourish newer intertribal ones in the coming decades.

Roots

Regardless of the purpose of travel, Indigenous movement alone was an act of resistance. It defied a colonial order built on the containment of Indians in isolated and remote reservations. With the creation of western reservations came a pass system used to monitor Indians on the move.[16] But pass systems were unevenly and often ineffectually enforced. As early as 1876, a Nebraska Indian Agent bemoaned the practice of intertribal visiting. "It is, without doubt," he wrote, "one of the most objectionable features among ancient customs, and calculated to perpetuate sentiments hostile to improvement and civilized life."[17] In 1876, only a handful of iron roads forked out into the West; most intertribal travel was horse-powered. But by the mid- to late 1880s, a new "horse" emerged, offering novel opportunities for migration.

By the mid-1880s, the railroad facilitated the expansion of significant spiritual revitalization movements that engulfed large swaths of Indian Country. Two religions—one drawn from the centuries-old ritual use of peyote, the other a product of Northern Paiute prophets and organized around a dance—fanned out across the West. Delegates from the Northern Plains and across Indian Territory traveled to the Kiowa Comanche Agency to visit with Quanah Parker (Comanche), a major figure in the rise of the nineteenth-century Peyote Religion. Meanwhile, in 1889, several delegations from the Great Basin and Northern and Southern Plains traveled, often by rail, to meet with the Ghost Dance prophet Wovoka at Walker River Reservation in Nevada.[18]

The Ghost Dance and the Peyote Religion built on intertribal networks that pre-dated the railroad age. Peyotism had established roots in pre-reservation and even pre-contact Indigenous spiritual practice that cut across tribal lines. The ritual use of peyote dates to pre-Colombian Mesoamerica, where communities used the dried cactus buttons for medicinal and religious purposes.[19] In the early nineteenth century, six tribes that lived in the ecological range of peyote in north-central Mexico and southern Texas knew of and used the button in ceremonial and healing practices. Carrizos, Lipan Apaches, Mescalero Apaches, Tonkawas, Karankawas, and Caddos lived and hunted in this area and often sourced their buttons from Hispanic *peyoteros* who harvested them for profit.[20] It is likely that Kiowas and Comanches, who often raided into northern Mexico, knew of peyote, though it did not become widespread in use and formalized in practice in their communities until the late nineteenth century.[21] Lipan Apaches were the primary purveyors of the ritual formalized by the Carrizos, and they brought the modern, all-night practice to tribal communities in New Mexico and Oklahoma when violent clashes with Mexican and US militaries and local settler militias forced them out of Texas and Mexico late in the century.[22]

The Modern Road

Migration—movement—was at the center of the modern Peyote Religion that emerged on the Southern Plains. Peyotists followed "the road," a term steeped in both physical and spiritual significance. In ceremony, peyote directed a spiritual journey, its visions revealing the path to God and to prosperous futures. Outside of the ceremony, following "the road" meant eschewing alcohol, protecting one's community, and working hard. Peyote roadmen also took to roads, many of them fastened in iron and wood, to spread the faith to other Indigenous communities. The Peyote Religion offered community, faith, and healing for reservation Indians confronting the combined forces of industrial-capitalism and settler colonization.[23] The road would expand and evolve considerably with the creation of rail lines. At the turn of the century, over eighteen distinct communities practiced variations of the Peyote Religion.[24] By the mid-twentieth century, the Peyote Religion touched Indigenous communities across the American West and into Canada.

In the summer of 1908, nearly one hundred Ho-Chunks left tribal lands in Nebraska to visit kin and share the good news in Black River Falls, Wisconsin. "They filled two train coaches with Indians," Mountain Wolf Woman (Ho-Chunk) (Figure 6.1) recalled, "they even had their drums and

Figure 6.1 Mountain Wolf Woman, ca. 1907. Charles Van Schaick Photographs and Negatives, Wisconsin Historical Society.

they sang in the train, drumming loudly."[25] Traveling to see their kin and former homelands was not new to the Ho-Chunks, but the religion they brought with them was. These travelers were followers of John Rave, a Ho-Chunk peyote roadman. They came to share the sacred Cross Fire ceremony with their relatives. Roadman Jesse Clay introduced another variation of the ceremony, the Half Moon, soon thereafter.[26]

The Peyote Religion relied on Indigenous roadmen who had the means to pay their railroad fare. Prominent peyotists such as Quanah Parker (Comanche) had ready cash, as did other Indian Territory and Central and Northern Plains travelers. As Indigenous homelands became economic hinterlands for growing urban centers, many Plains Indians earned wages as freighters and ranchers. Others received cash by leasing or selling their allotted lands to non-Indians. Mountain Wolf Woman recalled that the Ho-Chunk peyotists in Nebraska "had a lot of money from selling their land," which likely helped cover their fares to Wisconsin and elsewhere. Quanah Parker made his money leasing lands to Texas cattleman and was paid to advertise a short-line railroad—called the Quanah Route—that ran from the Red River to Floydada, Texas.[27] Other roadmen relied on the community collections, fees, and donations of their followers to earn a living. As is the case for many existing spiritual or cultural events, families or communities often pitched in to sponsor a meeting. The community collections often included a small fee for the roadman. Roadmen were also purveyors of the commodity that was central to the faith: the Peyote button.[28] A prominent follower of "the road," John Wilson (Caddo/Delaware), lived for twenty years solely as a roadman.[29] Often absent for months at a time, followers cared for Wilson's plot of land while he was gone and welcomed him back with a peyote ceremony when he returned.[30]

The expansion of the Peyote Religion relied not only on the movement of roadmen like Parker and Wilson, but also on the transport of peyote buttons from their growth region in north-central Mexico and southern Texas (Figure 6.2) to Indian Territory.[31] Ceremony participants—who were mainly men but included some women (depending on tribal variations of the ceremony)—would consume between 4 and 15 buttons over the course of the overnight ceremony. In addition to the buttons ingested, dried peyote was used for medicinal purposes and as sacred talismans. The expansion of the religion required a steady supply from harvest regions in south Texas, which was facilitated once the Texas-Mexican Railroad connecting Corpus Christi to Laredo was completed in December 1881. The line crossed the

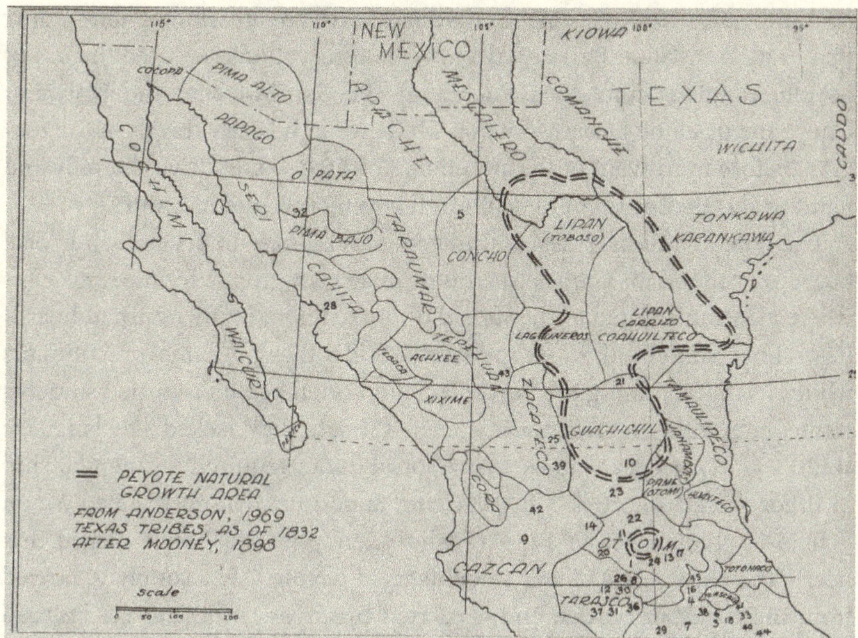

Figure 6.2 The peyote growth area extended south from Texas into Mexico. Map from Omer C. Stewart Collection, University of Colorado Boulder.

northern end of the most productive growing region for the plant, with a station Los Ojuelos, a village whose inhabitants had long harvested the cactus. From Laredo goods were shipped to Austin on the International and Great Northern Railroad, which later merged with the Missouri Kansas and Texas, offering continuous service from Laredo into Indian Territory through Denison. The Fort Worth and Denver City Railway was extended to Wichita Falls in 1883, connecting it to Vernon, Texas, only ten miles south of the Comanche-Kiowa reservation.[32] In 1888 alone, a Laredo resident reported that more than 30,000 buttons harvested by *peyoteros* were transported to a single reservation.[33]

From Oklahoma, the Peyote Religion traveled north to the Ho-Chunk through the work of John Rave, a roadman who learned the ceremony in Oklahoma from Otoes.[34] The Ho-Chunk became the principal agents for spreading the faith across the Central and Northern Plains and Upper Midwest in the early decades of the twentieth century, proselytizing among the Omahas, Lakotas, Dakotas, and Ojibwes. After the completion of the Northern Pacific Railroad, roadmen reached Crow Country in Montana.

And in early 1914, a Lakota roadman arrived at Uintah and Ouray Reservation in Utah. By 1916, twenty-one reservations reported the use of peyote, ranging from Taos Pueblo in the Southwest to the Northern Cheyenne in Lame Deer, Montana. These were the early travels of the religion, before the advent of the automobile, which would drive (literally and figuratively) the spread of the faith well into the twentieth century.[35]

The forced railcar rides of Indigenous children to federal and local boarding schools in Carlisle, Pennsylvania, Hampton, Virginia, and elsewhere also contributed to the spread of the religion. Many returned boarding school students became peyotists. Still others became practitioners while at school. Joining the Peyote Religion often helped returned students reintegrate with the community, even though they lacked the language skills, war experience, and extensive social duties required for membership in other sacred societies.[36] In 1916, the Superintendent at the Red Moon School in the Cheyenne and Arapaho Agency in Oklahoma alleged that nearly the entire class of 167 students used peyote. "The supply is carried from the Mexican border, and is carried by anyone who can get railroad fare."[37] The intertribal relationships developed in boarding schools also helped the faith spread across Indian Country. Older generations joined the returning students because following "the road" did not preclude practitioners from participating in other spiritual activities, which meant that longstanding faith traditions could be maintained and even incorporated into Peyote ceremony.[38] The flexibility of the practice allowed it to meet the needs of diverse communities, from boarding school students to elderly tribal leaders.

Practitioners relied on a steady supply of buttons, compelling roadmen to make regular visits to reservations. In early 1919, the Indian Office sent a questionnaire about peyote usage to every reservation agent, and their responses reveal the networks of kinship, commerce, and faith. Ho-Chunk regularly traveled south by rail to Ponca City, Oklahoma, to source their buttons, which would be brought back in trunks or carried in hand baggage onto trains.[39] "Sometimes two or three Indians will take a trip by rail," a carpenter at Uintah and Ouray Agency reported, "on a pretense of visiting their friends, no doubt bringing back a supply on their return." The agency carpenter also noted that peyotists would drive their horses over 100 miles to other camps for meetings and exchange.[40] Merian Mexican Cheyenne (Northern Cheyenne) noted that the community at Lame Deer received their supply from visiting Southern Cheyennes, who carried the buttons in trunks. "And when one of the Indians from this reservation visits Oklahoma," Cheyenne added, "he usually brings supply with him on his return."[41] The agency farmer in Cantonment, Oklahoma, shared that some used motor cars to drive to the Texas-Mexico border for supplies.[42]

The ceremony engaged in practices that referenced and reinforced Indigenous futures. Two major ceremonial versions prevailed: the Cross Fire and Half Moon. The Cross Fire ceremony incorporated Christian belief systems and included a Bible and crosses. In both ceremonies, peyotists sat in a circle, ingested peyote buttons, prayed, and sang songs over the course of one night. Peyote Religion expert Omer Stewart explained that "peyote protects; peyote allows one to see the future, or to find lost objects; peyote gives power to the user; peyote teaches."[43] The ceremony was meant to highlight purification, healing, and rebirth; the halfway point was marked by a midnight baptismal ceremony.[44] In addition, many peyote songs emphasize "a new dawn" and everlasting life.[45] The emphasis on rebirth and dawn signal the forward-looking nature of the ceremony. Peyote ceremony was designed, in part, to prepare followers for the future.

A shared emphasis on a specific lifestyle anchored the peyote ceremony, even as it evolved to suit different locales and sociocultural needs. Peyotists sought to build Indigenous worlds that would become prosperous by working within the economic systems entering tribal nations, while also maintaining a clear sense of spiritual purpose and direction. Peyotists preached abstention from alcohol and gambling, while promoting hard work. Self-reliance and the promise of prosperity were central teachings of the faith. Appearing before Oklahoma's state government to advocate for the repeal of a peyote ban in 1908, Quanah Parker stressed the faith's emphasis on work. "I tell all Indians to stop and not make it use [*sic*] for sickness all the time," he declared, "do your work; plowing your ground and build houses."[46] The Omaha anthropologist Francis La Flesche defended the Peyote Religion before Congress in 1918 by emphasizing the strong work ethic of many Peyotists. He noted that at a recent Omaha industrial fair, "many of the people who drew prizes were peyote people."[47] Fred Lookout (Osage) echoed La Flesche, stating "since the use of peyote amongst the Osages . . . they are prosperous; they are gaining; they are living a better life and making money."[48]

Despite the faith's core values, some roadmen engaged in less honest or well-meaning commercial practices. One of the most notorious profiteers of the Peyote Religion was Sam Lone Bear (Oglala) (Figure 6.3). The eminent

Figure 6.3 The notorious Samuel Lone Bear, ca. 1890. Gertrude Käsebier Photograph. Division of Work and Industry, National Museum of American History, Smithsonian Institution.

ethnographer of the Peyote Religion, Omer C. Stewart, dubbed him "a real scalawag."[49] Over the years, Lone Bear used his position as a roadman to extract considerable sums of money from followers. He had a reputation for traveling from reservation to reservation, leaving a raft of unpaid debts and several fatherless children in his wake. Followers of the Caddo leader John Wilson alleged that he died—his wagon struck by a train—because he had violated his duties as a spiritual leader and demanded a lofty sum of money to cure two Quapaw women.[50] Allegations of misconduct were also made against Quanah Parker before his death. He became sick on a train returning from a Cheyenne medicine feast, and died in February 1911.[51]

The exchange of peyote was part of a commercial exchange system, but the hosting of peyote ceremonies also incorporated tribal customs of gift-giving that persisted and evolved despite the rapid transformations in Indian Country. A report on peyote use compiled by the Indian

Office in 1922 makes this plain. Dr. Robert E. L. Newberne, hired by Commissioner of Indian Affairs Charles Burke, reported that "pilgrimages to peyote-land are an established feature among the users of the drug, the commercial consideration seems to be subordinate to the 'missionary spirit.'" He noted that a traveler would always divide his supply of peyote with another Indian, "and frequently the only purchase consideration is the 'strengthening the tie that binds.'"[52] Newberne, likely no fan of the faith, thus acknowledged that the building of spiritual community superseded commercial gain.

Peyote had long earned the ire of colonial officials who sought to regulate its consumption and trade. In 1803, President Thomas Jefferson asked Congress to pass legislation giving the president broad authority to regulate the sale of "spirituous liquors."[53] With the creation of the Office of Indian Affairs in 1832, Congress gave the Commissioner authority to police alcohol trafficking. Alcohol was prohibited in Indian Country through the Trade and Intercourse Acts that same year.[54] The legislation specified liquor, with no mention of peyote. Decades later, anti-peyotists lobbied to include peyote on the list of intoxicating substances banned from Indian Country. In 1888, the Kiowa, Comanche, and Wichita agent banned the use of peyote. By 1890, Commissioner of Indian Affairs T. J. Morgan ordered agents in Oklahoma to seize and destroy peyote, classifying it as an intoxicating liquor. This was an administrative law without foundation in existing legislation or judicial proceedings, but nevertheless aligned with the Indian Office's larger mission of assimilation.[55] Two court cases decided in 1897 that the suppression of liquor on reservations by the Indian Office did not in fact include peyote, but Indian agents often enacted their own policies on each reservation, confiscating buttons when they discovered them. In the first decade of the twentieth century, the agent at the Yankton Sioux Reservation, for example, jailed several members of the peyote community and continued his harassment of peyotists even after the Indian Office ordered their release.[56]

Without any clear-cut legislation, government crackdowns on peyote were haphazard. William E. Johnson and Henry A. Larson, both Indian Office employees tasked with liquor suppression, attacked peyotism with evangelical zeal. Johnson and Larson encouraged state governments to pass anti-peyote laws, which Oklahoma did in 1899. Violators there faced a fine of $200 and imprisonment for up to six months. However, Oklahoma law enforcement officials did not make their first arrest until 1907. In response, a coalition of followers including Quanah Parker met with the medical committee of the Oklahoma state Constitutional Convention and successfully convinced its members that peyote was not harmful and was central to their spiritual practice.[57] State officials repealed the law soon after, but across the country anti-peyote sentiment was on the rise, developing in tandem with an emerging Prohibition movement. As a result, various private organizations and the Indian Office pressured Congress to pass a comprehensive anti-peyote bill. Congressional officials introduced bills in 1916, 1917, and 1918.[58]

Peyotists across Indian Country began organizing in response to these threats. In January 1910, the Osage sent a petition via rail to the Indian Office defending the faith and requesting access to more peyote.[59] Five years later the Omaha Indian Peyote Society sent a petition to Commissioner of Indian Affairs Cato Sells to protest the department's restriction on peyote use. Society members highlighted the extent and magnitude of their faith, while invoking popular Progressive Era language of social and racial uplift. "The teaching of the Society extends beyond its own limits," the Omaha peyotists explained, "and constituted a marked factor in the physical, moral, and industrial advancement of the whole tribe."[60] It was a spiritual practice well-suited to the modern world, they explained, but also attentive to Indigenous traditions and healing customs. "We believe," they concluded, "that there is healing power in this peyote."[61] The contest over peyote would reach a fever pitch later in the decade and would involve another significant intertribal organization also born in the railroad age: the Society of American Indians.

Forum for Indigenous Futures

In October 1911, some fifty Indians disembarked from passenger cars in Columbus, stiff and groggy. They passed through the grand archways of Union Station onto the streets of Ohio's capital city, named after the alleged discoverer of the continent, Christopher Columbus. The Indigenous travelers convened the first gathering of an Indigenous-operated organization, the American Indian Association. The steering committee consisted of six prominent figures: Carlos Montezuma (Yavapai), Charles E. Dagenett (Peoria), Henry Standing Bear (Oglala), Thomas L. Sloan (Omaha), Charles Eastman

(Ohíye S'a, Santee Dakota), and Laura Cornelius Kellogg (Oneida). Their mission, not yet fully formed, crystallized over the course of the meeting.

The organization's *Quarterly Journal* later announced their plans to "develop race leaders, to give hope, to inspire, to lead outward and upwards."[62] The conference proceedings projected the ambitious and far-reaching goals the Indigenous members envisioned for the group, soon-after renamed the Society of American Indians (SAI).[63] The following January, the Executive Committee ratified the organization's statement of purpose, which contained the language of civil rights activism, tinged with a Progressive Era emphasis on social evolution and racial uplift. The SAI would "promote and cooperate with all efforts . . . that leave him [the Indian] free as a man to develop according to the natural laws." SAI activists also organized in response to the lingering legal uncertainties created by corporate and settler expansion into Indian Country, promising to "establish a legal department to investigate Indian problems." The SAI also set out to combat nefarious imagery of the anti-modern Indian, opting instead to "present in a just light the true history of the race." To do so, the organization instituted a bureau of information to collect data and manage publicity for the group.[64]

Many activists also celebrated the technological and material benefits of the modern age and sought to bring them to Indigenous communities.[65] "Any condition of living, habit of thought or racial characteristic that unfits the Indian for the modern environment," the SAI committee concluded at the first annual meeting, "is detrimental."[66] Scholars have pointed out that the SAI embraced an assimilationist ethos that regularly challenged or indirectly undermined tribal sovereignty.[67] The SAI advocated for US citizenship, not tribal independence, and yet, as Muskogee Creek historian K. Tsianina Lomawaima explains, the SAI was "fighting for an equitable, respected place in modern American society that descended from and remained connected to their indigeneity."[68] To protect individual and tribal interests, these activists argued, US citizenship was a vital shield. To accomplish their goals, SAI members fashioned lives in motion and circulated detailed visions of Indigenous futures. Kellogg, Sloan, Eastman, and other SAI members wrote powerful statements—letters, articles, and pamphlets to government officials and the US public—that chipped away at the endless cascade of anti-modern Indian imagery that saturated public life in the Progressive Era.

Several founding members first experienced industrialized travel on their harrowing journeys to boarding schools. Like peyotists, most early SAI leaders graduated from off-reservation institutions. Draconian federal policies plucked Native youth from their kin and community at a young age and consigned them to institutions far from their homes. Longtime SAI secretary Zitkála-Šá (Yankton Dakota) recalled her humiliating train ride to the Indiana Manual Labor Institute. "We had anticipated much pleasure from a ride on the iron horse," she wrote of her journey with other Indian pupils, "but the throngs of staring palefaces disturbed and troubled us."[69] White women looked on with concern for the parentless children clad in blankets and moccasins. "Large men, with heavy bundles in their hands, halted nearby, and riveted their glassy blue eyes upon us," she added. "I sank deep into the corner of my seat, for I resented being watched." But the sight of a familiar object, the telegraph poles lapping by her window, reminded Zitkála-Šá of the poles that cut through her homelands. "I sat watching for each pole that glided by to the last one," Zitkála-Šá recalled, "in this way I had forgotten my uncomfortable surroundings."[70] Charles Eastman recounted his trip to Beloit College in Wisconsin from Dakota Territory, a single journey among many Eastman made to white-run educational facilities. "[My] journey to Beloit College," Eastman wrote, "was an education in itself. I boarded the train for the first time in my life, but not before having made a careful inspection of the locomotive, that fiery monster." Eastman, too, noticed the telegraph poles ticking by as the locomotive moved at unprecedented speed. "Every hour brought new discoveries and thoughts," he wrote, "visions that came and passed like the telegraph poles as we sped by."[71] Kellogg, Sloan, and others likely carried their own stories of rail travel to off-reservation schools. Kellogg was educated at Grafton Hall, an Episcopal school in Fond du Lac, Wisconsin. Sloan studied at the Hampton Normal and Agricultural Institute in Virginia, over a thousand miles from his Omaha community in Nebraska. Parker and Montezuma attended US public schools, Parker in White Plains, New York, and Montezuma in Chicago, Illinois.

Montezuma would go on to offer critical support to Indigenous rail travelers while living in Chicago. In 1904, several Lakota performers for Bill Cody's Wild West show were killed when a mail train crashed into their railcar outside of Chicago.[72] A practicing physician, Montezuma was called in to care for injured passengers. The Pine Ridge Indian Agent had initially negotiated a settlement with the railroad company without the input of the injured parties and families of the deceased. A committee of concerned Lakotas, including Luther Standing Bear, contacted Montezuma and asked him to intervene on their behalf in the dispute. Montezuma sent a letter to the Indian Office protesting the handling of the case and filed a report detailing the extensive injuries the passengers suffered. The call fell on deaf ears, but Montezuma continued to be an ally to Indigenous travelers in other ways. He was known to meet traveling delegations at the train station and assist them in getting to connecting trains. When Indigenous travelers found themselves adrift in Chicago, Montezuma might help them find work or a hotel until they could make their way home. He became known as a crucial host and aid to Indians passing through Chicago.[73]

By the time Montezuma and the other Indigenous activists arrived in Columbus, they were seasoned travelers. SAI members planned their first conference to coincide with Columbus Day, a holiday steadily gaining in popularity since President Benjamin Harrison's 1892 proclamation promoting patriotic celebrations. The date and the location were deliberate choices by SAI members seeking to undermine the growing mythology of Christopher Columbus. Between October 12 and 15, 1911, speakers addressed a range of issues, from agriculture and industry to Indigenous art and education. Even in its infancy, the SAI put forth detailed visions that spelled out a distinctly Indigenous modernity. For instance, Laura Cornelius Kellogg had spent a large part of the year touring Indian Country, sharing her newly formed vision for Indigenous America. Her conference presentation, "Industrial Organization for the American Indian," outlined her bold plan to preserve reservations and recast them as industrial cooperatives owned and operated by tribal members. Kellogg proposed "organizing the Indians' holdings into a system of economic advantages," creating an "industrial village" where community members would live, work, and earn a living.[74] She at once endorsed corporate capitalism, while also critiquing the contemporary American economic system.

Drawing from agrarianism and Populist movements that argued for a reformation of the corporate order, Kellogg imagined a political economy tied to local leadership and local needs. "Instead of being fixtures in an industrial world, which is itself still largely problematic for the white man," Kellogg explained, "I maintain that the line of least resistance to the greatest possible good is to citizenize [*sic*] the possibilities and reorganize the opportunities of the Indian at home."[75] Throughout the conference, she stressed the need for a radical transformation in Indian policy and community organization. "The Indian should seek to organize something different and better for himself than already exists," she explained to the conference-goers.[76] Plow the field. Plant new seeds.

A central tenet of Kellogg's Lolomi Plan was the tribal control of economic and political resources. Non-Indian monopolists and the Indian Bureau would no longer supersede tribal interests. Tribal trusts, freed from the Indian Office's grasp, would fund Kellogg's industrial cooperatives. This economic model cut out white profiteers. "Instead of the white trader getting the 60 percent of the profits as he does in the white man's world of commerce," Kellogg explained, "let the Navajo so organize that he can sell his wares to the consumer direct."[77] Each tribal member would own shares in the corporation. Although individuals could acquire more stock, the Lolomi Plan instituted a "one man, one vote" policy to avoid creating a political economy in which those with the most wealth held the most power.[78] Economic authors agree that the greatest evil in the constitution of the corporations of the United States is their form of representation," Kellogg explained in *Our Democracy and the American Indian* (1920). The Lolomi Plan sought to remedy that evil by placing social and political value in community, not wealth accumulation.[79] Her plan also promoted self-government, albeit one that was still "protected" by the federal government. Kellogg did not make clear what the particulars of those protections would be, but she stressed that the federal government owed Native peoples continuing support and oversight. Indian industrial communities would be recognized by the federal government and tethered to the US capitalist marketplace.[80]

The Lolomi Plan imagined a modern Indigenous corporation freed from undemocratic hierarchies and attuned to local conditions.[81] Just as the Peyote Religion shifted to meet local community and tribe-specific needs, so too would the Lolomi Plan. The plan ensured that no single economic model or industry would be applied wholesale. Instead, community members would choose a certain industry based on available resources and tribal skills and experience. "In choosing the business of the organization, there are other things to be taken into the reckoning besides soil," Kellogg explained, "one is the natural bent of the group."[82] The plan was intertribal, yet adaptable to distinct tribal communities.

While Kellogg imagined an Indigenous future in which corporatization served tribal interests, Arthur Parker used modern technology to rethink

Indian education policy. Soon after Kellogg spoke, Parker, the secretary-treasurer of the organization, rose to comment on the state of Indian education. He began in the unlikeliest of places: Poughkeepsie, New York. Parker mentioned a railroad that once ran to Poughkeepsie, but could run no further because it operated on a narrow gauge track. "As fine as it was and great as was its capacity for taking on freight," he explained to the conference-goers, "it could not advance on a road meant for standard tracks." "Civilization today is the standard gauge," he intoned, "of what avail is it to load a splendid car with precious freight, and forgetting that its tracks are narrow gauge, to send it on over standard tracks? All is lost."[83] "The underpinning," Parker concluded, "that which is basic, that which a man runs on, must receive attention and must be standardized before the superstructure, as great as it is, may progress safely."[84] In Parker's mind, for the "trains" to run smoothly and on all the tracks available, the foundation of Indigenous life must first be addressed. That foundation, that "underpinning," was the long-neglected reservation. These spaces, in his view, "demanded immediate improvement, if not entire regeneration."[85]

Parker shared Kellogg's focus on a reimagining of tribal communities on reservations. He called for an Indian education system rooted on tribal lands, one that met the needs of Indian children and adults. His metaphor first appears to advocate for assimilation into white society. But it is the track that Parker sought to change, not the train, as "fine" and "great" as it was. Parker believed that education would provide Indian peoples with the tools to navigate a modern, industrial world.[86]

Like Parker and Kellogg, Thomas Sloan (Omaha) echoed a call for attention to tribal nations, though he—like many other SAI members—had spent considerable time off Indian agencies. Sloan's speech, "Reservation System Administration," advocated for giving Indian communities access to the US judicial system. Sloan believed that Indians could use the US courts to combat the wanton and unchecked political authority of the Indian Office and its agents. The legal uncertainties about the status of Indigenous peoples' land holding and their ability to negotiate with private and public interests often made it difficult for individuals and tribes to resist corporate overreach. Sloan believed that citizenship would grant unquestionable legal rights to Indians. "In the administration of Indian Affairs there should be such reforms," Sloan explained, "as will give the Indians in hearings an investigation into the rights which belong to him under the Constitution."[87] He excoriated the current system of Indian administration with its "star chamber proceedings" that excluded Indigenous input and often resulted in the dispossession of Indigenous peoples. He described a world in which "the most solemn safeguards of vested property rights are overridden by the very power that was designed to protect the Indian's rights."[88] He added that local farmers, politicians, and "railroad men" in the vicinity of a reservation "wish it open, not for the benefit of the Indian, but for a larger opportunity for each in his own line."[89] The only clear means of protecting tribal land bases from these self-interested land grabbers was to ensure the legal rights of Indigenous peoples.

To carry their ideas beyond the convention, SAI members relied on rail-powered mail systems that circulated their newspapers, letters, journals, and other publications across Indian Country and the United States. Parker was keenly aware of the importance of these information networks. He touted the SAI's first *Quarterly Journal*, published in 1913. "Just wait for the famous Journal," Parker wrote, "it will be a bombshell."[90] All members of the SAI, including non-Indian associate members, received copies of the *Journal*. Parker sent copies to public libraries across the United States, citing the publication's "unique contribution to the journalistic endeavor."[91] He placed galleys of the latest edition in the SAI's headquarters to expose the publication to tribal delegations visiting Washington. In an exhaustive letter to J. B. Hewitt of the Bureau of Ethnology later that year, Parker braided a critique of Hewitt's thinking with a celebration of the Society's journalistic endeavors. "With regard to the effect of the publications of this society," Parker wrote, "you would find that they have proven an inspiration to the Indians, who you term unlettered."[92] Contrary to Hewitt's belief, a generation of Indians had been taught to read and write in the English language in boarding schools. Indians on reservations also worked with local interpreters to transcribe letters and receive the latest updates in US newspapers.

SAI members contributed to the *Quarterly Journal* and to monthly newsletters sent to members, but also published their perspectives in mainstream media. Zitkála-Šá worked regularly with journalists to publish in American newspapers. Carlos Montezuma, who maintained a tenuous relationship with the SAI, started his own publication in 1916 dedicated to promoting the eradication of the Indian Office and the elimination of reservations. Eastman, Parker, Zitkála-Šá, and others published histories and autobiographies in the early decades of the twentieth century meant to educate white Americans about Indigenous issues.[93]

These information channels not only transported SAI ideas and initiatives to Indian agencies and non-Indian America, but also brought tribal concerns to the SAI's attention. Individuals from across Indian Country wrote to the SAI seeking assistance in legal and jurisdictional matters plaguing their communities. Elmer Wilson (Mescalero Apache) wrote to Parker in 1914 asking that the Society help promote the latest Indian Appropriations Bill before Congress that contained a clause for the purchase of cattle for his Apache Nation.[94] Wilson mentioned that SAI member Henry Roe Cloud had visited a few years earlier and advocated for cattle ranching on the reservation.[95] Others living in Indian Country sought the support of the SAI in obtaining or keeping allotments and in eradicating corrupt and coercive Indian Office activities. E. D. Prescott from Bend, Oregon, appealed to Parker for help seeking the patent to his deceased sister's land.[96] Pottawatomies in Kansas worked with Parker on overdue payments due to the tribe from land sales.[97] Indians wrote in from agencies in Montana, Oregon, South Dakota, Oklahoma, and Kansas for SAI support in other matters.[98] Parker, responding to a query penned by Goes-to-War (Lakota) regarding the role of the SAI in relation to the US government, explained that they were not connected to the government, but "the Government pays a great deal of attention to what we ask if it is right and can be done according to the law."[99] Just two years after the SAI's founding, Parker reported that the organization "has already received and slotted hundreds of complaints against superintendents and agents of the Interior Department and Indian Bureau."[100] As letters streamed into the SAI headquarters in DC, the shared plight of Indian communities came into focus.

The circulation of printed material was joined by Indigenous activists in motion who drew on a tradition of politically charged movement to promote their causes. Take for instance, Thomas L. Sloan, an Omaha attorney and founding member of the SAI. Sloan pieced together a life on the move between Washington, Nebraska, and sites across Indian Country, taking on clients and challenging the federal government's paternalistic Indian policies. He viewed his regular presence in Congress as a powerful antidote to the collusions between public officials and business sharks eager to profit from Indian lands. "Every Congress has before it legislation detrimental to the Indian," Sloan explained to Carlisle graduates during the school's commencement in 1912, "in nine cases out of ten the legislation is promoted by capitalists, speculators, and railroad men, who are more able than the

Indian to reach their Congressmen."[101] Thus Sloan made it a priority to physically represent Indigenous perspectives in Washington.

In 1913, Sloan took to the rails to investigate collusion between capitalists and the federal government on tribal land bases. Senator Joseph Robinson from Arkansas named Sloan as a special agent for a newly formed Joint Commission to Investigate Indian Affairs. As a special agent, Sloan traveled to the Crow, Blackfeet, and Yankton reservations to meet with local leaders and evaluate the status of land ownership and citizenship. Sloan explained to the committee how the Indian Office deemed Crow allottees incompetent and took from them critical grazing pasture for their commercial cattle industry.[102] He testified before Congress about the wanton imprisonment of tribal members, the theft of resources at the hands of Indian agents, and the Indian Office practice of simply transferring troublesome or incompetent Indian Agents to other postings, where, Sloan explained, "they are inflicted upon some other poor Indians."[103]

He traveled back and forth from Omaha in the second decade of the century working on a tribal disenrollment case that brought him to the Supreme Court in 1917. He also served as an official tribal delegate sent to the District of Columbia to open up several Omaha cases to the US Court of Claims. By 1920, Sloan was a fixture in Washington, president of the Society of American Indians, and a recognized expert on Indian law and policy. He made his presence known in the colonial governing spaces that made major decisions for Indigenous peoples. "I have been engaged in fighting grafters," he explained in 1912. Indeed, he made a life traveling from reservations back and forth to the capital to ensure that legislation and US Courts protected Indigenous lands and freedoms.[104]

Many other SAI members were incredibly mobile in their campaigns for citizenship and Indian rights. "The combination of my state of work with my interests in this organization," Arthur Parker wrote in 1913, "keep me moving quite rapidly over the country."[105] Zitkála-Šá, working for the Indian Service, moved repeatedly over the course of her life, though she settled for considerable time in DC in an effort to shape policy decisions and public opinion. Charles Dagenett, also an Indian Service employee, frequently relocated for new assignments and, as overseer of the Department of Indian Employment, traveled to reservations across the West to recruit Indians for off-reservation work, often on track gangs and in railroad shops. He negotiated with corporations to secure pay and protections for

Indigenous laborers. Reverend Sherman Coolidge (Arapaho) headlined lecture tours in Missouri and Iowa and traveled to Oklahoma, Utah, and Washington, DC, for public talks and missionary work.[106] Traveling back and forth from reservations, speaking in front of public audiences across the country, and visiting Washington, DC, on official business, these leaders made homes on the move in an effort to realize their visions for Native America. Their activities built on a tradition of politically charged movement that raised white public awareness and pushed legislative issues for which tribal delegates and activists such as Sara Winnemucca (Paiute), Coleman Cole (Choctaw), and others had advocated beginning in the 1880s.

The SAI also worked with railroad officials to promote attendance at their annual meetings. Parker reported ahead of the 1913 meeting in Denver, Colorado, that the SAI's "publicity committee" was preparing to circulate reading material to generate interest in the conference. He encouraged an industrial school superintendent to send him a list of the institution's students and graduates. "This will allow the Railroad Companies to place information in the hands of your former and present students," Parker explained.[107] Union Pacific officials reported that same year that two passenger agents in New York, two in New England, and one in Philadelphia scoured the Northeast looking for potential Native and non-Native attendees for the Denver Conference. The Agent reported that the company was "very anxious to secure the business for the Union Pacific system," but so far no one had expressed interest in attending. The UP agent then beseeched Parker to provide an additional list of those who planned to attend so they could undertake more targeted marketing.[108]

Kellogg, Sloan, and other SAI members' status as middle-class Indians who could afford their railroad fare made industrialized travel accessible to them, and they had learned the skills needed to enter colonial spaces that had long been cordoned off to their ancestors. From the League of Nations to the meetings of the Congressional Subcommittee on Indian Affairs, Sloan, Kellogg, Dagenett, and others used their knowledge of the English language, financial means, and industrial transportation to speak truth to power in the Progressive Era. Following a century of dispossession of their people, the SAI used modern technologies to promote Indigenous issues in US society, educate non-Indian America about Native peoples, and espouse visions for an Indigenous future.

The Confrontation

Cracks in the foundation of the Society were visible at the first Columbus meeting, though SAI leaders labored tirelessly over the years to hold the membership together in pursuit of a greater goal of improving the conditions for Native peoples. But mounting public and US government concern over the use of peyote irreparably damaged the organization. In 1918, Congressman Carl V. Hayden from Arizona introduced an amendment to an existing bill that would label peyote as an "intoxicant" and ban it from Indian lands and reservations. The debate over the labeling was not only about whether peyote was in fact an intoxicant, but it also dealt with the question of citizenship that so occupied the SAI.[109]

Several legal cases decided in the early decades of the twentieth century dealt with the extent to which Congress and the Indian Office still had authority to regulate Indian affairs after Indians were no longer federal wards and were instead citizens. This debate extended into the peyote hearings, because select Indigenous activists (including Sloan) believed that federal liquor laws could no longer apply to Indian citizens. A letter of support from the Indian Office for the Hayden Bill discussed the various lawsuits addressing the question of whether or not liquor and intoxicant suppression laws applied to Indians deemed US citizens. The Indian Office letter claimed that guardianship "is in full force as to property rights and personal rights, at least as long at the tribal relation continues, except insofar as Congress has relinquished it," though the Office also noted that the courts were divided on the issue.[110] The letter cited Supreme Court case *U.S. v. Noble* (1915) and Circuit Court of Appeals cases in which judges concluded that Indian allottees still fell under guardianship and therefore the existing liquor laws. Another Supreme Court Case, *United States v. Nice* (1916), argued that allotees before holding fee patent to their land were not subject to liquor laws, though it contended that Congress could still exercise plenary power over Indians recognized as citizens, thereby limiting their citizenship rights.[111] "Citizenship is not incompatible with tribal existence or continued guardianship," Justice Van DeVanter explained in the majority opinion, "and so may be conferred without completely emancipating the Indians, or placing them beyond the reach of congressional regulations adopted for their protection."[112] Montezuma, Sloan, and others dedicated themselves to the emancipation of Indigenous peoples from "the reach of congressional regulations." Clearly more was at stake in the debating of the Hayden bill than peyote usage.

The contest over peyotism brought peyote roadmen and SAI leaders onto the congressional stage with other Indian policy stakeholders, including the leader of the Indian Rights Association, celebrated ethnologist James Mooney, and doctors and scientists from across North America. For several SAI members, peyote was not part of the Indigenous future they imagined for their communities. It was a corrupting intoxicant, destined to consign Indians to a life of dependency. For others, including SAI leader and peyotist Thomas Sloan, the Peyote Religion offered direction and acted as a curative for social and physical ills. Francis La Flesche, an Omaha anthropologist and SAI member, put the pro-peyote position bluntly in the 1918 congressional hearings: "I am thoroughly convinced that these Indians are worshipping God in their own simple way, and if their religion is interfered with by the Government or anybody else, and it is suppressed, the consequences will be very grave."[113] The implications, La Flesche suggested, would extend beyond the suppression of a faith tradition and speak to a more critical matter: What right did the federal government have to meddle in these issues if all Indians would soon be US citizens?

Dakota political activist, social reformer, and SAI member Zitkála-Šá (Figure 6.4) led the charge against peyotism in the 1918 hearings. In addition to her repeated claims about its narcotic effects and the moral degradation it caused, Zitkála-Šá's testimony against the Peyote Religion addressed the economic exploitation of unwitting followers. She had likely witnessed the nefarious acts of peyote roadman Sam Lone Bear on the Uintah and Ouray Reservation, where she was living with her husband when Lone Bear arrived by rail in 1912. She wrote to the office to try to remove him from the reservation, but to no avail.[114] At the congressional Peyote hearings in 1918, she would give accounts of a certain "Cactus Pete" who appeared among the Utes selling small crosses with alleged spiritual properties. If the crosses tarnished (which they all did), the carrier was to seek out more peyote to cleanse themselves. "Money is gotten under false pretenses," she stressed in her request to Congress to pass legislation that would add the cactus to a federal list of intoxicants.[115]

Though the Hayden bill did not pass the Senate, the threat of federal action led a group of Peyotists to seek legal protections as a nonprofit corporation. Shortly after the conclusion of the hearings, a gathering of

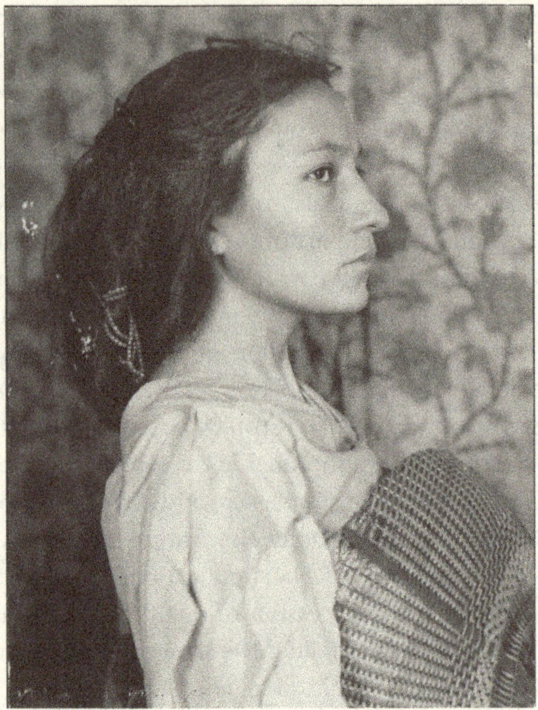

Figure 6.4 Zitkála-Šá, a member of the Society of American Indians, advocated against peyotism. Gertrude Käsebier Photograph ca. 1898. Division of Work and Industry, National Museum of American History, Smithsonian Institution.

Oklahoma Peyotists with representatives from six different tribes met in El Reno and drew up a charter for the Native American Church. By the end of the 1920s, over thirteen articles of incorporation had been filed in six states.[116] Out of this world in motion emerged one of the most significant intertribal Indigenous institutions of the twentieth century, boasting over 300,000 members today, representing a coalition of churches in Canada, the United States, and Mexico.[117]

But the networks of relations that the SAI had built from their lives on the move could not act as a sufficient bulwark against the factionalism that saturated the organization. The Peyote hearings had a corrosive effect. By the time Thomas Sloan took the presidency in 1920, the SAI was all but defunct. It would hold its last conference in 1923, a year before the passage of the Indian Citizenship Act, which granted birthright US citizenship to all Indigenous peoples. Debates over federal responsibilities to Indigenous communities continued in US courtrooms, in Congress, and in Indian Country well into the twentieth century.

From the very start of the railroad age in the West, Indigenous peoples actively engaged in the worlds the railroad made and unmade. From the earliest negotiations over rights-of-way granting free travel on lines, to the movement—forced and willing—of Native men, women, and children along the tracks, Indigenous peoples regularly came into contact with trains. It was a colonial technology that proved pivotal to the rise of the intertribal Peyote Religion, as dried buttons of the peyote plant traveled by rail to reservations and believers congregated in the halls of Congress and in camps across Indian County to maintain and defend their religious practice. By taking the physical road, roadmen and other Peyote followers fostered new ties of friendship and community. The spiritual road, meanwhile, offered men and women a metaphysical escape from the confines of the reservation and the opportunity for renewal amidst the disruptive forces of colonization and modernization.

For many SAI activists, their early migrations shaped their audacious visions for an Indigenous future in a settler society. The Progressive Era intertribal organization relied on industrial infrastructure to maintain and develop its organization between 1911 and 1923, and its core members traveled regularly across Indian Country and the United States, calling for legal protection, US citizenship, and economic independence. Their vision for a modern Indian future involved regular engagement with corporations and the industrial and information technologies that swept through their communities in the Progressive Era. Kellogg's vision and the peyotists' decision to incorporate also spotlight the unique ways in which Indigenous communities refashioned the corporate model to serve their interests. Kellogg, Sloan, Zitkála-Šá, and others participated in the shared practice of migration to meet with local Indigenous communities and enter the corridors of colonial power that had long excluded Indian peoples. From the League of Nations to the Supreme Court, SAI activists carved out space in colonial enclaves and pushed for public discussion of Indigenous issues in the Progressive Era.

Wodziwob's colorful vision of a train bringing Indians back to life did not materialize, but the central message embedded in the image—of renewal in Indian Country—did take hold in the late nineteenth and early twentieth centuries. As Indians traveled to dance, participate in ceremonies, work, and "talk back" to the colonial government, Native organizations adapted to and refashioned the widespread and far-reaching changes that gripped Indian Country and the United States in the railroad age. Writing in the *Quarterly Journal* in 1915, SAI leader Arthur Parker called on the colonial government to provide for "the restitution of seven stolen rights." He indicted colonial officials who long attempted to strip Indians of "an intellectual life"; "social organization": "economic independence"; "moral standards he can trust"; "the right of assured [legal] status"; "the right of freedom"; and "a good name among nations."[118] It was an ambitious set of goals that the SAI and the Peyote Religion began to address at the turn of the century. Through these organizations, Indians realized visions for economic independence, advocacy for legal protections, and journeys toward freedom. By World War I, over thirty claims by Native peoples had entered the US Court of Claims.[119] By the end of the 1920s, the Native American Church had incorporated in several states to protect Indigenous religious freedoms and safeguard the spiritual revitalization offered by its ceremonies. Many of the futurist visions advocated by Kellogg and other SAI members would take root in the Indian New Deal programs of the next decade, which promoted local control over tribal political and economic affairs. A century of activism and cultural and spiritual resurgence had just begun.

The Iron Horse in Indian Country: Native Americans and Railroads in the US West. Alessandra La Rocca Link, Oxford University Press. © Alessandra La Rocca Link 2025. DOI: 10.1093/9780197674437.003.0009

Railway Journeys

Kiowa Travels

With deep-set eyes conveying a kind of stern melancholy, Satanta (Kiowa) (Figure RJ 3.1) peered out over the Jackboro-Belknap road. A prominent Kiowa chief, Satanta joined a war party of over 100 Comanches and Kiowas, intent on looting wagon trains passing through the North Texas causeway. Earlier that spring, he, along with Kiowa leaders Big Tree and Santank, decided to raid south of the Red River. In 1871, Satanta watched as the second large wagon train rolled across the dirt thoroughfare. He descended on the wagons with his allies, killing seven men, capturing over forty mules, and making off with various goods.[1]

Two months later, Satanta approached another wagon, this time with his wrists bound. US Army General William T. Sherman arrested Satanta, along with Santank and Big Tree, at Fort Sill, Indian Territory in July. Santank did not survive the journey. Officers shot him when he threw himself out of the cart, attempting to escape. When Big Tree and Satanta arrived in Jacksboro, Texas, they were swiftly sentenced to hang by a Jack County Court. Concerned that an execution of prominent leaders would set off violent reprisals by Kiowas, the Texas governor eventually commuted their sentences to life imprisonment.[2]

Satanta and Big Tree were incarcerated in a state penitentiary in Huntsville, Texas, where they were set to work on a chain gang, laying track. But their tracklaying days proved to be short-lived. A year into their imprisonment, US officials plucked them from the gang and sent them by rail to meet with Kiowa leaders heading to Washington, DC.[3] Kiowa chief Lone Wolf had negotiated with US officials for the meeting, promising to send a delegation to Washington to discuss land cessions and peace with President Grant only if they were able to meet with the Kiowa leaders Satanta and Big Tree beforehand. The Indian Office complied with their request and made arrangements for the prisoners' travel to Atoka, Indian Territory.

RJ 3.1 William S. Soule, photograph of Satanta, Kiowa chief, between 1870 and 1875. Library of Congress.

On September 26, 1872, US military officials placed the two men on a Missouri, Kansas, and Texas railway car at Atoka, but kept their presence a secret from the official tribal delegation traveling in a separate car. Army officers recognized that the Kiowa leaders were "still in a country known to them" and feared they might attempt an escape. The soldiers also reasoned that had the delegation known of the prisoners' presence, "there is no doubt they would have dictated terms which could not be complied with."[4] A year after the St. Louis meeting, Lone Wolf succeeded in securing the release on parole of Satanta and Big Tree from the Texas governor Edmund Davis, so long as they promised to cease their raids into the state. The governor's move outraged both Texas settlers and General Sherman.[5]

For Satanta, roads meant many things. Roads carried wagons of goods—goods that offered much-needed sustenance for Kiowas recently confined to a reservation near Fort Sill. Roads were also scenes of appalling violence: the death and mutilation of freighters at the hands of Satanta and his allies;

the lead bullet slicing through Santank's flesh along a wagon road. In the span of a few months, Satanta grew intimately aware of the new roads that would radically alter his homelands. As a prisoner, he worked building an iron road that cut through Texas. He then traveled, bound, on tracks to St. Louis. There he conferred with a Kiowa delegation that relied on railroads to meet with US officials and make their claims in the heart of US empire.

The tremors unleashed by rail expansion drew Satanta to violence yet again. In the summer after his release, Satanta was present when Kiowas, allied with Comanches and Plains Apaches, clashed with bison hunters in the west Texas town of Adobe Walls. The growing number of Euro-American bison hunters in the region owed in part to expanding rail networks in Texas and Indian Territory, which provided ready access to hide markets in the east. Satanta's presence at the battle cost him his freedom. He was arrested and sent back to the Huntsville prison, where he laid track for the Missouri, Kansas, and Texas Railroad until 1878 when, utterly broken, he jumped to his death from a high window in the prison hospital.[6]

Railroads formed the backbone of a carceral program Satanta could not escape. A year after his death, the US government opened Carlisle Indian Industrial School. Eighty-two children arrived at Carlisle by train on October 6, 1879, in the dead of night—an effort by Carlisle employees to avoid the large crowds of whites gathering to view the Indigenous travelers. US officials designed Carlisle—a deserted military barrack repurposed as a school—for the assimilation of Native peoples into white culture. Railroads were the circulatory system of these schools, funneling students in and out, from across North America. Luther Standing Bear (Sicangu/Oglala Lakota), one of the first students, recalled riding on "little houses." "We held our blankets between our teeth," Standing Bear wrote, "because our hands were so busy hanging on our seats, so frightened were we."[7] Officials hoped federal boarding schools like Carlisle, which proliferated in the following years, would rid Indigenous peoples of their cultural distinctiveness and erode tribal sovereignty.

In coming years, as rail lines expanded, trains carted in US soldiers to quell Indigenous resistance campaigns in the West and sent Indigenous freedom fighters to prison camps like Fort Marion (Figure RJ 3.2). The role of railroads in this carceral program of containing and "reforming" Indigenous peoples animated Indigenous policy from Satanta's time well into the early twentieth century.

RJ 3.2 Chiricahua Apache prisoners, including Geronimo (first row, third from right), 1886. Photographs of American Military Activities, National Archives and Records Administration.

Two decades after Satanta's death, several of his tribal descendants woke before dawn to take the six-mile trek from Rainy Mountain Boarding School to the rail depot in Harrison, Oklahoma. They arrived by wagon and waited for the coming train, hands taut with cold.[8] The locomotive lurched to halt just as the sun cut through the horizon. The Kiowa children filed in and took their seats. "At first I was afraid and would not look out the window," Helen Esrago recalled.[9] Alma Big Tree wedged herself between her cousin Louis and playmate Maurice Blue Bird. Convinced that the sheer speed of the machine would thrust her from her seat, Alma clung tightly to the cushion below her.[10] Before long the children relaxed, having discovered the ease with which they could charge across the landscape. Helen gazed out the window, rapt, as the bald cypress and water oak of eastern Oklahoma gave way to tallgrass prairies. "I coulded [*sic*] not keep my head in the room," she remembered.[11]

Writing about their journey the next day, Helen, Alma, and their travel companions mentioned little about their first train ride, a 200-mile trip from Harrison west to Anadarko, Oklahoma. The highlight of their journey was not the train, but the people waiting for them when they arrived. Children from St. Patrick's Mission School—friends and relatives of the Rainy Mountain students—met Helen and her classmates on the platform. They spent the morning moseying about in town shops before congregating at the Mission School for a meal. Afterward, the Kiowa children boarded the iron steed once again to return to Rainy Mountain.

Helen, Alma, and their classmates rode on the Chicago and Rock Island Railroad, whose owner, Hilon A. Parker, paid for the school trip after giving a talk at Rainy Mountain the previous month. Parker came to the Kiowa-Comanche Agency to ensure that tribal leaders would grant his company rights-of-way through their reservation.[12]

Though neither the Kiowa children nor Satanta had ever traveled to Chicago or Rock Island, they came from a people born in motion. The Kiowas, according to an origin story recounted by Kiowa author N. Scott

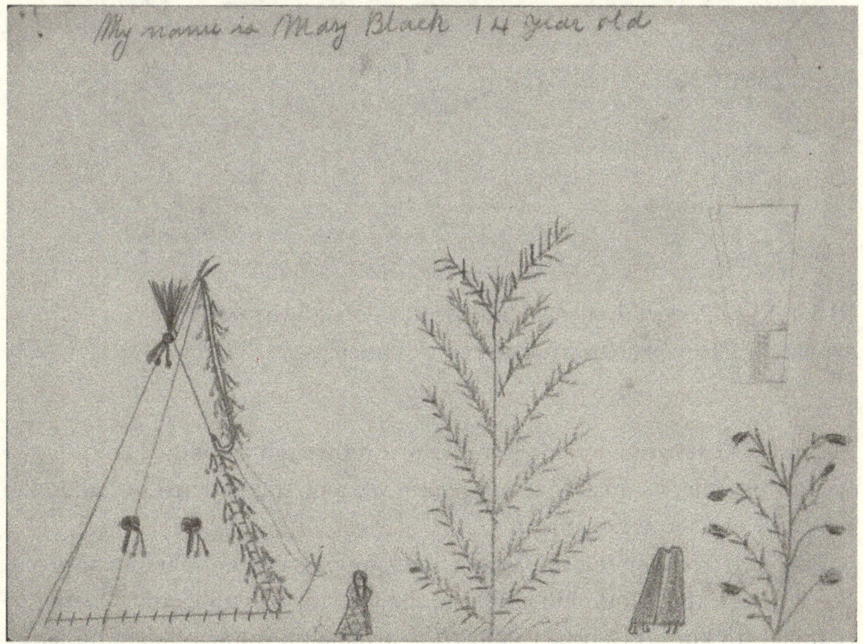

RJ 3.3 Kiowa ledger drawing. Hilon A. Parker family papers. William L. Clements Library, University of Michigan.

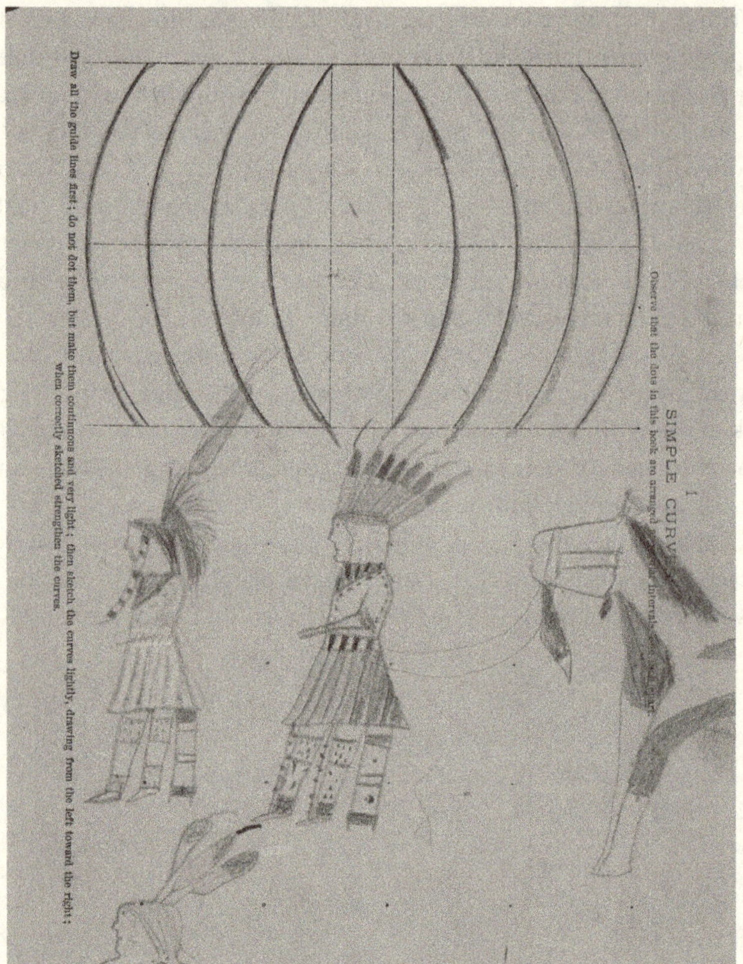

RJ 3.4 Kiowa ledger drawing. Hilon A. Parker family papers. William L. Clements Library, University of Michigan.

Momaday, "came one by one into the world through a hollow log." It was a narrow passage, so small that a pregnant woman, trapped inside, halted the flow of Kiowas into existence.[13]

Parker arrived among the Kiowas seeking passage in the name of profit. But for the Rainy Mountain children, the journey was a welcome chance to reunite with kin, and a brief respite from a demanding and often humiliating school environment. Tasked with writing Parker thank you notes after their journey, many children sent drawings (Figures RJ 3.3 and 3.4). The images thanking him for the “good long ride of kindness” were not of the train, not of the “white ways” modeled at school, but of Kiowa culture and custom.[14] Their message was clear. What was born on the journey from the hollow log would not perish in the halls of Rainy Mountain.

The Iron Horse in Indian Country: Native Americans and Railroads in the US West. Alessandra La Rocca Link, Oxford University Press. © Alessandra La Rocca Link 2025. DOI: 10.1093/9780197674437.003.0010

Conclusion

Trickster Tales of Indians and Technology

Native people migrate in modern times as well.
—Scott Richard Lyons (Dakota/Ojibwe)[1]

On a bone-chilling January evening in 1946, a small crowd gathered at Lodge Grass Station in southeastern Montana. Pendleton blankets, arranged neatly from the iron road to a group of vocalists, established a path of honor for a returned warrior. "I was supposed to walk along the row of blankets and start dancing as I reached the singers," Joseph Medicine Crow (Crow) recalled. He had decided to stop for a "dime hamburger" at Louie's in nearby Sheridan. Immersed in the greasy Sheridan delight, Medicine Crow missed his connecting train. After receiving news that he'd been spotted at the burger joint, Medicine Crow's mother sent the crowd home. He arrived that evening to the deafening silence of the deserted station.[2]

Other Crow World War II veterans traversed the Pendleton pathway at Lodge Grass in the winter of 1945–1946, though some may have been carried over the sacred causeway, their lifeless bodies a tragic reminder of the costs of war. During these moments, Lodge Grass Station became a Crow space for ceremony and reunion. Crows congregated along the tracks drew from traditions that reached deep into their tribe's history and culture, just as they incorporated mass-produced blankets and coal-powered transportation technologies.[3]

By 1946, Crows—like peoples throughout Indian Country—had integrated trains into their daily lives and customs. Indians had also acclimated to the newest industrial interloper: the automobile. Beginning in the late 1910s and early 1920s, Indians began purchasing used cars. The vehicles carried the quirks of old age that Indian filmmakers and writers still feature with heavy doses of humor and irony. Most famously, a vehicle in the celebrated film *Smoke Signals* (1998), written by Sherman Alexie (Spokane/Coeur d'Alene), runs only in reverse. To this day, "Indian cars"—also known as "rez runners"—tend to be decrepit machines, castaways from a consumer-driven society that left Indigenous communities behind. Automobile manufacturers touted the "freedom" offered by the open road, but that freedom came at a cost. Cars contributed to the atomization of American and American Indian societies alike, sending individuals off on isolated sojourns. Cars also brought increased financial instability to Indian Country. Unlike a rail ticket, cars required substantial financial investments, often locking Native peoples into cycles of debt.[4]

Automobiles needed paved pathways, just as iron horses called for mile upon mile of wood, iron, and steel. Indian laborers contributed to the construction of roads and highways on their lands in the early decades of the twentieth century, even as major decisions about the location and distance of roads fell under the explicit authority of the US federal government. The 1921 Federal Highway Act funded highways across Indian Country, leaving choices about location to the Indian Office. Not until Red Power activists in the 1960s and 1970s demanded local control of infrastructure and development projects did tribal leaders and later tribal councils wrest some authority over road-building from US officials.[5]

The federal government maintained control over the pathways required for automobiles, but car companies crafted the Indigenous imagery that sold their products. Motor vehicle advertising drew on the legacy of railroad marketing schemes, deploying images of Indians to boost their bottom lines. Over the course of the twentieth century, car buyers contemplated joy rides in vehicles such as the Jeep Cherokee, Pontiac Chieftain, and Ford Thunderbird. Recurring tropes juxtaposing the latest in car technology with the primitive Indian flooded the media. These depictions underscored the gap between seemingly anti-modern Indians and the high-powered technology catapulting American consumers to freedom on the open road.[6]

The legacy of this anti-modern imagery is far-reaching. Depictions of anti-modern Indians continue to saturate American public life and inflect Indian and non-Indian attitudes toward Native peoples. A 2015 study of media representations found that historical imagery of Indian peoples prevails on the Internet. Other recent studies conclude that these images affect not only the traction Native peoples are able to gain for important policy initiatives, but also how Natives, especially Native children, view themselves.[7] This imagery has also overlooked interactions between Native peoples and technology. Recent scholarship in urban Indigenous history has begun to unravel the knots of misrepresentation about Native peoples and urban and industrial spaces, but ample opportunity remains to illuminate the ways in which Native peoples utilized, created, and refashioned modern technologies, including new media and information systems, to sustain, advance, and protect kin and community.[8]

In recounting histories of dispossession and road-building in the American West, this book traces some of the stories behind the advertisements of stoic warriors and steel-encased locomotives. One story outlines how the paths that many Native peoples helped surveyors map became sites of large-scale compulsory land purchases. To justify the mass transfer of Indigenous lands to private corporations, US colonial agents relied on a critical legal scaffold: eminent domain. Railroad-induced dispossession rested on the assumption that railroads were critical infrastructure that inherently served a public good. Indigenous leaders and activists contested both the nature of the "public" and "good" from the very start.

Another set of stories obscured by this corporate imagery explore the ways in which Native peoples shaped the course of their cultural, spiritual, political, and material lives by harnessing modern technologies. From the opening scenes of the railroad saga in the West, Native peoples took leading roles, guiding railroad surveyors along future railroad routes, all the while marking their claims to land and negotiating the terms of expansion. Euro-American surveyors relied on Indigenous knowledge and goods as they charted the course of iron roads in Indian Country. When construction crews descended on the Plains and Great Basin in the mid-nineteenth century, Indians responded with a wide array of strategies. Some Plains communities, wracked by disease and dwindling resources, formed intertribal alliances to resist US expansion. Other communities adopted programs of accommodation, often securing free passage on trains in exchange for rights-of-way. The mobility offered by rail travel meant that Indians could continue long-standing migrations to other tribes and also undertake sojourns to Washington, DC, to negotiate on behalf of their tribes. Individuals left reservations by taking up work on railroads and in railroad-related industries. Still others took to trains for political activism and cultural and spiritual revival. Two intertribal movements, the Peyote Religion and the Society of American Indians, emerged out of a railroaded world. Their participants reimagined colonial institutions and processes long associated with railroads—mobility, the corporation, and the US legal system—in order to articulate vibrant and diverse Indigenous presents and futures.

Rail lines continue to be sites of Indigenous resistance and imagination, even as corporate power continues to threaten Indigenous interests across the globe. In the winter of 2020, Tyendinaga Mohawk activists blocked railroad tracks in eastern Canada, impacting over 1 billion Canadian dollars in freight traffic and disrupting passenger travel for an estimated 24,000 people. The Mohawk activists disrupted this critical infrastructure in a show of solidarity with the Wet'suwet'en peoples of British Columbia who were in an ongoing battle to block oil and gas pipeline construction through their territories.[9] The COVID-19 pandemic's disproportionate impact on Indigenous communities, paired with the immense wealth and political capital of the corporation behind the pipeline, TC Energy, ultimately stymied the movement. The Coastal GasLink pipeline was completed in the fall of 2023 despite the protests of the Wet'suwet'en and other First Nations.

Native activists also use new technologies to combat static representations of their communities and advocate for reform. Activist movements such as Idle No More and Rising Hearts call for positive and accurate depictions of Indigenous pasts and presents and demand that Euro-American consumers discontinue derogatory misrepresentations. On December 13, 2017, Rising Hearts—a coalition of Indigenous women living in Washington, DC—took to the internet for a "culture jam." They circulated fictional headlines claiming that corporate officials for the Washington football team, which had long been known by a racist Indian term, had elected to change the team's name to the Redhawks. The buzz from the culture jam generated considerable coverage in the mainstream media, bringing a wider audience of Americans into a public conversation about Indian mascots. In 2020, the team officially dropped the racist name and re-branded as The Commanders.[10] The First Nations advocates behind Idle No More are challenging the corporate takeover of Indigenous resources and promoting the adoption of new, sustainable technologies. In the United States, an intertribal Indigenous activist organization founded by Winona LaDuke (Ojibwe), Honor the Earth, is investing in solar power and other alternative energy technologies on reservations.[11] These strategies—tapping new technologies, focusing attention on the nation's capital, and fostering intertribal alliances—draw on legacies of political organizing that can be traced to the Society of American Indians and other Indigenous mobilizations in the railroad age.

Still others turn to old media to comment on Indigenous issues of the past, present, and future. Cree artist Kent Monkman's *Iron Horse* (2015)

Figure C.1 Kent Monkman, *Iron Horse*, 2015. Acrylic on canvas, 84 in. × 126 in. Image courtesy of the artist.

(Figure C.1) is one potent example. Adopting the romantic, luminist style of nineteenth-century painters who famously depicted anti-modern Indians and unpeopled landscapes, Monkman situates Native peoples firmly at the center of the railroad scene. Showcasing Monkman's embrace of the trickster tradition, the painting shocks viewers just as it invites a critical engagement with central themes in the history of Canadian colonization, a story that has much in common with events unfolding south of the border. In the painting, Monkman's alter-ego—a two-spirit time traveler—holds a hand over her heart as Indigenous men pull a giant horse statue across the tracks. On the sidelines, in the darkness and shade of the wilderness, settlers stand idly by in their frocks and top hats. Native peoples take center stage and are on the move in this painting, and yet the horse, the "gift" from colonists, contains within it the forces that would wreack devastating havoc on Indigenous communities. Just as the fabled Trojan horse spelled disaster for the city of Troy, so, too, did this colonial technology ultimately unleash terribly destructive forces: disease, settlement, violence, dispossession, and ecological destruction.[12]

Monkman's painting directs viewers to this colonial past, just as it subverts the colonial gaze and places Native peoples at the center of the historical scene. Elsewhere, Monkman has emphasized that his work looks to highlight resilience in the face of these colonial realities. “Despite all of these theories of the ‘vanishing Indian’” he explains, “we are still innovative cultures...we are still moving forward.”[13] *Iron Horse* is a painting in which a confrontation with historical realities becomes a means of engaging with possible futures, just as the famous *Smoke Signals* car drove backward in order to move forward. In both cases, modern peoples are engaging with modern technologies, confronting destructive and corrosive forces while finding ways to move forward. *The Iron Horse in Indian Country* is but one chapter in a larger anthology of this practice—a practice that continues today and will persist into the future.

The Iron Horse in Indian Country: Native Americans and Railroads in the US West. Alessandra La Rocca Link, Oxford University Press. © Alessandra La Rocca Link 2025. DOI: 10.1093/9780197674437.003.0011

Notes

Acknowledgments

1. Mary Oliver, *Upstream: Selected Essays* (New York: Penguin Random House, 2016), 8.

Introduction

1. Tony Gremo, "Narcotic Seized in Indian Raid on Hogan," *San Bernardino (Calif.) Country Sun*, April 29, 1962, 37.
2. The Native American Church of California was incorporated in 1958. At the time of the Nez, Woody, and Anderson arrests, nineteen states recognized Native American Church corporate charters. See Gremo, "Narcotic Seized in Indian Raid," *San Bernardino (Calif.) Country Sun*, April 29, 1962, 37.
3. "Coast Navajos Win Right to Use Peyote in Religious Rites," *New York Times*, August 25, 1964, 35. See also Omer C. Stewart, *Peyote Religion: A History* (Norman: University of Oklahoma Press, 1987), 308–310.
4. For more on the details of peyote ceremonies, see Stewart, *Peyote Religion*; Thomas C. Maroukis, *The Peyote Road: Religious Freedom in the Native American Church* (Norman: University of Oklahoma Press, 2010). See also Alexander S. Dawson, *The Peyote Effect: From the Inquisition to the War on Drugs* (Los Angeles: University of California Press, 2018).
5. Leon Wall and William Morgan, *Navajo-English Dictionary* (Lawrence, KS: Haskell Indian Junior College, 1958), 18.
6. See Stewart, *Peyote Religion*, 61; Mountain Wolf Womanand Nancy Oestreich Lurie, eds. *Mountain Wolf Woman: Sister of Crashing Thunder: The Autobiography of a Winnebago Indian* (Ann Arbor: University of Michigan Press, 1961), 48, and Chapter 6, "Mobilizing for Indigenous Futures."
7. For more on "sacred companies," see N. J. Demerits, Peter Dobbin Hall, Terry Schmidt, and Rhys H. Williams, eds., *Sacred Companies: Organizational Aspects of Religion and Religious Aspects of Organizations* (New York: Oxford University Press, 1998); and Maroukis, *The Peyote Road*, 5.
8. Danika Medak-Saltzman, "Coming to You from the Indigenous Future: Native Women, Speculative Film Shorts, and the Art of the Possible," *Studies in American Indian Literatures* 29, no. 1 (Spring 2017): 143.
9. Grace Dillon, *Walking the Clouds: An Anthology of Indigenous Science Fiction* (Tucson: University of Arizona Press, 2012); Tarren Andrews, "Indigenous Futures and Medieval Pasts," *English Language Notes* 58, no. 2 (October 2020): 1–16; Audra Mitchell and Aadita Chaudhury, "Worlding Beyond 'the 'End of 'the Word': White Apocalyptic Visions and BIPOC Futurisms," *International Relations* 34, no. 3 (2020): 32; Kyle Whyte, "Indigenous Science (Fiction) in the Anthropocene," *Environment and Planning E: Nature and Space* 1 (2018): 224–242; Suzanne Newman Fricke, "Indigenous Futurisms in the Hyperpresent Now," *World Art* 9, no. 2 (2019): 107–121; William Lempart, "Indigenous Media Futures: An Introduction," *Cultural Anthropology* 33, no. 2 (2018): 173–179; and Medak-Saltzman, "Coming to You from the Indigenous Future."
10. "Iron Horse," November 1839, *The Knickerbocker, or New York Monthly Magazine*, vols. 13–14 (New York: Clark and Edson Proprietors, 1839), 413–415.
11. "Statistics and Speculations Concerning the Pacific Railroad," *Putnam's Monthly Magazine* II (Sept. 1853), 271.
12. For scholarship on the anti-modern Indian, see Jean O'Brien, *Firsting and Lasting: Writing Indians Out of Existence in New England* (Minneapolis: University of Minnesota Press, 2012); and Philp J. Deloria, *Indians in Unexpected Places* (Lawrence: University Press of Kansas, 2004). See also Erika Marie Bsumek, *Indian-Made: Navajo Culture in the Marketplace, 1868–1940*

(Lawrence: University Press of Kansas, 2008); Leah Dilworth, *Imagining Indians in the Southwest: Persistent Visions of a Primitive Past* (Washington, DC: Smithsonian, 1997); Roy Harvey Pierce, *Savagism and Civilization: The Study of the Indians and the American Mind* (Baltimore, MD: Johns Hopkins University Press, 1953); Richard Slotkin, *Regeneration Through Violence: The Mythology of the American Frontier 1600–1860* (Norman: University of Oklahoma Press, 2000); Coll Thrush, *Native Seattle: Histories from the Crossing-Over Place* (Seattle: University of Washington Press, 2008); and David Wrobel, *Promised Lands: Promotion, Memory, and the Creation of the American West* (Lawrence: University Press of Kansas, 2002).

13. Pierce, *Savagism and Civilization*, 239.
14. These estimates were drawn from Charles O. Paullin's *Atlas of the Historical Geography of the United States*, which includes maps of Indian Reservations for several years. As Jimmy Sweet rightly points out, these government documents are not entirety reliable, but the estimates presented here drive home the alarming rate of physical removal and dispossession in these years. These maps have been digitized by the University of Richmond's Digital Scholarship Lab. Special thanks to Rebecca Wingo for directing me to this source. You can find the maps here: https://dsl.richmond.edu/historicalatlas/108/c/?about=show. Accessed April 26, 2021.
15. "According to most American narratives," historian Philip J. Deloria states, "Indian people, corralled on isolated and impoverished reservations, missed out on modernity—indeed, almost dropped out of history itself." Deloria, *Indians in Unexpected Places*, 5–6.
16. Marquerite S. Shaffer, *See America First: Tourism and National Identity, 1880–1940* (Washington, DC: Smithsonian Books, 2001). See also Katrina Philips, *Stating Indigeneity: Salvage Tourism and the Performance of Native American History* (Chapel Hill: University of North Carolina Press, 2021); David Wrobel, *Promised Lands, and Seeing and Being Seen: Tourism in the American West* (Lawrence: University Press of Kansas, 2001); Dilworth, *Imagining Indians in the Southwest*; and Bsumek, *Indian-Made.*
17. Hal Rothman, *Devil's Bargains: Tourism in the Twentieth-Century American West* (Lawrence: University Press of Kansas, 2000), 11. Railroad companies were still actively involved in the acquisition of Indigenous lands and resources and were architects of a national narrative about Native peoples that wrote them out of modern American life.
18. Wrobel, *Seeing and Being Seen*, 47.
19. Scholarship that touches on the "modern" construction of railroads includes Alfred D. Chandler, *The Visible Hand: The Managerial Revolution in American Business* (Cambridge, MA: Harvard University Press, 1977); Scott Huffard, *Engines of Redemption: Railroads and the Reconstruction of Capitalism in the New South* (Chapel Hill: University of North Carolina Press, 2019); T. C. McLuhan, *Dream Tracks: The Railroad and the American Indian, 1890–1930* (New York: Random House, 1987); George Revill, *Railway* (London: Reaktion Books, 2012); Wolfgang Schivelbusch, *A Railway Journey: The Industrialization of Time and Space in the 19th Century* (Los Angeles: University of California Press, 1977); David Walker, *Railroading Religion: Mormons, Tourists, and the Corporate Spirit of the West* (Chapel Hill: University of North Carolina Press, 2019); Alan Trachtenberg, *The Incorporation of America: Culture and Society in the Gilded Age* (New York: Hill and Wang, 2007). Richard White, *Railroaded: The Transcontinentals and the Making of Modern America* (New York: W. W. Norton, 2012); and Barbara Welke, *Recasting American Liberty: Gender, Race, Law, and the Railroad Revolution, 1865–1920* (Cambridge: Cambridge University Press, 2001). See also Carlos A. Schwantes and James P. Ronda, *The West the Railroads Made* (Seattle: University of Washington Press, 2008), 30–31, 37; Richard H. Frost, *The Railroad and the Pueblo Indians: The Impact of the Atchison, Topeka, and Santa Fe on the Pueblos of the Rio Grande, 1880–1930* (Salt Lake City: University of Utah Press, 2016); and Paul N. Edwards, "Infrastructure and Modernity: Force, Time, and Social Organization in the History of Sociotechnical Systems," in *Technology and Modernity: The Empirical Turn* (Cambridge, MA: MIT Press, 2002), 185–225.
20. For more on railroads as technologies of empire that perpetuated racial difference, see Manu Karuka, *Empire's Tracks: Indigenous Nations, Chinese Workers, and the Transcontinental Railroad* (Oakland: University of California Press, 2019); and Julia H. Lee, *The Racial Railroad* (New York: New York University Press, 2022). See also Daniel Headrick, *Power over Peoples: Technology, Environments, and Western Imperialism 1400 to the Present* (Princeton, NJ: Princeton University Press, 2012); and Leo Marx, *The Machine in the Garden: Technology and the Pastoral Ideal in America* (Oxford: Oxford University Press, 2000). See also Marian Aguiar, *Tracking Modernity: India's Railway and the Culture of Mobility* (Minneapolis: University of Minnesota Press, 2011); Clarence B. Davis, Ronald B. Robinson, and Kenneth Wilburn, eds.,

Railway Imperialism (Westport, CT: Praeger, 1991); Marta Macedo and Jaume Valentines-Alvarez, "Technology and Nation: Learning from the Periphery," *Technology and Culture* 57, no. 4 (October 2016): 989–997; and Kate McDonald, "Asymmetrical Integration: Lessons from a Railway Empire," *Technology and Culture* 56, no. 1 (January 2015): 115–149.

21. "In nineteenth-century western America," historian Richard White exclaims, "the railroad and the modern state were co-productions. The litany of work they did together is impressive." White's illuminating study spotlights the transformations in the nation's political economy that resulted from the toxic relationship between Gilded Age railroad monopolies and the US government, but his statement extends just as easily to the settler colonial program in the American West. White, *Railroaded*, 511.
22. Patrick Wolfe, "Settler Colonialism and the Elimination of the Native," *Journal of Genocide Research* 8, no. 4 (2009): 387–409.
23. US Senate, Committee on the Pacific Railroad, Report on the Pacific Railroad, Report No. 219, 40th Cong., 3d. sess. (1869), 15.
24. White, *Railroaded*, 458.
25. Here I draw from the work of Jodi Byrd, especially her concept of "colonial cacophony." See Jodi Byrd, *The Transit of Empire: Indigenous Critiques of Colonialism* (Minneapolis: University of Minnesota Press, 2011).
26. Numerous books in Native American and railroad history reference the destructive effects of railroad expansion. A few relevant examples include Robert Utley and Wilcomb E. Washburn, *Indian Wars* (New York: Mariner Books, 2002), 236, 299; White, *Railroaded*, 25, 59–62, 465, 489–490; David La Vere, *Contrary Neighbors: Southern Plains and Removed Indians in Indian Territory* (Norman: University of Oklahoma Press, 2000), 137–138; H. Craig Miner, *The Corporation and the Indian: Tribal Sovereignty and Industrial Civilization in Indian Territory, 1865–1907* (Columbia: University of Missouri Press, 1976); Dee Brown, *Bury My Heart at Wounded Knee: An Indian History of the American West* (New York: Henry Holt, 1970), 441; and Margaret Jacobs, *White Mother to a Dark Race: Settler Colonialism, Maternalism, and the Removal of Indigenous Children in the American West and Australia* (Lincoln: University of Nebraska Press, 2009), 155.
27. James L. Smith to Thomas L. Kimball, July 8, 1881, WA MSS S-3183 Sm683, Beinecke Rare Book and Manuscript Library, Yale University, New Haven, CT. Thanks to Justin Gage for locating this exchange.
28. Hannaford to Elliot, January 13, 1908, Opening of Indian Reservations, file no. 534, 137.D.4.7.B, President Subject Files, Northern Pacific Railroad Collection, Minnesota History Center, Minneapolis, MN.
29. See Thomas McGraw, *Prophets of Innovation: Joseph Schumpeter and Creative Destruction* (Cambridge, MA: Harvard University Press, 2007); and White, *Railroaded*, xxv; 455–495.
30. Julian Lim, *Porous Borders: Multiracial Migrations and the Law in the U.S. Mexico Borderlands* (Chapel Hill: University of North Carolina Press, 2018), 17.
31. Secondary material that touches on these issues includes Brown, *Bury My Heart at Wounded Knee*; Herman Viola, *Diplomats in Buckskin: A History of Indian Delegations in Washington City* (Washington, DC: Smithsonian Institution Press, 1981); and Frank R. Rzeczkowski, *Uniting the Tribes: The Rise and Fall of Pan-Indian Community on the Crow Reservation* (Lawrence: University Press of Kansas, 2012).
32. See "hearing story" in Margaret Kovach, *Indigenous Methodologies: Characteristics, Conversations, and Contexts*, 2nd ed. (Toronto: University of Toronto Press, 2021), 150–165. See also Thomas King, *The Truth About Stories: A Native Narrative* (Minneapolis: University of Minnesota Press, 2008).
33. Patrick Wolfe, "Settler Colonialism and the Elimination of the Native," *Journal of Genocide Research* 8, no. 4 (2009): 387–409.
34. Laura Cornelius Kellogg, *Our Democracy and the American Indian: A Comprehensive Presentation of the Indian Situation as It Is Today* (Kansas City, MO: Burton Publishing Co., 1920), 34.
35. Ibid., 41.
36. See Medak-Saltzman, "Coming to You from the Indigenous Future"; and Dillon, ed., *Walking the Clouds.*
37. This project is influenced by the work of Marisa Elena Duarte, who has invited scholars to consider the relationship between Indians and technology not solely as one of exploitation, but also as one of possibility. See Marisa Elena Duarte, *Network Sovereignty: Building the Internet Across Indian Country* (Seattle: University of Washington Press, 2017).

Chapter 1

1. Clifford E. Trafzer, *A Chemehuevi Song: The Resilience of a Southern Paiute Tribe* (Seattle: University of Washington Press, 2015), xvi, 12, 32.
2. Ibid., 21.
3. See Amiel Weeks Whipple notebook, entry for February 22, 1854, folder 22, box 2, Amiel Weeks Whipple Collection, mss. 1892.091, Oklahoma Historical Society, Oklahoma City, OK.
4. W. J. Keeler, *Notes to Accompany Keeler's Map of the U.S. Territory, from the Mississippi River to the Pacific Ocean...* (Washington, DC: Government Printing Office, 1867), box 6, Christopher C. Augur Papers, Everett D. Graff Collection, Newberry Library, Chicago, Illinois [hereafter Augur Papers, Graff Collection, Newberry Library], 1.
5. Ibid., 1.
6. For recent studies on the Civil War and the West, see Virginia Scharff, ed., *Empire and Liberty: The Civil War and the West* (Oakland: University of California Press, 2015); and Adam Arenson and Andrew R. Graybill, *Civil War Wests: Testing the Limits of the United States* (Oakland: University of California Press, 2015).
7. "The Public Land Survey System," *National Atlas*, online at https://web.archive.org/web/20120607063232/http://www.nationalatlas.gov/articles/boundaries/a_plss.html, accessed June 8, 2021.
8. Hannah B. Higgins, *The Grid Book* (Cambridge, MA: MIT Press, 2009), 6.
9. Joseph M. Pierce explains that settler colonialism "demands that our sacred bonds of recognition and reciprocity be converted into estrangement." See Joseph M. Pierce, "Allotment Speculations: The Emergence of Land Memory," in Daniel Heath Justice and Jean M. O'Brien, eds., *Allotment Stories: Indigenous Land Relations Under Settler Siege* (Minneapolis: University of Minnesota Press, 2021).
10. Here I draw from the work of Jodi A. Byrd, Alyohsa Goldstein, Jodi Melamed, and Chandan Reddy, who contend that "economies of dispossession" like that of the settler colonial United States, require "rationalities of abstraction." See Jodi A. Byrd, Alyohsa Goldstein, Jodi Melamed, and Chandan Reddy, "Predatory Value: Economies of Dispossession and Disturbed Relationalities," *Social Text* 36, no. 2 (June 2018): 1–18.
11. Robert Nichols, *Theft Is Property: Dispossession and Critical Theory* (Durham, NC: Duke University Press, 2020), 31–35; Aileen Moreton-Robinson, *The White Possessive: Property, Power, and Indigenous Sovereignty* (Minneapolis: University of Minnesota Press, 2015); and Karuka, *Empire's Tracks.*
12. See Jodi Byrd, especially her concept of "colonial cacophony." Jodi Byrd, *The Transit of Empire: Indigenous Critiques of Colonialism* (Minneapolis: University of Minnesota Press, 2011).
13. Carl I. Wheat, *Mapping the Trans-Mississippi West, 1540–1861* (San Francisco: Institute of Historical Cartography, 1957–1963); Paul E. Cohen, *Mapping the West America's Westward Movement, 1524–1890* (New York: Rizzoli, 2002); Bill Hubbard, *American Boundaries: The Nation, the States, the Rectangular Survey* (Chicago: University of Chicago Press, 2009); Paul Mapp, *The Elusive West and the Contest for Empire, 1713–1763* (Chapel Hill: University of North Carolina Press, 2011); Susan Schulten, *Mapping the Nation: History and Cartography in Nineteenth-Century America* (Chicago: University of Chicago Press, 2012); and David Bernstein, *How the West Was Drawn: Mapping, Indians, and the Construction of the Trans-Mississippi West* (Lincoln: University of Nebraska Press, 2019). Colonial maps of the West also claimed ownership of land that the United States held in name only through the Louisiana Purchase; see Robert Lee, "Accounting for Conquest: The Price for the Louisiana Purchase of Indian Country," *Journal of American History* 103, no. 4 (March 2017): 921–942.
14. Keeler, *Notes to Accompany Keeler's Map...*, 1.
15. William H. Goetzmann, *Army Exploration in the American West, 1803–1863* (Austin: Texas State Historical Association, 1991), 274.
16. Goetzmann, *Army Exploration*, 274–275; and William Goetzmann, *Exploration and Empire: The Explorer and the Scientist in the Winning of the American West* (New York: Alfred Knopf, 1966), ch. 4.
17. Goetzmann, *Army Exploration*, 278–279; and Kent D. Richards, *Isaac A. Stevens: A Young Man in a Hurry* (Provo, UT: Bringham Young University Press, 1979), ch. 6.
18. Goetzmann, *Army Exploration*, 275–292.
19. Ibid., 292.

20. See Goetzmann, *Army Exploration*, and *Exploration and Empire*; Richard A. Bartlett, *Great Surveys of the American West* (Norman: University of Oklahoma Press, 1980); Thomas R. Hietala, *Manifest Design: American Exceptionalism and Empire* (Ithaca, NY: Cornell University Press, 1985); Michael A. Morrison, *Slavery and the American West: The Eclipse of Manifest Destiny* (Chapel Hill: University of North Carolina, 1997); and Carlos D. Schwantes, ed., *Encounters with a Distant Land: Exploration and the Great Northwest* (Moscow: University of Idaho Press, 1994); see also Richards, *Isaac I. Stevens*; Hazard Stevens, *The Life of Isaac Ingalls Stevens*, 2 vols. (Boston: Houghton and Mifflin, 1900); and Jeremy Vetter, *Field Life: Science in the American West During the Railroad Era* (Pittsburgh, PA: University of Pittsburgh Press, 2016).
21. Balduin Möllhausen, *Diary of a Journey from the Mississippi to the Coasts of the Pacific...* (London: Longman, Brown, Green, Longmans, and Roberts, 1858), 2:194.
22. William Cronon, *Changes in the Land: Indians, Colonists, and the Ecology of New England* (New York: Hill and Wang, 1983); William Cronon, "The Trouble with Wilderness, or, Getting Back to the Wrong Nature," in William Cronon, ed., *Uncommon Ground: Rethinking the Human Place in Nature* (New York: W. W. Norton, 1995), 69–90; Shepard Krech III, *The Ecological Indian: Myth and History* (New York: W.W. Norton, 2000).
23. On sketches, see "Appendix A: Diary of the Expedition by J. H. Byrne, Assistant Surveyor," March 15, 1854, in Reports of Explorations and Surveys, suppl. to vol. 2, 63.
24. See Rachel St. John, "Contingent Continent: Spatial and Geographic Arguments in the Shaping of the Nineteenth-Century United States," *Pacific Historical Review* 86, no. 1 (February 2017): 47–49; and Vetter, *Field Life*.
25. *Reports of Explorations and Surveys to Ascertain the Most Practicable and Economic Route for a Railroad from the Mississippi River to the Pacific Ocean...* (Washington, DC: William A. Harris, 1859), supplement to vol. 1, 31.
26. Ibid., 21.
27. Anne Hyde, *Empires, Nations, and Families: A New History of the American West, 1800–1860* (Omaha: University of Nebraska Press, 2011), 458; and Will Bagley, *Blood of Prophets: Brigham Young and the Massacre at Mountain Meadows* (Norman: University of Oklahoma Press, 2004).
28. Hyde, *Empires*, 436–438.
29. Damon B. Akins and William J. Bauer, *We Are the Land: A History of Native California* (Berkley: University of California Press, 2022), 127–138; and Boyd Cothran, *Remembering the Modoc War: Redemptive Violence and the Making of American Innocence* (Chapel Hill: University of North Carolina Press, 2017).
30. Hyde, *Empires*, 421–423.
31. Ibid., 315.
32. Ibid., 126–127.
33. Ibid., 452.
34. Ibid., 419.
35. Ibid., 417. Charles J. Kappler, "Treaty of Fort Laramie with the Sioux, Etc.," in Indian Affairs: Laws and Treaties, vol. II (Washington, DC: Government Printing Office, 1904), 594–595.
36. July 24, 1853, in "Lieutenant A. W. Whipple's Transcontinental Railroad Survey Across the Panhandle of Texas, ed. Ernest A. Archambeau, » *Panhandle Plains Historical Review* 44 (1971): 37.
37. July 26, 1853, Archambeau, "Whipple's Transcontinental Railroad Survey Across the Texas Panhandle."
38. Edward G. Beckwith, September 21, 1853, journal, June 14 to September 26, box 8, Edward G. Beckwith and John Laurence Fox Papers, mssBF, The Huntington Library, San Marino, CA. Dr. James Schiel, surgeon and naturalist employed with the Gunnison-Beckwith expedition noted earlier that September that local Indians ignited a grass fire with which, he wrote, "the Indians signal the presence of strangers." See Frederick W. Bachmann and William Swilling Wallace, eds., *The Land Between: Dr. James Schiel's Account of the Gunnison-Beckwith Expedition into the West, 1853–1854* (Los Angeles: Westernlore Press, 1975), 80–81.
39. Mary McDougall Gordon, ed., *Through Indian Country to California: John P. Sherburne's Diary of the Whipple Expedition* (Stanford, CA: Stanford University Press, 1988), 201–202.
40. Edward G. Beckwith to Corneilia Williamson Beckwith, July 17, 1853, box 1, Beckwith and Fox Papers. For an account from the Whipple survey, see Archambeau, "Whipple's Transcontinental Railroad Survey Across the Texas Panhandle, 1853," p. 71.

41. Lesley Wischmann, *Frontier Diplomats: Alexander Culbertson and Natoyist-Siksina' Among the Blackfeet* (Norman: University of Oklahoma Press, 2000), 221.
42. Ibid., 221; and *Annual Report of the Commissioner of Indian Affairs* (Washington, DC: Government Printing Office, 1855), 196.
43. *Report near the Thirty-Fifth Parallel, Under the Command of Lieutenant A.W. Whipple...*, vol. 3, *Reports on Explorations and Surveys...* (Washington, DC: A. O. Nicholson, 1855), 73.
44. *Reports on Explorations and Surveys*, suppl. to vol. 1, 73.
45. Ibid.
46. *Narrative of Final Reports of Explorations for a Route for a Pacific Railroad...*, vol. 12, (Washington, DC: A. O. P. Nicholson, 1855), 93.
47. *Report of Explorations in California for Railroad Routes*, vol. X in *Reports on Explorations and Surveys* (Washington, DC: Government Printing Office, 1855), 96.
48. Richards, *Isaac I. Stevens*, 112–113.
49. *Reports on Explorations and Surveys*, suppl. to vol. 1, 75.
50. Ibid.
51. A. W. Whipple, journal, August 26 and August 30, 1853, "Whipple's Transcontinental Railroad Survey Across the Texas Panhandle, 1853," ed. Archambeau. John P. Sherburne, the surgeon and geologist assigned to the Whipple survey, also notes the fires of Paiutes in eastern California on March 6, 1854, near the base of the Sierra Nevadas. See Gordon, ed., *Through Indian Country to California*, 201–202.
52. Walter Scribner Schulyer to Matilda Scribner Schulyer, July 16, 1876, box 1, Walter Scribner Schulyer Papers, mssWS 1-106, The Huntington Library, San Marino, CA.
53. Gordon, ed., *Through Indian Country to California*, 206–207.
54. Hyde, *Empires*, 457–459; Bagley, *Blood of the Prophets*, 44.
55. Robert Kent Fielding and Dorothy S. Fielding, eds., *The Journal of Lt. Edward G. Beckwith Compared to the Final Report of the Gunnison Expedition in Utah Territory Including Trail and Campsite Descriptions* (Higganum, CT: Gunnison Memorial Associates, 2003), 51.
56. Ibid., 51; see also Edward G. Beckwith to Corneilia Williamson Beckwith, November 22, 1853, box 1, Beckwith and Fox Papers.
57. Archambeau, "Whipple's Transcontinental Railroad Survey Across the Texas Panhandle, 1853," 53–54.
58. Ibid., 54.
59. For scholarship on the arid region and western water history, see Walter Prescott Webb, *The Great Plains.* (Boston, Mass.: Ginn and Company, 1931); Wallace Stegner, *Beyond the Hundredth Meridian: John Wesley Powell and the Second Opening of the West* (Boston, Mass.: Houghton Mifflin, 1953); Norris Hundley's trilogy of scholarship: *Dividing the Waters* (Berkeley: University of California Press, 1966), *Water and the West: The Colorado River Compact and the Politics of Water in the American West* (Berkeley: University of California Press, 1975), *The Great Thirst: Californians and Water, 1770s–1990s* (Berkeley.: University of California Press, 1992); Donald Worster, *Rivers of Empire: Water, Aridity, and the Growth of the American West* (New York: Oxford University Press, 1985); Donald Pisani, *Water, Land, and Law in the West: The Limits of Public Policy, 1850–1920* (Lawrence: University Press of Kansas, 1996) and *To Reclaim a Divided West: Water, Law, and Public Policy, 1848–1902* (Albuquerque: University of New Mexico Press, 1992).
60. Rachel St. John explains the concern about the Rockies and other geographic imaginings of the region. See Rachel St. John, " Contingent Continent," 47–48. For more on the transcontinentals and Pacific trade, see Sean Fraga, " 'An Outlet to the Western Sea': Puget Sound, Terraqueous Mobility, and Northern Pacific Railroad's Pursuit of Trade with Asia, 1864–1892," *Western Historical Quarterly* 51, no. 4 (Winter 2020): 439–458.
61. Not all the guides were Indigenous. Mexican herders often provided critical cartographic knowledge on the Whipple expedition. Prominent Anglo traders and trappers also joined survey parties as special agents. See *Report Near the Thirty-Fifth Parallel, Under the Command of Lieutenant A.W. Whipple...*, vol. 3, *Reports on Explorations and Surveys...*, (Washington, DC: A. O. Nicholson, 1855), 48.
62. John C. Ewers, *Indian Life on the Upper Missouri* (Norman: University of Oklahoma Press, 1968), 61–63.
63. *Annual Report of the Commissioner of Indian Affairs* (Washington, DC: Government Printing Office, 1855), 195–196.

64. Ryan Hall, *Beneath the Backbone of the World: Blackfoot People and the North American Borderlands, 1720–1877* (Chapel Hill: University of North Carolina Press, 2020), 111–113, 128.
65. Ibid., 128.
66. Stevens quoted in Wischmann, *Frontier Diplomats*, 223–224.
67. *Reports on Explorations and Surveys*, suppl. to vol. 1, 88.
68. Ibid.
69. *Report of Explorations in Çalifornia for Railroad Routes*, vol. X in *Reports on Explorations and Surveys* (Washington, DC: Government Printing Office, 1855), 96, 102.
70. E. G. Beckwith, Journal entries for May 10, 1854 and May 11, 1854, box 8, Beckwith and Fox Papers.
71. Gordon, ed., *Through Indian Country to California*, 193–196.
72. *Report near the Thirty-Fifth Parallel, Under the Command of Lieutenant A. W. Whipple*, 71–72.
73. Ibid.
74. Octavius Seowtewa, ArcGis Map, Grand Canyon Trust, https://storymaps.arcgis.com/stories/86f31b6724ef40ac981753096cada6f0, accessed June 29, 2022.
75. *Report Near the Thirty-Fifth Parallel, Under the Command of Lieutenant A. W. Whipple*, 71–72.
76. Ibid., 75.
77. *Report Near the Thirty-Fifth Parallel, Under the Command of Lieutenant A. W. Whipple*, 97–98. Thanks are due to Maurice Crandall for tracking down the Yavapai name for the river.
78. E. G. Beckwith, Journal entries for June 14 to September 26, 1853, Edward G. Beckwith, box 8, Beckwith and Fox Papers.
79. Arhcambeau, ed., *Whipple's Transcontinental Railroad Survey Across the Texas Panhandle*, 93. From the Pope expedition, see *Reports on Explorations and Surveys*, suppl. to vol. 2, 2.
80. Archambeau, ed., *Whipple's Transcontinental Railroad Survey Across the Texas Panhandle*, 93. From the Pope expedition, see *Reports on Explorations and Surveys*, suppl. to vol. 2, 81.
81. Fielding, Kent R., and Dorothy S. Fielding. *The Journal of Lt. Edward G. Beckwith Compared to the Final Report of the Gunnison Expedition in Utah Territory Including Trail and Campsite Descriptions*. (Higganum, CT: Gunnison Memorial Associates, 2003), 14.
82. Gordon, ed., *Through Indian Country to California*, 192.
83. *Reports on Explorations and Surveys*, suppl. to vol. 1, 71.
84. Ibid., 79.
85. Ibid., 76–79.
86. For more on the Blackfoot Confederacy, see D'Arcy Jenish, *Indian Fall: The Last Great Days of the Blackfoot Confederacy* (New York: Viking Press, 1999); and Hana Samek, *The Blackfoot Confederacy, 1880–1920: A Comparative Study of Canadian and U.S. Indian Policy* (Albuquerque: University of New Mexico Press, 2011).
87. Gordon, ed., *Through Indian Country to California*, 206–207.
88. Stevens mentions carting an entire wagon full of goods to distribute to Indians. See *Reports on Explorations and Surveys*, suppl. to vol. 1, 33.
89. Major-General Grenville M. Dodge, *How We Built the Union Pacific Railway and Other Railway Papers and Addresses* (Council Bluffs, IA: Monarch Printing Co., n.d.), The Everett D. Graff Collection of Western Americana, The Newberry Library, Chicago, 7–8. Richard White points out that Dodge was a first-rate self-promoter who participated in Union Pacific corruption schemes. See Richard White, *Railroaded: The Transcontinentals and the Making of Modern America* (New York: W. W. Norton, 2011), 30–31.

Chapter 2

1. Stanford quoted in George Kraus, *High Road to Promontory: Building the Central Pacific Across the High Sierra* (Palo Alto, CA: American West, 1969), 59.
2. Dee Brown, *Hear That Lonesome Whistle Blow: Railroads in the West* (New York: Holt Rinehart, and Winston, 1977), 50.
3. Kraus, *High Road to Promontory*, 59.
4. John Hoyt Williams, *A Great and Shining Road: The Epic Story of the Transcontinental Railroad* (New York: Times Books, 1988); 72.
5. E. C. Lockwood, "With the Casement Brothers While Building the Union Pacific," *The Union Pacific Magazine* February 1931, p. 24. See also Wesley S. Griswold, *A Work of Giants: Building the First Transcontinental Railroad* (New York: McGraw Hill, 1962), 174–175.
6. Griswold, *A Work of Giants*, 174–175.

7. Richmond L. Clow, *Spotted Tail: Warrior and Statesman* (Pierre: South Dakota Historical Society Press, 2019), 38–39.
8. George Bent and George E. Hyde, *Life of George Bent Written from his Letters* (Norman: University of Oklahoma Press, 1968), 165. For more on Sand Creek and the resulting Black Hawk War, see Robert Scott, *Blood at Sand Creek: The Massacre Revisited* (Caldwell, ID: Caxton Press, 1994); Elliott West, *The Contested Plains: Indians, Goldseekers, and the Rush to Colorado* (Lawrence: University Press of Kansas, 1998); and Ari Kelman, *A Misplaced Massacre: Struggling over the Memory of Sand Creek* (Cambridge, MA: Harvard University Press, 2015).
9. "The Indian War. Fort at Julesburg Attacked," *Evening Star* (Washington, DC), February 4, 1865, 1; "Indian Affairs," *Cleveland Daily Leader*, January 27, 1865, 1.
10. For more on Spotted Tail, see Pekka Hämäläinen, *Lakota America: A New History of Indigenous Power* (New Haven, CT: Yale University Press, 2019); and Clow, *Spotted Tail.*
11. See Brown, *Hear That Lonesome Whistle Blow*; John Carson, *The Union Pacific: Hell on Wheels!* (New Mexico: Press of the Territorian, 1968); Kraus, *High Road to Promontory*; Griswold, *A Work of Giants*; Lynne Rhodes Mayer and Kenneth E. Vose, *Makin"Tracks: The Story of the Transcontinental Railroad in the Pictures and Words of the Men Who Were There* (New York: Praeger, 1975); Williams, *A Great and Shining Road*; David Haward Bain, *Empire Express: Building the First Transcontinental Railroad* (New York: Penguin Books, 2000); and Richard White, *Railroaded: The Transcontinentals and the Making of Modern America* (New York: W. W. Norton, 2011).
12. I received permission from the University of Utah to reproduce the Castleton image of a site north of Roosevelt, Utah. I contacted the Ute Tribe and the Utah Division of Indian Affairs for any available information about whether or not the site was sacred. My research does not indicate that it is, and these entities did not respond to my outreach. For the Ute sites near Mill Creek and Roosevelt, Utah, see Kenneth B. Castleton, *Petroglyphs and Pictographs of Utah* (Salt Lake City: Utah Museum of Natural History, 1984), 60; and for the site in the Green River Basin, see James D. Keyser and George Poetschat, *Warrior Art of Wyoming's Green River Basin: Biography Petroglyphs Along the Seedskadee* (Portland: Oregon Historical Society, 2005), 55–57.
13. White, *Railroaded*, 23.
14. Ibid., 24.
15. Dodge, Grenville Melen. *How We Built the Union Pacific Railway, and Other Papers and Addresses.* (Council Bluffs, IA: Monarch Printing Co., 1910), 35.
16. Pacific Railway Act, sec. 2.
17. Stacy Leeds, "By Eminent Domain or Some Other Name: A Tribal Perspective on Taking Land," *Tulsa Law Review* 41 (Fall 2005): 6–8.
18. Meredith Alberta Palmer, "Rendering Settler Sovereign Landscapes: Race and Property in the Empire State," *Environment and Planning D: Society and Space* 38, no. 5 (2020): 793–810.
19. Eric Kades, "The Dark Side of Efficiency: *Johnson V. M'Intosh* and the Expropriation of American Indian Lands," *University of Pennsylvania Law Review* 148 (April 2000): 1186.
20. Leeds, "By Eminent Domain," 5.
21. For more on the Marshall Trilogy, see David Wilkins, *American Indian Politics and the American Political System* (New York: Rowman and Littlefield, 2017).
22. Henry Edmund Mills, *Mills on the Law of Eminent Domain* (Ithaca, NY: Cornell University Press, repr. 2009), 61.
23. White, *Railroaded.*
24. Leeds, "By Eminent Domain,"1.
25. Kades, "The Dark Side of Efficiency," 1190.
26. Colin G. Calloway, *Pen and Ink Witchcraft: Treaties and Treaty-Making in American Indian History* (New York: Oxford University Press, 2013), 174–175.
27. John Stands in Timber, *Cheyenne Memories* (Lincoln: University of Nebraska Press, 1972), 161–162.
28. Charles J. Kappler, *Indian Affairs: Laws and Treaties* (Washington, DC: GPO, 1904), vol. 2, 594. See also Le Roy R. Hafen and Francis Marion Young, *Fort Laramie and the Pageant of the West, 1834–1890* (Lincoln: University of Nebraska Press, 1938); Paul L. Hedren, *Fort Laramie and the Great Sioux War* (Norman: University of Oklahoma Press, 1876).
29. Francis Paul Prucha, *American Indian Treaties: The History of a Political Anomaly,* (Berkeley: University of California Press, 1994), 238.
30. Stands in Timber, *Cheyenne Memories*, 162.

31. Kappler, *Indian Affairs: Laws and Treaties*, vol. 2, 600–602. Accessed online at digital.library.okstate.edu; Prucha, *American Indian Treaties*, 240. See also Paul W. Gates, *Fifty Million Acres: Conflict over Kansas Land Policy 1854–1890* (Ithaca, NY: Cornell University Press, 1954); Stan Hoig, *White Man's Paper Trail: Grand Councils and Treaty-Making on the Central Plains* (Boulder: University Press of Colorado, 2006); and H. Craig Miner, *The End of Indian Kansas: A Study of Cultural Revolution, 1854–1871* (Lawrence: Regents Press of Kansas, 1978).
32. Excerpt from Prucha, *American Indian Treaties*, 242.
33. Prucha, *American Indian Treaties*, 243–246; and Kappler, *Indian Affairs*, vol. IV, 1081–1085. For more on California Indians, see Damon B. Atkins and William J. Bauer, *We Are the Land: A History of Native California* (Berkeley: University of California Press, 2021).
34. Gregory Michno, *The Deadliest Indian War in the West: The Snake Conflict, 1864–1868* (Caldwell, ID: Caxton Press, 2007), 5.
35. Kappler, *Indian Affairs: Laws and Treaties*, vol. 2, 849, 852, 859.
36. See *Shoshone Tribe of Indians v. United States*, 299 U.S. 476 (1937); and *Northwestern Shoshone v. United States*, 324 U.S. 335, 1945.
37. *Annual Report of the Secretary of War to the President* (Washington, DC: GPO, 1868), 43, 45.
38. Kerry R. Oman, "The Beginning of the End of the Peace Commission of 1867–1868," *Great Plains Quarterly* 22, no. 1 (Winter 2002): 33–51.
39. Alfred Banitz quoted in Calloway, *Pen and Ink Witchcraft*, 212; see also 209–211. See also Jill St. Germain, *Indian Treaty-Making Policy in the United States and Canada 1867–1877* (Lincoln: University of Nebraska Press, 2001); and Pekka Hämäläinen, *Comanche Empire* (New Haven, CT: Yale University Press, 2009), 324.
40. *Lone Wolf v. Hitchcock*, 187. U.S. 553 (1903). See also David Wilkins and K. Tsianina Lomawaima, *Uneven Ground: American Indian Sovereignty and Federal Law* (Norman: University of Oklahoma Press, 2001); and Walter Echo-Hawk, *In the Courts of the Conqueror: The 10 Worst Indian Law Cases Ever Decided* (Golden, CO: Fulcrum, 2010).
41. Clow, *Spotted Tail*, 46.
42. Col. Henry R. Carrington, *AB-SA-RA-KA, Land of Massacre: Being the Experience of an Officer's Wife on the Plains. With an Outline of Indian Operations and Conferences from 1865 to 1878*, 5th ed. (Philadelphia: J. B. Lippincott and Co., 1879), The Everett D. Graff Collection of Western Americana, The Newberry Library, Chicago, 79–80.
43. The abandonment of the Bozeman Trail was seen as a victory for Red Cloud, but Peace Commissioners knew that the railroad could provide miners access to the Black Hills through another route. See St. Germain, *Indian Treaty-Making Policy in the United States and Canada 1867–1877*, 36.
44. Grenville M. Dodge, "Biography of Grenville M. Dodge from 1831 to 1871," mss MFILM 00721, 1022–1023, Huntington Library, San Marino, CA. Thanks to Mary E. Mendoza for copying these files.
45. Rebecca Solnit, *Savage Dreams: A Journey into the Hidden Wars of the American West* (Berkeley: University of California Press, 2014), 136.
46. See Ferol Egan, *Sand in a Whirlwind: The Paiute Indian War of 1860* (Reno: University of Nevada Press, 1972); John M. Townley, *The Pyramid Lake Indian War* (Reno, NV: Great Basin Studies Center, 1984); Martha C. Knack and Omer C. Stewart, *As Long as the River Shall Run: An Ethnohistory of Pyramid Lake Indian Reservation* (Reno: University of Nevada Press, 1999).
47. Crocker quoted in Williams, *A Great and Shining Road*, 182.
48. Collis Potter Huntington biographical material for H. H. Bancroft's Chronicles of the Builders of the Commonwealth, 1880–1890, BANC MSS, C-D773, 775–778, microfilm, Bancroft Library, University of California, Berkeley.
49. C. P. Huntington to Charles Crocker, May 2, 1868, *Letters from Colis P. Huntington to Mark Hopkins, Leland Stanford, Charles Crocker, E. B. Crocker, Charles F. Crocker and D. D. Cotton*, vol. 1. 1869, New York, 1892, Huntington Library, San Marino, CA.
50. Caxton [W. H. Roads, *San Francisco Chronicle*] quoted in George Kraus, *High Road to Promontory*, 204, 208.
51. Manu Vimalassery, "The Prose of Counter-Sovereignty," in Alyosha Goldstein, ed., *Formations of United States Colonialism* (Durham, NC: Duke University Press, 2014), 101; Kraus, *High Road to Promontory*, 204, on berries, 186.
52. W. B. Dodoridge, quoted in Mayer and Vose, *Makin' Tracks*, 92.
53. Great Northern officials conversed about such arrangements with the Union Pacific years later. See Ralph Budd to J. T. Maher, September 1, 1924, and J. T Maher to Ralph Budd, September 2,

1924, Citizenship Question, 133.K.12.3b, box 529, 11231, President Subject Files, Great Northern Railway Company Records, Minnesota History Center, Minneapolis, MN.

54. Calloway, *Pen and Ink Witchcraft*, 217.
55. Porcupine quoted in George Bird Grinnell, *The Fighting Cheyennes* (Norman: University of Oklahoma Press, 1983), 265.
56. Bent and Hyde, *Life of George Bent*, 277.
57. Grinnell, *The Fighting Cheyennes*, 267–268; and Bent and Hyde, *Life of George Bent*, 277.
58. Andrew Isenberg, *The Destruction of the Bison: An Environmental History 1750–1920* (London: Cambridge University Press, 2000); Hämäläinen, *Comanche Empire*, 299; and West, *Contested Plains*, 243. See also Theodore Binnema, *Common and Contested Ground: A Human and Environmental History of the Northwest Plains* (Norman: University of Oklahoma Press, 2001); and Dan Flores, *American Serengeti: The Last Big Animals of the Great Plains* (Lawrence: University Press of Kansas, 2016).
59. Elliott West, *Continental Reckoning: The American West in the Age of Expansion* (Lincoln: University of Nebraska Press, 2023), 198–199.
60. Henry Stanley, *My Early Travels and Adventures in America and Asia* (London: Gerald Duckworth and Co., 1895), 220.
61. Luther Standing Bear, *My People the Sioux* (1928; New York: Bison Books, 2006), 87–88.
62. Ibid.
63. Grenville M. Dodge, *How We Built the Union Pacific Railway and Other Railway Papers and Addresses* (Washington, DC: GPO, 1910), 18.
64. *Annual Report of the Secretary of War to the President* (Washington, DC: GPO, 1868), 22–23.
65. Andrew C. Isenberg, *Destruction of the Bison*; Dodge, *How We Built the Union Pacific*, 116.
66. "Samuel B. Reed to wife, August 17, 1864, Samuel Benedict Reed Letters, 1864–1870, The Huntington Library, San Marino California.
67. Dodge, *How We Built the Union Pacific*, 16.
68. Stephen Casement to Frances Marion Jennings Casement, April 26, 1868, John Stephen Casement Papers, mssFAC 714, The Huntington Library, San Marino, California.
69. For other interpretations of this image and event, see Glenn Gardner Willumson, *Iron Muse: Photographing the Transcontinental Railroad* (Berkeley: University of California Press, 2013); Martha A. Sandweiss, *Print the Legend: Photography and the American West* (New Haven, CT: Yale University Press, 2002); Thomas Weston Fels, *Destruction and Destiny: The Photographs of Alfred J. Russell, Directing American Energy in War and Peace* (Pittsfield, MA: Berkshire Museum, 1987); T. C. McLuhan, *Dream Tracks: The Railroad and the American Indian* (New York: Random House, 1987); and Barry Combs, *Westward to Promontory: Building the Union Pacific Across the Plains and Mountains, a Pictorial Documentary* (Palo Alto, CaA: Oakland Museum, 1969).
70. Sherman, quoted in Dodge, *How We Built the Union Pacific*, 17.
71. US Senate, Committee on the Pacific Railroad, Report on the Pacific Railroad, Report No. 219, 40th Cong., 3d. sess, (1869), 15.
72. *New York Times*, June 2, 1870, June 3, 1870.

Railway Journeys: Iron Roads to Washington

1. Oliver Otis Howard, *My Life and Experiences Among Our Hostile Indians* (Hartford, CT: A. D. Worthington and Company, 1907), 173–74.
2. Ibid., 175–177.
3. ARCIA, 1872, 125.
4. Red Cloud and Spotted Tail's 1870 visit included a similar tour. See Katherine C. Turner, *Red Men Calling on the White Father* (Norman: University of Oklahoma, 1951), 120–122.
5. "I was once a prisoner and kept a whole year, in a prison like this, in Santa Fe. I was innocent of any crime. I was very lonely and sad, and I don't want another man to be so unhappy." Miguel to O. O. Howard, *My Life and Experiences Among Our Hostile Indians*, (Hartford, Conn.: A. D. Worthington and Co., 1907), 175.
6. See Neil Irvin Painter, *Exodusters: Black Migration to Kansas After the Civil War* (New York: W. W. Norton, 1992).
7. Keokuk quoted in Herman Viola, *Diplomats in Buckskin: A History of Indian Delegations in Washington City* (Washington, DC: Smithsonian Institution Press, 1981), 47.
8. Viola, *Diplomats in Buckskin*, 48.

9. *Reports of Cases Argued and Determined in the Supreme Court of the State of Kansas* (1872), vol. 6 (Topeka: Kansas State Printing Plant, 1873), 101.
10. Viola, *Diplomats in Buckskin*, 48.
11. Turner, *Red Men Calling*, 161–182. For more on Sara Winnemucca, see Cari M. Carpenter and Carolyn Sorisio, eds., *The Newspaper Warrior: Sara Winnemucca Hopkins's Campaign for American Indian Rights, 1864–1891* (Lincoln: University of Nebraska Press, 2015). See also Sara Winnemucca Hopkins, *Life Among the Piutes: Their Wrongs and Claims* (Lincoln: University of Nebraska Press, 1883; repr. 1994).
12. McGillycudy to Price, J., December 30, 1883, Office of the Bureau of Indian Affairs, Record Group 75, Pine Ridge Agency, South Dakota, box 36, Copies of Correspondence and Reports Sent to the Office of Indian Affairs, August 10, 1883–Sept. 30 1889, NARA, Kansas City, Missouri; and Viola, *Diplomats in Buckskin*, 58.
13. C. J. Aktins to McLaughlin, May 6, 1886, in Miscellaneous Correspondence Received, 1865–1910, box 30, Standing Rock Agency, Fort Yates, North Dakota, RG 75, Records of the Bureau of Indian Affairs, National Archives and Records Administration, Kansas City, Missouri.
14. C. N. Bliss to all U.S. Indian Agents, Circular Letter, July 3, 1897, in Official Letters and Telegrams Received, 1897–1906, box 1, February 1895–December 1898, Crow Agency Records, RG 75, Records of the Office of Indian Affairs, National Archives and Records Center, Denver, CO.
15. Viola, *Diplomats in Buckskin*, 109.

Chapter 3

1. Osage Council Proceedings, May 25, 1868, Great and Little Osage Indians, box 36, Lester Hargrett Collection, Gilcrease Museum, Library and Archives, Tulsa, Oklahoma. 26 [hereafter Hargrett Collection, Gilcrease].
2. J. N. Bowman, "Driving the Last Spike at Promontory, 1869," *California Historical Society Quarterly* 36, no. 2 (June 1957): 96–106; and 36, no. 3 (September 1957): 263–274. Accessed online at http://cprr.org/Museum/Bowman_Last_Spike_CHS.html, February 13, 2017.
3. Joseph Medicine Crow, *From the Heart of Crow Country: The Crow Indians' Own Stories* (Lincoln: University of Nebraska Press, 1992), 44.
4. H. Craig Miner is the first scholar to tackle the impact of corporations in Indian Country. See H. Craig Miner, *The Corporation and the Indian: Tribal Sovereignty in Indian Territory, 1865–1907* (Norman: University of Oklahoma Press, 1989).
5. Ely S. Parker, Commissioner of Indian Affairs, to Department of the Interior, *Annual Report of the Commissioner of Indian Affairs*, 1870 (Washington, DC: Government Printing Office, 1871), 10–11 [hereafter ARCIA, (year), page].
6. ARCIA, 1851, 16.
7. ARCIA, 1860, 5.
8. ARCIA, 1869, 1.
9. *Annual Report of the Secretary of War*, 1869, xi.
10. See Elliott West, *The Contested Plains: Indians, Goldseekers, and the Rush to Colorado* (Lawrence: University Press of Kansas, 1998).
11. "Initial Letter Dividing the Indian Agencies Among the Christian Societies," August 11, 1870, Vincent Colyer Sect. of Board, p. 98, appendix 25, ARCIA, 1870. For more on Grant's "Peace Policy," see R. R. Levine, "Indian Fighters and Indian Reformers: Grant's Indian Peace Policy and the Conservative Consensus," *Civil War History* 31, no. 4 (December 1985): 329–352; Cathleen D. Cahill, *Federal Fathers and Mothers: A Social History of the United States Indian Service, 1869–1933* (Chapel Hill: University of North Carolina Press, 2013); C. Joseph Genetin-Pilawa, *Crooked Paths to Allotment: The Fight over Federal Indian Policy After the Civil War* (Chapel Hill: University of North Carolina Press, 2012). For a recent local study, see David S. Trask, "Episcopal Missionaries on the Santee and Yankton Reservations: Cross Cultural Collaboration and President Grant's Peace Policy," *Great Plains Quarterly* 33, no. 2 (Spring 2013): 87–101.
12. ARCIA, 1885, xxxv.
13. Clara Sue Kidwell, *The Choctaws in Oklahoma: From Tribe to Nation, 1855–1970* (Norman: University of Oklahoma Press, 2007), 89.
14. For more on the role of railroads in the settlement of the West, see Paul W. Gates, *History of Public Land Law Development* (Washington, DC: GPO, 1968), and *Fifty Million*

Acres: Conflicts over Kansas Land Policy, 1854–1890 (Norman: University of Oklahoma Press, 1997); Maury Klein, *Union Pacific, Volume 1: 1862–1893* (Minneapolis: University of Minnesota Press, 2006); Richard J. Orsi, *Sunset Limited: The Southern Pacific Railroad and the Development of the American West, 1850–1930* (Berkeley: University of California Press, 2007); and Richard White, *Railroaded: The Transcontinentals and the Making of Modern America* (New York: W. W. Norton, 2011).

15. John Joseph Matthews, *The Osages, Children of the Middle Waters* (Norman: University of Oklahoma Press, 1981), 693.
16. James R. Christiansen, "A Study of Osage History Prior to 1876," (PhD diss., Brigham Young University, 1962), 228.
17. Ibid., 227; and Executive Department, Topeka, Kansas, "Remonstrance Against the Treaty with the Great and Little Osage Indians. . . ," box 36, "Osages," Hargrett Collection, Gilcrease, 6. For more complaints from Kansas officials about the Sturgis treaty, see George H. Hoyt, "Kansas and the Osage Swindle" (Washington, DC: Gibson Brothers Printers, 1868), Hargrett Collection, Gilcrease.
18. Superintendent Thomas Murphy to Commissioner of Indian Affairs, November 15, 1867, box 36, "Osage Indians," Hargrett Collection, Gilcrease.
19. G. C. Snow to Superintendent Murphy, February 16, 1868, box 36, "Osage Indians," Hargrett Collection, Gilcrease.
20. Penny T. Linsenmayer, "Kansas Settlers on the Osage Diminished Reserve: A Study of Laura Ingalls Wilder's *Little House on the Prairie*," *Kansas History* 24, no. 2 (Autumn 2001), 171.
21. I. E. Quastler, "Charting a Course: Lawrence, Kansas, and Its Railroad Strategy," *Kansas History* 18, no. 1 (Spring 1995): 27.
22. Ibid., 28.
23. G. C. Snow to Superintendent Murphy, February 26, 1868, box 36, "Osage Indians," Hargrett Collection, Gilcrease.
24. Lisnenmayer, "Kansas Settlers on the Osage Diminished Reserve,"172.
25. Thomas Murphy to Commissioner of Indian Affairs, March 5, 1868, box 36, "Osage Indians," Hargrett Collection, Gilcrease; and Thomas Murphy to Commissioner of Indian Affairs, March 26, 1868, Hargrett Collection, Gilcrease.
26. Thomas Murphy to Commissioner of Indian Affairs, March 5, 1868, box 36, "Osage Indians," Hargrett Collection, Gilcrease; and Thomas Murphy to Commissioner of Indian Affairs, March 26, 1868, Hargrett Collection, Gilcrease.
27. Also cited as "Sturgis" or "Sturges" treaty and the Drum Creek treaty. See David Parsons, "The Removal of the Osages from Kansas," (PhD diss., University of Oklahoma, 1940), 22, fn. 1. On the allegation that the council meetings were private from May 20 onward, see Parsons, "The Removal of the Osages," 28.
28. Sidney Clarke, Report, "Osage Indian Treaty," June 18, 1868, box 36, Hargrett Collection, Gilcrease.
29. *Congressional Globe*, 40th Cong., 2d sess., 1868, 3259.
30. "Osage Council Ground, May 23, 1868," printed with "Message of the President of the United States in answer to a resolution. . . ," in box 36, "Osage Indians," Hargrett Collection, Gilcrease, 11–18; Hard Rope quoted on p. 13.
31. Lisenmayer, "Kansas Settlers on the Osage Diminished Reserve," 172–173; and Parsons, "The Removal of the Osages from Kansas," 40–42. Parsons states that the first report can be found in the Jesuit archives for the province of Missouri. See Paul Mary Ponziglione, "The Osages and Father John Schoemakers, S.J.," chapter XXXIV, book IV, 340–347. The second report is in the Jesuit House history of the Osage mission. See "Historia Domus, Missionis Osaginae ad. S. Franciscum de Hieronymo, A.D. 1868," ms. no. 3755, 10–13, The Jesuit Archives for the Province of Missouri, St. Louis University. Thanks to Alexandria Gough for the Latin translation of this document.
32. *Congressional Globe*, 40th Cong., 2d sess., 1868, 3256–3258.
33. Ibid., 3256.
34. Clarke quoted in Prucha, *The Great Father*, 293.
35. Ibid.
36. *Congressional Globe*, 40th Cong., 2nd sess., 1868, 3257.
37. Richard White explores how "friendship was lucrative" in Gilded Age America. See White, *Railroaded*, 63, 93.

38. Gates, *History of Public Land Law Development*, 341–371.
39. William Lawrence, "The Osage Ceded Lands: Who Owns Them? The Settler vs. The Railroads, Views of Judge Lawrence of Ohio," June 5, 1871, "Osage Indians," box 36, Hargrett Collection, Gilcrease.
40. Parsons, "The Removal of the Osage from Kansas," 47.
41. Wilkins, *American Indian Sovereignty and the U.S. Supreme Court*, 27–29.
42. Marshall quoted in Wilkins, *American Indian Sovereignty and the U.S. Supreme Court*, 32.
43. Wilkins, *American Indian Sovereignty and the U.S. Supreme Court*, 22.
44. Parsons, "The Removal of the Osages from Kansas," 47; and U.S. Const. art. 4, sec. 3, cl. 2.
45. Sidney Clarke, Report, "Osage Indian Treaty," June 18, 1868, box 36, "Osage Indians," Hargrett Collection, Gilcrease, 1–3.
46. In 1869, Congress, led by Rep. William S. Holman of Indiana and Rep. Julian Harlan and Sen. James Harlan of Iowa, tried to pass a resolution opposing land grants and reserving public lands for "actual settlers." Yet the resolution did little to stop the passage of several acts granting lands to railroad corporations in the West. In March 1870, Holman brought forth a resolution declaring that Congress would cease providing railroads land grants that passed unanimously. Just two weeks later a land grant bill would enter and ultimately pass Congress for an Oregon railroad company. The 41st Congress granted nearly 20 million more acres to railroads. See Darwin P. Roberts, "The Legal History of Federally Granted Railroad Rights-of-Way and the Myth of Congress's '1871 Shift,'" *Colorado Law Review* 82 (2011): 131–134.
47. Chas. W. Blair, President, Missouri, Fort Scott, and Santa Fe Railroad Co., "Statement Relative the Osage Treaty," in Clarke, Report, Hargrett Collection, Gilcrease Center, 8–9.
48. Quastler, "Charting a Course," 31, n. 31.
49. "Ibid., 31.
50. "Public Opinion and National Policy on Our Indian Relations," *Frank Leslie's Illustrated Newspaper*, August 21, 1869, issue 725.
51. Similar treaties with the Kaws, Sac and Foxes, Missouria and Iowas, all provided sale of ceded lands to corporations. See Prucha, *American Indian Treaties*, 284–285. See also Vine Deloria Jr. and Raymond DeMallie, eds., *Documents of American Indian Diplomacy: Treaties, Agreements, and Conventions, 1775–1979*, vol 1. (Norman: University of Oklahoma Press, 1999), 514–544.
52. *The Second Annual Report of the Board of Indian Commissioners, 1870* (Washington, DC: Government Printing Office, 1871), 79.
53. Ibid.
54. Ibid.
55. Prucha, *American Indian Treaties*, 291.
56. See Cahill, *Federal Fathers and Mothers*; and Genetin-Pilawa, *Crooked Paths to Allotment*.
57. Prucha, *American Indian Treaties*, 298–299.
58. *Congressional Globe*, 41st Cong. 3rd sess., March 1, 1871, 1812.
59. Ibid.

Chapter 4

1. ARCIA, 1869, 99–100.
2. For more on the history of Oklahoma, see Arrell Morgan Gibson, *Oklahoma: A History in Five Centuries* (Norman: University of Oklahoma Press, 1981); and David A. Chang, *The Color of the Land: Race, Nation, and the Politics of Landownership in Oklahoma, 1832–1929* (Chapel Hill: University of North Carolina Press, 2010).
3. ARCIA, 1871, 566.
4. Warren, Lous. *God's Red Son: The Ghost Dance Religion and the Making of Modern America*, (New York: Basic Books, 2017), 96.
5. "American Indians," *The Encyclopedia of Oklahoma History*, Oklahoma Historical Society, www.okhistory.org, accessed April 25, 2017.
6. White, Richard. *Railraoded: The Transcontinentals and the Making of Modern America* (New York: W. W. Norton, 2012), 24.
7. John Bartlett Meserve, "Chief Coleman Cole," *Chronicles of Oklahoma*, vol. 14, no. 1, March 1936, Oklahoma State University Digital Collections. Accessed April 24, 2017, 15–16.
8. Ibid., 18.
9. Known as the "Net Proceeds Claim"; ibid., 19. See also H. B. Cushman, *History of the Choctaw, Chickasaw, and Natchez Indians* (Greenville, TX: Headlight Print. House, 1899), 275.

10. Coleman Cole to President Grant, February 19, 1877, Choctaw Nation Agency Records, CTN 74, Oklahoma Historical Society, Oklahoma City, OK [hereafter Oklahoma Historical Society].
11. For more on the Fort Smith Treaties, see William G. McLoughlin, *After the Trail of Tears: The Cherokee's Struggle for Sovereignty, 1839–1880* (Chapel Hill: University of North Carolina Press, 1994); and Minnie Thomas Bailey, *Reconstruction in Indian Territory: A Story of Avarice, Discrimination, and Opportunism* (Port Washington, NY: Kennikat Press, 1972).
12. Article 6, 1886, Treaty with the Choctaw and Chickasaws; Charles J. Kappler, *Indian Affairs: Laws and Treaties* (Washington, DC: GPO, 1904), vol. 2, 920–921.
13. Ibid. All of the tribes in the eastern portion of the Indian Territory were to trade some of their land holdings for stock in the railroad companies, except for the Cherokee. See H. Craig Miner, *The Corporation and the Indian: Tribal Sovereignty and Industrial Civilization in Indian Territory, 1865–1907* (Columbia: University of Missouri Press, 1976), 14.
14. Kappler, *Indian Affairs*, 2:921.
15. *The Congressional Globe*, 39th Cong., 1st sess., March 1, 1866, 1102.
16. Ibid.
17. "An Act Granting Land to Kansas to Aid in the Construction of the Kansas and Neosho Valley Railroad and Its Extension to Red River," quoted in Kidwell, *The Choctaws in Oklahoma*, 90.
18. *The Congressional Globe*, 39th Cong., 1st sess., June 22, 1866, 3334–3336.
19. James Baker, attorney for the Atlantic and Pacific Railroad, would later testify that the company preemptively issued bonds to the United States assuming that the company would receive title to alternate sections of land in Indian Territory. See "Testimony before the Subcommittee of the Committee on Territories," March 22, 1878, Choctaw Nation Agency Records, CTN 67, Oklahoma History Center, p. 3
20. Kidwell, *The Choctaws in Oklahoma*, 96; and *M. K. & T. Ry. Co. v. U.S.*, 235 U.S. 37 (November 9, 1914).
21. Miner, *The Corporation and the Indian*, 24; and Bill No. 7, Choctaw National Council, October 10, 1870, Choctaw Nation File, CTN 74, Oklahoma History Center [hereafter Choctaw Nation File, OHC].
22. Bill No. 7, Choctaw National Council, October 10, 1870, Choctaw Nation File, OHC.
23. Miner, *The Corporation and the Indian*, 26–27.
24. ARCIA,1870, 292.
25. Ibid., 287.
26. Miner, *The Corporation and the Indian*, 22–23, 42.
27. "Journal of the General Council of the Indian Territory," September 30, 1870, vol. 3, no. 1, 42.
28. Ibid.
29. Memorial of the Indian Delegates to Congress…, Railroad File box 38, Lester Hargrett Collection, Gilcrease.
30. Ibid.
31. Miner, *The Corporation and the Indian*, 97–98; and ARCIA, 1871, 184–185.
32. ARCIA, 1871, 575.
33. Ibid.
34. James D. Morrison, "The Union Pacific Southern Branch," *Chronicles of Oklahoma* 14, no. 1 (March 1936): 181.
35. Morrison, "The Union Pacific, Southern Branch," 182.
36. "Railroads," *Encyclopedia of Oklahoma History*, Oklahoma Historical Society, accessed April 24, 2017.
37. ARCIA, 1871 566; "Under the impression derived from current reports, as well as from my own surmises, that the company in question has mainly in view getting possession of the Indian lands valuable from the extreme fertility of a large portion, the abundance of the supply of water, their mineral resources, and the unrivaled climate of the territory." ARCIA, 1870, 287.
38. The Seminole nation was not crossed by either railroad, and the MKT passed through only ten miles of the Chickasaw nation. The locus of the assault was in Cherokee and Choctaw territories. The Cherokee in particular were concerned about land grants because the MKT cut along the Grand River Valley—the heart of their country. See Morrison, "The Union Pacific Southern Branch," 175.
39. The Choctaw Tribal Council also passed an act to address the sale of timber and stone to railway companies. Missouri Kansas and Texas RR through Choctaw Nations, Special Case 136, Special Cases, 1821–1907, Records of the Bureau of Indian Affairs, RG 75, Box 117, SC-1361.2 to SC-137, NARA DC.

40. Kidwell, *The Choctaws in Oklahoma*, 97.
41. Miner, *The Corporation and the Indian*, 52.
42. Ibid.
43. ARCIA, 1870, 287.
44. Kidwell, *The Choctaws in Oklahoma*, 96.
45. "Protest of Coleman Cole," *Indian Journal*, February 6, 1878, 1.
46. Kidwell, *The Choctaws in Oklahoma*, 100.
47. Ibid.
48. Kidwell, *The Choctaws in Oklahoma*, 100.
49. Miner, *The Corporation and the Indian*, 114.
50. Kidwell, *The Choctaws in Oklahoma*, 97.
51. For more on Cherokee institutions, see Julie L. Reed, *Serving the Nation: Cherokee Sovereignty and Social Welfare, 1800–1907* (Norman: University of Oklahoma Press, 2016).
52. Peter Gallagher to Commissioner of Indian Affairs, June 3, 1889, Utah and Northern Railway through Fort Hall Reservation, Also Oregon Short Line, Special Case 99, box 74, SC-99, Special Cases, RG 75, NARA, DC.
53. Peter Ronan to Commissioner of Indian Affairs, August 25, 1881, Northern Pacific through Flathead Reservation, Special Case 55, box 52, Special Cases, RG 75, NARA DC.
54. Ibid.
55. In addition to following examples, see also John C. Indian Agent, to Commissioner of Indian Affairs, August 20, 1890; Commissioner of Indian Affairs Atkins to Secretary of the Interior, January 19, 1887; Howard, Indian Agent at Gila River, to Atkins, CIA, January 22 1887; and Colvan, Agent to CIA, May 12, 1887, Special Case 145, St. Paul, Minnesota, and Manitoba RR through Blackfeet, Ft Berthold, Ft. Peck, and White Earth Reservations, box 1128, Special Cases, RG 75, NARA DC.
56. Thomas noted that this particular reservation was the second one set aside for the Jicarilla and they had not been taken to either of them. Ben M. Thomas to Commissioner Price, April 27, 1881, Denver and Rio Grande Railroad through Ute Reservation and Jicarilla Reservation, Special Case 68, box 61, Special Cases, NARA DC.
57. Telegram to W. J. Palmer, President of Denver and Rio Grande RR, from S. J. Kirkwood, Secretary of the Interior, May 3, 1881, Special Case 68, Denver and Rio Grande Railroad through Ute Reservation and Jicarilla Reservation, box 61, Special Cases, NARA DC.
58. Iron Nation, Medicine Bull, Little Pheasant to President James A. Garfield, November 13, 1880, Special Case 20, Chicago, Milwaukee, and St. Paul Railroad Right of Way through Sioux Reservation, box 8, Special Cases, NARA DC.
59. Ibid.
60. Jack Daugherty to Assistant Secretary of Interior, January 3, 1881, Chicago, Milwaukee, and St. Paul Railroad Right of Way through Sioux Reservation, Special Case 20, box 8, Special Case Files, NARA DC.
61. Little No Heart via Brown, Acting Indian Agent to Commissioner of Indian Affairs, Cheyenne River Indian Agency, June 30, 1880, Chicago, Milwaukee, and St. Paul Railroad Right of Way through Sioux Reservation, Special Case 20, box 8, Special Cases, NARA DC.
62. J. J. Moore to J. J. Dodge, November 10, 1880, Northern Pacific Railroad through Crow Reservation, Special Case 82, box 66, Special Cases, NARA, DC; and Frederick E. Hoxie, *Parading Through History: The Making of the Crow Nation in American, 1805–1935* (New York: Cambridge University Press, 1997), 120.
63. ARCIA 1872, 75–76.
64. ARCIA, 1884, xxx. The Denver and Rio Grande also built through the Great Sioux Reservation without consent. ARCIA, 1882, 18. The Carson and Colorado Railroad Company also built through the Walker River Reserve without obtaining consent from the tribe or approval from the government. ARCIA, 1882, xxviii. See also Oregon Railway and Navigation Company through the Umatilla Reserve, ARCIA 1883, xxii.
65. President Rutherford B. Hayes, Statement, May 12, 1880. Denver and Rio Grande Railroad Through Ute Reservation and Jicarilla Reservation, Special Case 68, box 61, Special Cases, RG 75, NARA DC.
66. ARCIA, 1882, xxvii. The DRG also built through the Great Sioux Reservation without consent. ARCIA, 1882, 18. The Carson and Colorado Railroad Company built through the Walker River Reserve without obtaining consent from the tribe or approval from the government,

ARCIA, 1882, xxviii. See also Oregon Railway and Navigation Company through the Umatilla Reserve, ARCIA, 1883, xxii. In other cases, smaller corporations often attempted to negotiate directly with the tribal leaders and not involve Congress or the Indian Office. Such was the case on the Papago reserve in 1882, when representatives for the Arizona Southern Railroad Company offered to build a schoolhouse for the Papago on the reservation in exchange for a right of way through their lands. Hearing that congressional consent to the stipulations was required, the Indian Office instead paid monies to put in tribal trusts and controlled by Department of the Interior. ARCIA, 1882, xxii.

67. They paid a mere $3,290 for the right of way. ARCIA, 1905, 91.
68. Congress approved the agreements and then the railroad company was allowed to begin building, though in some instances railroad companies had already built lines or proceeded with building without consulting with Congress, the Indian Office, or the tribes. Congress and the Indian Office was often slow to collect the rents on rights-of-way. See Vine Deloria Jr. and Raymond DeMallie, eds., *Documents of American Indian Diplomacy: Treaties, Agreements, and Conventions, 1775–1979*, vol 1. (Norman: University of Oklahoma Press, 1999), 514.
69. The Cherokee National Fund and the Delaware General fund both invested in the Union Pacific Railroad, eastern division. ARCIA, 1885, 286–287. See also Emilie Connolly, "Fiduciary Colonialism: Annuities and Native Dispossession in the Early United States," *American Historical Review* 127, no. 1 (March 2022): 223–253.
70. Proceedings of a Council held at Lower Brulé Agency on Tuesday, November 8, 1880, and November 10, 1880, Chicago, Milwaukee, and St. Paul Railroad Right of Way through Sioux Reservation, Special Case 20, box 8, Special Cases, 1821–1907, RG 75, NARA DC.
71. Robert S. Gardner, Indian Inspector to C. Schurz, November 15, 1880, ibid.
72. Proceedings of a Council at Rosebud Agency November 1, 1880, ibid.
73. Proceedings of a Council at Crow Creek, November 12, 1880, ibid.
74. Agreement with Paiute Indians and Carson and Colorado RR Co., August 9, 1882, Carson and Colorado RR Right of Way through Walker River Reservation, Special Case 90, box 68, Special Cases, 1821–1907, RG 75, NARA DC; and ARCIA, 1883, xxii.
75. On the Crow arrangement, see Special Case 82; see also Hoxie, *Parading Through History*, 20–21. For the Laguna agreement see Kurt M. Peters, "Continuing Identity: Laguna Pueblo Railroaders in Richmond, California, "*American Indian Culture and Research Journal* 22, no. 4, (1998):187–198; and Myla Vicenti Carpio, *Indigenous Albuquerque* (Lubbock: Texas Tech University Press, 2011).
76. Author said he held a meeting in the town of Isleta and the officers and leading men say there is no objection, but ask that damages be paid to farmed lands that the railroad would pass through. Tome Relles Padilla (Gov of Isleta) and Juan Felipe Jolja (captain of war), Addressed to Mr. Don Armbrosio Armijo, requested by railway leaders to discuss right of way through Isleta lands. Letter from Isleta officials granting right of way to railroad, box 1, folder 7, 1879 Indian Affairs Collection, University of New Mexico, Center for Southwest Research, Albuquerque, New Mexico.
77. Lee Marmon and Tom Corbett, *Laguna Pueblo: A Photographic History* (Albuquerque: University of New Mexico Press, 2015), 41.
78. ARCIA, 1882, XX.
79. See Cherokee Nation Agency Records, Railroad File, 1881–1910, mss. CHN 96, Oklahoma History Center, Oklahoma City, Oklahoma. See also H. J. Armstrong to CIA Hiriam Price, May 24 1883, Northern Pacific Railroad through Crow Reservation, Special Case 82, box 66, Special Cases, 1821–1907, RG 75, NARA DC.
80. Russell B. Harrison to J. W. Noble, Secretary of Interior, Washington, DC, Special Case 145, Special Cases, 1821–1907, Records of the Bureau of Indian Affairs, RG 75, Box 1128, SC-144 to SC-145 NARA DC.
81. In addition to these requests, Salish and Kootenai tribal leaders proposed extending the Flathead reservation boundary north to the Canadian border to enable the tribe to move away from the NP line. Their final request was never realized, and the relationship between the Salish Kootenai and the NPRR remained fraught well over the next decade. Robert Harris, President, NPRR, to William Teller, May 22, 1884, Northern Pacific through Flathead Reservation, Special Case 55, box 52, Special Cases, 1821–1907, RG 75, NARA DC.
82. Letter from Ronan to Assistant Attorney Gen, Nov 7, 1882; and H. Villard, NP President, to SofI, M. L. Joslyn, October 28, 1882, Northern Pacific through Flathead Reservation, Special Case 55, box 52, Special Cases, 1821–1907, RG 75, NARA DC.

83. Letter from W. H. Parkland, Indian Agent, Lower Brulé Agency, to CIA, April 8, 1882, Chicago, Milwaukee, and St. Paul Railroad Right of Way through Sioux Reservation, Special Case 20, box 8, Special Cases, 1821–1907, RG 75, NARA DC.
84. ARCIA, 1889, 37–38, Crow and ARCIA, 1890, 118; Puyallup, ARCIA, 1889, 40. The Chippewa at Red River also refused entreaties for year from the Duluth, Superior, and Michigan Railroad agents, initially requesting $25 per acre for the right of way, which the company refused. See ARCIA, 1887, 231, and ARCIA 1889, 37.
85. P. Gallagher to CIA Jno. N. Oberly, CIA, November 17, 1888, Utah and Northern Railway through Fort Hall Reservation, Also Oregon Short Line, Special Case 99, box 74, Special Cases, 1821–1907, RG 75, NARA DC.
86. J. M Buckley to C. H. Mitchell, March 11, 1885, Northern Pacific through Flathead Reservation, Special Case 55, box 52, Special Cases, 1821–1907, RG 75, NARA DC.
87. Leonard Whitney to CIA J. D. Atkins, Feb. 15, 1886; and Peter Ronan to CIA, March 5, 1886, ibid.
88. Gallagher to CIA Oberly, June 3, 1889, Utah and Northern Railway through Fort Hall Reservation. Also Oregon Short Line, Special Case 99, box 74, Special Cases, 1821–1907, RG 75, NARA DC.
89. Henry N. Capp to Hiram Price, CIA, March 14, 1885, Chicago, Milwaukee, and St. Paul Railroad Right of Way through Sioux Reservation, Special Case 20, box 8, Special Cases, NARA DC.
90. H. J Armstrong to CIA Hiram Price, May 24, 1883, Northern Pacific Railroad through Crow Reservation, Special Case 82, box 66, Special Cases, 1821–1907, RG 75, NARA DC.
91. Wilkins, David E. *American Indian Sovereignty and the U.S. Supreme Court: The Masking of Justice*, (Austin: University of Texas Press, 1997), 81.
92. "Protest of D. W. Bushyhead, Principal Chief, and Other Cherokee and Creek Indians . . ." March 7, 1884, Senate misc. doc. 62, 48th Cong., 1st sess., in Cherokee Nation Agency Records, Railroads Vertical File, 1881–1910, mss. CHN96, Oklahoma History Center,
93. Wilkins, *American Indian Sovereignty*, 84; and ARCIA, 1884, xxxii.
94. ARCIA, 1885, 184; and ARCIA, 1889, 293.
95. ARCIA, 1889, 184.
96. Judge Parker's Decision, *Cherokee Nation v. Southern Kansas Railway Company*, in "Cherokees, 1870–1891," box 4, Hargrett Collection, Gilcrease.
97. "Reply to Brief of Appellant," *Cherokee Nation v. Southern Kansas Railway Company*, "Cherokees, 1870–1891," box 4, Hargrett Collection, Gilcrease Center, 1–2.
98. De Witt Clinton Duncan, "The Indian's Hard Lot," in Bernd C. Peyer, ed., *American Indian Nonfiction: An Anthology of Writings, 1760s–1930s* (Norman: University of Oklahoma, 2007), 163.
99. D. W. Bushyhead, "Seventh Address to Senate and Council of the Cherokee Nation," "Cherokees, 1870–1891," box 4, Hargrett Collection, Gilcrease, 17.

Railway Journeys: Heart Work

1. A. B. Meacham, *Wi-ne-ma (the Woman Chief) and Her People* (Chicago: American Publishing Co., 1875), 94–95.
2. Ibid., 103.
3. Ibid., 105.
4. Ibid.
5. *Chicago Daily Inter Ocean*, September 17, 1875.
6. Meacham, *Wi-ne-ma*, 102.
7. Ibid., 103; and "The Kidnapped Klamath," *New York Times*, September 14, 1875.
8. See Boyd Cothran, *Remembering the Modoc War: Redemptive Violence and the Making of American Innocence* (Chapel Hill: University of North Carolina Press, 2017), 87–92.
9. *Milwaukee Sentinel*, September 22, 1884, 4; *Bismarck Daily Tribune*, January 23, 1885, issue 64; and *Frank Leslie's Illustrated Weekly*, Saturday October 4, 1884, 103, issue 1515.
10. Saturday, October 20, 1883, *Frank Leslie's Illustrated Newspaper*, issue 1, no. 465, 131.

Chapter 5

1. John Joseph Flinn, *Official Guide to the World's Columbian Exposition* (Chicago: Columbian Guide Co., 1893), 54.

2. Ibid., 55. For more on Indigenous experiences of the World's Fair, see Paige Raibmon, "Theatres of Contact: The Kwakwaka'wakw Meet Colonialism in British Columbia and at the Chicago's World Fair," *The Canadian Historical Review* 81, no. 2 (2000): 157–190 and *Authentic Indians: Episodes of Encounter from the Late-Nineteenth-Century Northwest Coast* (Durham, NC: Duke University Press, 2005).
3. *Annual Report of the Commissioner of Indian Affairs for the Year 1894* (Washington, DC: Government Printing Office, 1895), 408 [hereafter ARCIA, year, page]; Robert A. Trennert, "From Carlisle to Phoenix: The Rise and Fall of the Indian Outing System, 1878–1930," *Pacific Historical Review* 52, no. 3 (January 1983): 267–291; Kevin Whalen, "Labored Learning: The Outing System at Sherman Institute, 1902–1930," *American Indian Culture and Research Journal* 36, no. 1 (January 2012): 151–176; and David Wallace Adams, *Education for Extinction: American Indians and the Boarding School Experience, 1875–1925* (Lawrence: University Press of Kansas, 1995).
4. Quoted in Brenda J. Child, *Boarding School Sessions: American Indian Families, 1900–1940* (Lincoln: University of Nebraska Press, 2000), 82.
5. James C. Bush, ed. *Journal of the Military Service Institution of the United States* (New York: Clark and Zugalla, 1896), 521.
6. Fred Kaye interview, Black Mountain, AZ, interviewer: Tom Ration, tape #361, side 1, Inventory of the American Indian Oral History Collection, 1967–1972, Center for Southwest Studies, University of New Mexico, Albuquerque, NM.
7. "Interview with Alex and Grover Splitlog," Miami, OK, by Nannie Lee Burns, Indian-Pioneer History, S-149, December 3, 1937, Oklahoma History Center, Oklahoma City, OK [hereafter Splitlog Interview, Indian Pioneer History, OHC], 17.
8. ARCIA, 1903, 145.
9. *The Problem of Indian Administration. Report of a Survey Made…* (Baltimore, MD: Johns Hopkins Press, 1928), 671.
10. ARCIA, 1905, 5.
11. Harmon, O'Neill, and Rosier note major gaps in scholarship on the economy in Indian Country in the nineteenth and twentieth centuries. Colleen O'Neil, *Working the Navajo Way: Labor and Culture in the Twentieth Century* (Lawrence: University Press of Kansas, 2005); and Alexandra Harmon, Colleen O'Neill, and Paul C. Rosier, "Interwoven Economic Histories: American Indians in Capitalist America," *The Journal of American History* 98, no. 3 (December 2011): 698–722. See also Brian Hosmer, Colleen O'Neill, and Donald J. Fixico, eds., *Native Pathways: American Indian Culture and Economic Development in the Twentieth Century* (Boulder: University Press of Colorado, 2004); Alice Littlefield and Martha C. Knack, *Native Americans and Wage Labor: Ethnohistorical Perspectives* (Norman: University of Oklahoma Press, 1996); and Brian Hosmer, *American Indians in the Marketplace: Persistence and Innovation Among the Menominees and Metlakatlans, 1870–1920* (Lawrence: University Press of Kansas, 1999). Similar transformations were unfolding north of the US border as well. See Rolf Knight, *Indians at Work: An Informal History of Native Labour in British Columbia, 1858–1930* (Vancouver, BC: Newstar Books, 1996); Andrew Parnaby, *Citizen Docker: Making a New Deal on the Vancouver Waterfront, 1919–1939* (Toronto: University of Toronto Press, 2008); and Douglas C. Harris, *Landing Native Fisheries: Indian Reserves and Fishing Rights in British Columbia, 1849–1925* (Vancouver: University of British Columbia Press, 2008) and *Fish, Law, and Colonialism: The Legal Capture of Salmon in British Columbia* (Toronto: University of Toronto Press, 2005).
12. J. Diane Pearson, "Developing Reservation Economies: Native American Teamsters, 1857–1921," *Journal of Small Business and Entrepreneurship* 18, no. 2 (2005): 158–159.
13. Pearson, "Developing Reservation Economies," 160.
14. *Report of the Special Commission Appointed to Investigate the Affairs of the Red Cloud Indian Agency*, July 1875 (Washington, DC: GPO, 1875) 20, 830. See also Hyde, *Spotted Tail's Folk: A History of the Brule Sioux* (Norman: University of Oklahoma Press, 1976), 183, 189, 150.
15. ARCIA, 1878, 58; and ARCIA, 1880, xii–xiii.
16. "And whenever practicable wagon transportation may be performed by Indian labor"; ch. 101, *An Act Making Appropriations for the Current and Contingent Expenses of the Indian Department…*, March 3, 1877, 44th Cong., sess. 11, 1877, 291.
17. ARCIA, 1880, xii–xiii.
18. ARCIA, 1880, xiii.

19. J. W. Daniels to Commissioner of Indian Affairs, June 24, 1875, Council of 1875, Records of the Bureau of Indian Affairs, Pine Ridge Agency, Box 779, National Archives and Records Center, Kansas City, Kansas [hereafter, NARA, Kansas City]; and Hyde, *Spotted Tail's Folk*, 217.
20. Mike Cowdry, "A Winter Count of the Wajaje Lakota 1758–59 to 1885–86," *Tribal Art Magazine* 77 (Autumn 2015): 128–133. Many thanks to Justin R. Gage for bringing this winter count to my attention.
21. Pearson, "Developing Reservation Economies," 157.
22. Luther Standing Bear, *My People the Sioux* (1928; New York: Bison Books, 2006), 98–99.
23. Ibid., 104.
24. ARCIA, 1889, 516–527.
25. I am indebted to J. Pearson for her compilation of this data. See Pearson, "Developing Reservation Economies," 156.
26. ARCIA, 1878, 39.
27. Crows lobbied heavily for contracts to freight flour from the train station at Custer to their reservation, Hopis repaired roads to ensure they could transport goods from Flagstaff, and reports of Cheyenne eager to take any and all work. See Pearson, "Developing Reservation Economies," 160–162.
28. For more on Indigenous communication networks in the later decades of the nineteenth century, see Justin Gage, *We Do Not Want the Gates Closed Between Us: Native Networks and the Spread of the Ghost Dance* (Norman: University of Oklahoma Press, 2020).
29. Indian Freighter Receipt Rolls, third quarter, 1892, 27 June 1892 and 20 July 1892, box OS 9, Record Group 75, Records of the Bureau of Indian Affairs, Pine Ridge Agency, NARA, Kansas City.
30. Jeffrey Ostler, "'The Last Buffalo Hunt' and Beyond: Plains Sioux Economic Strategies in the Early Reservation Period," *Great Plains Quarterly* 21, no. 2 (Spring 2001): 119.
31. Pearson, "Developing Reservation Economies," 160.
32. Ostler, "'The Last Buffalo Hunt,'" 126.
33. Payroll of Indian Freighters, 1886–1921, Standing Rock Agency, Fort Yates, North Dakota, RG 75, Records of the Bureau of Indian Affairs, Box OS 26, NARA, Kansas City.
34. Petition of a Council Held on White Clay District, ca. 1902. Petitions, 1875–1907, Records of the Bureau of Indian Affairs, Pine Ridge Agency, Box 779, NARA Kansas City.
35. D. M. Browning to Chas. G. Penney, August 16, 1895, Freighter and Receipt Rolls, Box OS4, Indian Freighter and Receipt Rolls, 1st Quarter 1894 to 3rd Quarter FY 1897, Records of the Bureau of Indian Affairs, Pine Ridge Agency, NARA Kansas City.
36. ARCIA, 1888, 218.
37. ARCIA, 1883, 41.
38. Ibid.
39. ARCIA, 1878, 20.
40. Ostler, "'The Last Buffalo Hunt,'" 121.
41. Pearson, "Developing Reservation Economies," 163.
42. McGillycuddy to Commissioner of Indian Affairs Price, February 27, 1883, Bureau of Indian Affairs, Record Group 75, Pine Ridge Agency, South Dakota, box 35, Copies of Correspondence and Reports Sent to the Office of Indian Affairs, August 18, 1875 to August 23, 1883, NARA, Kansas City.
43. Pearson, "Developing Reservation Economies," 155.
44. ARCIA, 1885, 87.
45. ARCIA, 1901, 355.
46. ARICA, 1884, 38.
47. Louise Udall, *Me and Mine: The Life Story of Helen Sekaquaptewa* (Tucson: University of Arizona Press, 1969), 175–176.
48. Pearson, "Developing Reservation Economies,"161.
49. O. Vance Hawkins, "Grand River Empire 'Visioned in '89," *The Tulsa Daily World*, July 21, 1941.
50. Velma Nieberding, "Chief Splitlog and the Cayuga Mission Church" Splitlog, Oklahoma History Center Vertical File, Oklahoma History Center, Oklahoma City, OK [hereafter OHC], p. 22.
51. Hawkins, "Grand River Empire,"; on building of church, ARCIA, 1896, 146 and ARCIA, 1897, 137.
52. Pete Dublin, "In Kansas City, Splitlog Coffee Honors Strawberry Hill History," *Feast Magazine*, May 22, 2017. Accessed online September 17, 2017. https://www.feastmagazine.com/travel/

kansas-city/splitlog-coffee-co-is-steeped-in-kansas-city-kansas-history/article_1dcdc32a-875c-11e7-b084-0baa898ba481.html.

53. Splitlog Interview, Indian Pioneer History, OHC, 2.
54. Alexandra Harmon, *Rich Indians: Native People and the Problem of Wealth in American History* (Chapel Hill: University of North Carolina Press, 2010), 135, 144.
55. Cherokee Advocate, August 24, 1887, clipping from box 33, vol. 67, Grant Foreman Collection, Gilcrease Center, Tulsa, OK; and Nieberding, "Chief Splitlog," OHC.
56. "A Rich Redskin, an Indian Who Is Building a Railroad Out West," *The Londonderry (Vt.) Sifter*, September 22, 1887, vol. 1v, no. 3. Nieberding, "Chief Splitlog," OHC, 19; and "Alex and Grover Splitlog," Indian Pioneer History, OHC, 2.
57. See Mary Stockwell, *The Other Trail of Tears: The Removal of the Ohio Indians* (Yardley, PA: Westholme Press, 2016); and John T. Bowes, *Land Too Good for Indians: Northern Indian Removal* (Norman: University of Oklahoma Press, 2016).
58. Splitlog Interview, Indian Pioneer History, OHC, 3.
59. Indian Territory would not undergo allotment until the passage of the Curtis Act in 1898, two years after Splitlog's death.
60. Nieberding, "Chief Splitlog," 18.
61. Nieberding, "Chief Splitlog," 20; and Treaty of 1817, 197, Foreman Collection, Gilcrease Museum, Library and Archives, Tulsa, OK. The group of Senecas allegedly included not only Senceas, but a mixed group from the Iroquois Confederacy called "Mingoes," who tended to be more hostile to settlers than Iroquois Confederacy members. See James H. Howard, "Cultural Persistence and Cultural Change as Reflected in Oklahoma Seneca-Cayuga Ceremonialism," *Plains Anthropologist* 6, no. 11 (February 1961): 21.
62. Splitlog Interview, Indian Pioneer History, OHC, 5; the Seneca Reservation was established in the 1830s, comprised 51,958 acres in 1876. Roughly half (21,821.55 acres) was allotted to tribal members. Quapaw Agency, Introduction, QA6, Quapaw Agency Records, OHC.
63. For more on this system of land ownership among the Cherokee, see Khaled J. Bloom, "An American Tragedy of the Commons, Land and Labor in the Cherokee Nation, 1870–1900," *Agricultural History* 76, no. 3 (Summer 2002): 497–523.
64. See James Hamill, "Being Indian in Northeast Oklahoma," *Plains Anthropologist* 45, no. 173 (August 2000): 291–303.
65. The combined population of the eight NEO nations in 1900 was 1,515. ARCIA, 1900, 224. For a recent study of social intuitions in the Cherokee Nation, see Julie L. Reed, *Serving the Nation: Cherokee Sovereignty and Social Welfare, 1800–1907* (Norman: University of Oklahoma Press, 2016). 212,298 acres of combined reservation land in 1891. ARCIA, 1891, 235.
66. ARCIA, 1898, 149.
67. ARCIA 1892, 243–244.
68. ARCIA, 1896, 149.
69. ARCIA, 1904, 202.
70. Hawkins, "Grand River Empire 'Visioned in '89."
71. Ibid.
72. Ibid.
73. Ibid.
74. Boudinot quoted in William G. McLoughlin, *After the Trail of Tears: The Cherokees' Struggle for Sovereignty* (Chapel Hill: University of North Carolina Press, 1994), 269–270. The monies were to be taken from each nation's trust fund. It was a measure that had support among traditionalists and progressives. The Cherokee delegates spent three years pushing the bill.
75. Ibid., 265–266. It was short-lived after producers in the South caught on and convinced Congress to enforce an 1868 law taxing liquor and tobacco products leaving Indian Territory.
76. White, *Railroaded: The Transcontinentals and the Making of Modern America* (New York: W. W. Norton, 2011), 139.
77. ARCIA, 1896, 148. See also ARCIA, 1895, 150.
78. Rezin W. McAdam, "An Indian Commonwealth," *Harper's Monthly* 0087, no. 522 (November 1893): 895.
79. Harmon, *Rich Indians*, 141.
80. ARCIA, 1898, 149.
81. Nieberding, "Chief Splitlog," 23.
82. Nieberding, "Chief Splitlog," 21; and Splitlog Interview, Indian Pioneer History, OHC, 17.
83. Keith Bryant, *History of the Atchison, Topeka, and Santa Fe* (Lincoln: University of Nebraska Press, 1992), 90–92.

84. ARCIA, 1898, 112.
85. Peter Nabokov, *Where the Lightning Strikes: The Lives of American Indian Sacred Places* (New York: Penguin Books, 2010), 230–238.
86. See Erika Bsumek, *Indian-Made: Navajo Culture in the Marketplace, 1868–1940* (Lawrence: University Press of Kansas, 2008); Brian Hosmer and Colleeen O'Neill, eds., *Native Pathways: American Indian Culture and Economic Development in the Twentieth Century* (Boulder: University Press of Colorado, 2004).
87. John Adair, *The Navajo and Pueblo Silversmiths* (Norman: University of Oklahoma Press, 1944), 56, 138. Special thanks to The Wheelwright Museum in Santa Fe for the reference.
88. Howell Jones to Peter Paquette, Superintendent, Navajo Indian Agency, August 16, 1924. Southern Navajo Agency Subject Files, 1900–1935, For Defiance Arizona, box,2; and Howell Jones to Peter Paquette, March 12, 1924, box 6, and Peter Paquette to Howell Jones, April 5, 1924, box 6, Southern Navajo Agency Subject Files, 1900–1935, Fort Defiance Arizona, RG 75, NARA, Riverside.
89. The Southern Pacific employed Yumas on west side of the Colorado River; ARCIA, 1890, 15. Pimas worked on the Pima and Maricopa Reservation after their signed right-of-way agreement ensured that Pima laborers would be paid for construction. The company promised to give the Pima the first chance to work on the road. See Railroads thru Pima and Maricopa Reservations, Arizona, Special Case 16, Special Cases, 1821–1907, Records of the Bureau of Indian Affairs, RG 75, Box 7, SC 12 to SC 20, NARA, DC. For the Hualapai work on the railroad, see Jeffrey P. Shepard, *We Are an Indian Nation: A History of the Hualapai People* (Tucson: University of Arizona Press, 2010), 75. For Indigenous labor on the Southern Pacific, see "The Indian as Workman," August 2, 1896, *The Arizona Republican*, 8. See also ARCIA 1896, 115; and Myla Vincent Carpio, *Indigenous Albuquerque* (Albuquerque: University of New Mexico Press, 2011).
90. ARCIA, 1893, 120.
91. Ibid.
92. Shepard, *We Are an Indian Nation*, 76.
93. Eric Meeks, *Border Citizens: The Making of Indians, Mexicans, and Anglos in Arizona* (Austin: University of Texas Press, 2007), 34.
94. ARCIA, 1900, 192.
95. Charles E. Dagenett to Philip T. Lonergan, June 3, 1911, Colorado River Agency Subject Files, 1904–1922, box 21, RG75, NARA, Riverside.
96. Tom Ration, Medicine Man, Crownpoint, New Mexico, American Indian Oral History Collection, 1967–1972, The University of New Mexico, University Libraries, Center for Southwest Research, 27.
97. Ibid., 25, 28–31.
98. Meeks, *Border Citizens*, 50.
99. ARCIA 1901, 189.
100. Charles E. Daguett to Horton Miller, Supt Indian School, Keams Canyon, February 18, 1909, Moqui Indian Agency, Bureau of Indian Employment, Moqui Agency Subject Files, 1907–1920, box 10, RG 75, NARA, Riverside.
101. ARCIA, 1890, 2.
102. ARCIA, 1899, 147.
103. Abraham Lincoln to Supt. A. F. Duclos, April 9, 1921, Colorado River Agency Subject Files, 1904–1922, "Outing Students," box 208, RG 75, NARA, Riverside.
104. Mojave Indian Welfare Committee to Leo Crane, March 11, 1923; and Leo Crane to Mojave Indian Welfare Committee, March 19, 1923, box 19, Central Classified Correspondence, 1924–1951, Colorado River Agency Records, Record Group 75, Records of the Bureau of Indian Affairs, National Archives and Records Center, Riverside, CA [hereafter, RG 75, NARA, Riverside].
105. Colin John Davis, *Power at Odds: The 1922 National Railroad Shopmen's Strike* (Chicago: University of Illinois Press, 1997), 84; for more on Mexican railroad work, see Jeffrey Marcos Garcílazo, *Traqueros: Mexican Railroad Workers in the United States, 1870–1930* (Denton: University of North Texas Press, 2012).
106. "President Will Promise the Railroads Protection," *The Ocala (Fl.) Daily Star*, August 15, 1922; and "Striking Santa Fe Trainmen Outlawed by the Union Chiefs," *The Coconino (Az.) Sun*, August 18, 1922, 6.
107. "Says Big Four Plotted Train Tie Up in Desert," *The New York Herald*, August 14, 1922.
108. T. C. McLuhan, *Dream Tracks: The Railroad and the American Indian, 1890–1930* (New York: Henry N. Abrams, 1985); David Wrobel, *Promised Lands: Promotion, Memory, and the*

Creation of the American West (Lawrence: University Press of Kansas, 2002); and Stephen Fried, *Appetite for America: Fred Harvey and the Business of Civilizing the American West—One Meal at a Time* (New York: Bantam, 2011).

109. ARCIA, 1901, 208.
110. ARCIA, 1900, 436.
111. ACRIA 1903, 240.
112. Ibid.
113. ARCIA 1906, 281.
114. Tape 416, side 1, Fred Brown, Tohatchi, NM, February 1969. American Indian Oral History Collection, 1967–1972, Center for Southwest Research, University of New Mexico Libraries, Albuquerque.
115. ARCIA, 1909, 5.
116. For more on railroad labor, see Gerald Eggert, *Railroad Labor Disputes: The Beginnings of Federal Strike Policy* (Detroit: University of Michigan Press, 2016); Eric Arnesen, Brotherhoods of Color: Black Railroad Workers and the Struggle for Equality (Cambridge, MA: Harvard University Press, 2001); Theresa A. Case, *The Great Southwest Railroad Strike and Free Labor* (College Station: Texas A&M University Press, 2010); and Shelton Stromquist, *The Pattern of Railroad Labor Conflict in Nineteenth-Century America* (Chicago: University of Illinois Press, 1987).
117. Three Bears, White Calf, Long Time Sleeping, Eagle Fish Calf, Wolf Plume, Bird Rattler, Medicine Owl, and Lazy Boy to L. W. Hill, March 6, 1914, Glacier Indians Going to Fairs and Conferences, 132.F10.5b, 5814, President Subject Files, Great Northern Railway Company Records, Minnesota History Center, Minneapolis, MN.
118. "Blackfeet Indians at Big Chicago Land Show," *The Times (Va.) Dispatch*, May 31, 1914, 40.
119. "The Red Man in the Air," *The Wilmington (N.C.) Dispatch*, June 16, 1914, 2. See also L. W. Hill to W. P. Kenney, April 22, 1914; H. H. Parkhouse to Chas. Griffin, April 22, 1914; H. H. Parkhouse to L. W. Hill, March 25, 1914; and H. H. Parkhouse to Fish Wolf Robe, April 13, 1914, Glacier Indians Going to Fairs and Conferences, 132.F10.5b, 5814, President Subject Files, Great Northern Railway Company Records, Minnesota History Center, Minneapolis, MN.

Chapter 6

1. Cora DuBois, *The 1870 Ghost Dance* (Lincoln: University of Nebraska Press, 2007), 5; and Louis S. Warren, *God's Red Son: The Ghost Dance Religion and the Making of Modern America* (New York: Basic Books, 2017), 93–94.
2. Lee D. Baker, *Anthropology and the Racial Politics of Culture* (Durham, NC: Duke University Press, 2010), 14.
3. Timothy Egan, *Short Nights of the Shadow Catcher: The Epic Life and Immortal Photographs of Edward Curtis* (New York: Houghton Mifflin, 2012).
4. "An Indian Girl and Glad of It: Miss Cornelius Here to Study Law at Barnard," *New York Sun*, February 11, 1906, 7.
5. Patrick Wolfe, "Settler Colonialism and the Elimination of the Native," *Journal of Genocide Research* 8, no. 4 (2006): 387–409.
6. See Warren, *God's Red Son.*
7. Audra Mitchell and Aadita Chaudhury, "Worlding Beyond 'the 'End" of 'the Word': White Apocalyptic Visions and BIPOC Futurisms," *International Relations* 34, no. 3 (2020): 321. For more in Indigenous Futurism, see Grace Dillon, *Walking the Clouds: An Anthology of Indigenous Science Fiction* (Tucson: University of Arizona Press, 2012); Kyle Whyte, "Indigenous Science (Fiction) in the Anthropocene," *Environment and Planning E: Nature and Space* 1 (2018): 224–242; Suzanne Newman Fricke, "Indigenous Futurisms in the Hyperpresent Now," *World Art* 9, no. 2 (2019): 107–121; and Danika Medak-Saltzman, "Coming to You from the Indigenous Future: Native Women, Speculative Film Shorts, and the Art of the Possible," *Studies in American Indian Literatures* 20, no. 1 (2017): 139–171.
8. *Report of the Executive Council on the Proceedings of the First Annual Conference of the Society of American Indians* (Washington, DC, 1912), 5.
9. "Indian Woman in Capital to Fight Growing Use of Peyote by Indians," *Washington Times* (Washington, DC), February 17, 1918, 9.
10. Alan Trachtenberg, *The Incorporation of America: Culture and Society in the Gilded Age* (New York: Hill and Wang, 2007); and Robert H. Wiebe, *The Search for Order, 1877–1920* (New York: Hill and Wang, 1966).

11. Thomas C. Maroukis, *The Peyote Road: Religious Freedom and the Native American Church* (Norman: University of Oklahoma Press, 2012), 46–58.
12. Two organizations filed in Oklahoma, two in Nebraska, one in North Dakota, Montana, Colorado, and Idaho, and five in South Dakota. Some articles specifically called out the use of peyote as a sacrificial object, others did not. All stressed Christian influence and church organization. See Omer C. Stewart, *Peyote Religion: A History* (Norman: University of Oklahoma, 1993), 223–238.
13. *Peyote: Hearings Before a Subcommittee of the Committee on Indian Affairs of the House of Representatives on H.R. 2614 to Amend...* (Washington, DC: Government Printing Office, 1918).
14. This analysis is informed by Marisa Elena Duarte's *Network Sovereignty: Building the Internet Across Indian Country*. Duarte's study focuses on how "Native and Indigenous peoples leverage information and technology to subvert the legacies and processes of colonization as it manifests over time across communities." See Duarte, *Network Sovereignty*, 15.
15. "Protest of the Pueblos," *The Evening Times*, November, 15, 1899; and ARCIA, 1900, 697.
16. Justin Gage, "Intertribal Communication, Literacy, and the Spread of the Ghost Dance," (PhD diss., University of Arkansas, 2015), 159–162.
17. ARCIA, 1876, 96.
18. Warren, *God's Red Son*, 111; and James Mooney, *The Ghost-Dance Religion and the Sioux Outbreak of 1890* (Lincoln: University of Nebraska Press, 1991), 797, 894.
19. See Thomas C. Maroukis, *The Peyote Road: Religious Freedom and the Native American Church* (Norman: University of Oklahoma Press, 2010), 15; and Stewart, *Peyote Religion*, 17–30.
20. Los Ojuelos was a major center for peyote commerce. *Peyoteros* harvested buttons along the slopes or the bordas escarpment, less than a quarter mile from Los Ojuelos. George Robert Morgan, "Man, Plant, and Religion: Peyote Trade on the Mustang Plains of Texas" (PhD diss., 1976, University of Colorado at Boulder), box 37, Omer C. Stewart Collection, mss. COU-1518, University of Colorado Boulder Archives, 4.
21. Stewart, *Peyote Religion*, 45–47.
22. See Nancy McGowan Minor, *The Light Grey People: An Ethno-History of the Lipan Apaches of Texas and Northern Mexico* (Lanham, MD: University Press of America, 2009); and Sherry Robinson, *I Fought a Good Fight: A History of the Lipan Apaches* (Denton: University of North Texas Press, 2013), 338–345.
23. Peyotism has long been a subject of ethnographic research. See Stewart, *Peyote Religion*; Thomas C. Maroukis, *The Peyote Road: Religious Freedom and the Native American Church* (Norman: University of Oklahoma Press, 2010); James S. Slotkin, *The Peyote Religion: A Study in Indian-White Relations* (Glencoe, IL: Free Press, 1956); and Weston La Barre, *The Peyote Cult* (Norman: University of Oklahoma Press, 1976). See also N. J. Demeritis III, Peter Dobbin Hall, Terry Schmidt, and Rhys H. Wiliams, eds., *Sacred Companies: Organizational Aspects of Religion and Religious Aspects of Organizations* (New York: Oxford University Press, 1998).
24. Maroukis, *Peyote Road*, 67–72.
25. Mountain Wolf Woman and Nancy Oestreich Lurie, eds., *Mountain Wolf Woman: Sister of Crashing Thunder: The Autobiography of a Winnebago Indian* (Ann Arbor: University of Michigan Press, 1961), 48.
26. Stewart, *Peyote Religion*, 161.
27. See Stewart, *Peyote Religion*, 74; Charles Henry Sommer, *Quanah Parker: Last Chief of the Comanches, a Brief Sketch* (St. Louis, 1945), 39–45; and Clyde L. Jackson and Grace Jackson, *Quanah Parker Last Chief of the Comanches: A Study in Southwestern Frontier History* (New York: Exposition Press, 1963), 141.
28. When US officials attempted to cut off the supply of peyote buttons from south Texas/Mexico, Quanah Parker sent a Kickapoo and Comanche to Mexico to procure buttons. See Stewart, *Peyote Religion*, 76.
29. Ibid., 87.
30. August 29, 1898, to Maj. W. J. Walker from J. W. Ijams, agency famer, box 41, Omer C. Stewart Collection.
31. Maroukis, *The Peyote Road*, 5.
32. Stewart, *Peyote Religion*, 61.
33. With the completion of the Texas-Mexican Railroad, demand increased, forcing harvesting to move from the gravel hills of the Mirando Valley to the Rio Grande Valley; see George Robert Morgan, "Man, Plant, and Religion," box 37, Omer Stewart Collection.

34. John Rave's account in Paul Radin, *The Winnebago Tribe* (Lincoln: University of Nebraska Press, 1970), 371.
35. Stewart, *Peyote Religion*, Lakota, 175; Crow, 187; Ute, 197; Blackfeet, 253; Navajo, 293; and Canada, 257, 258; and H. Larson BIA Chief Special Officer to CIA December 18, 1916, box 43, Omer C. Stewart Collection. Enclosed within the letter are responses to a 1916 survey of peyote usage.
36. Loretta Fowler discusses this in the context of the Arapaho longhouse system. Loretta Fowler, *Wives and Husbands: Gender and Age in Southern Arapaho History* (Norman: University of Oklahoma Press, 2010), 242; and Maroukis, *The Peyote Road, 34.*
37. Willis E. Dunn to H. A. Larson, December 9, 1916, box 43, Omer Stewart Collection.
38. Slotkin, *The Peyote Religion*, 21.
39. L. W. Tingley of Ponca City, to CIA, April 30, 1919, box 43, Omer C. Stewart Collection.
40. Wallace Stark to CIA, August 22, 1919, box 43, Omer C. Stewart Collection.
41. "Statements of Merian Mexican Cheyenne Relative to the Use of Peyote Among the Northern Cheyenne Indians," enclosed in John A. Buntin to Commissioner of Indian Affairs, May 6, 1919, box 43, Omer C. Stewart Collection.
42. Jay Johnson to Supt. Robert E. E. Daniel, April 17, 1919, box 43, Omer C. Stewart Collection.
43. Stewart, *Peyote Religion*, 41.
44. Ibid., 37–42.
45. See Maroukis, *The Peyote Road*, 181–182. For more on Peyote Music, see Edward S. Curtis, *The North American Indian: Tribes of Oklahoma, the Wichita, Southern Cheyenne, Oto, and Comanche*, vol. 19 (Norwood, MA: Plimpton Press, 1930), 199–214.
46. Transcription, January 21, 1908, "Liquor Traffic and Peyote/Mescal Use, 1871–1933," Cheyenne and Arapaho Agency, roll CAA50, Indian Archives Division, Oklahoma Historical Society, Oklahoma City, Oklahoma, 29.
47. Frederick Hoxie, ed., *Talking Back to Civilization: Indian Voices in the Progressive Era* (New York: Bedford/St. Martin's, 2001), 84.
48. Ibid., 85.
49. Stewart, *Peyote Religion*, 178.
50. Ibid., 93.
51. Ibid., 78.
52. Dr. Robert E. L. Newberne, "Peyote: An Abridged Compilation from the Files of the Bureau of Indian Affairs" (Washington: GPO, 1922), box 44, Omer C. Stewart Collection.
53. Jill E. Martin, "'The Greatest Evil': Interpretations of Indian Prohibition Laws, 1832–1953," *Great Plains Quarterly* 23 (Winter 20013): 37.
54. Ibid., 37–38.
55. Omer C. Stewart, "Peyote and the Law," box 68, Omer C. Stewart Collection.
56. Maroukis, *The Peyote Road*, 104.
57. Stewart, *Peyote Religion*, 137–141.
58. Maroukis, *The Peyote Road*, 104.
59. Stewart, *Peyote Religion*, 142.
60. Petition, Omaha Indian Peyote Society, box 43, Omer C. Stewart Collection.
61. Ibid.
62. *Quarterly Journal of the Society of American Indians*, quoted in Frederick E. Hoxie, *This Indian Country: American Indian Activists and the Place They Made* (New York: Penguin, 2012), 225.
63. *Report of the Executive Council on the Proceedings of the Annual Conference of the Society of American Indians* (Washington, DC, 1912), 5–8.
64. *The Society of American Indians Statement of Purpose...*, January 25–27, 1912, The Papers of the Society of the American Indians, 1911–1923, Personal Collection of John Lemer, Series I: Correspondence, 1911–1923 [hereafter SAI Papers].
65. *Report of the Executive Council*; and "To Help Race: Indian Congress Wrestles with Industrial Problems," *Maysville Journal-Tribune*, October 13, 1911.
66. "Ibid., 14.
67. Hazel Hertzberg, *The Search for American Indian Identity: Modern Pan-Indian Movements* (Syracuse, NY: Syracuse University Press, 1971); and "The Society of American Indians and its Legacies, a Special Combined Issue of *SAIL* and *AIQ*," *Studies in American Indian Literatures* 25, no. 2 (Summer 2013).
68. K. Tsianina Lomawaima, "The Mutuality of Citizenship and Sovereignty," *American Indian Quarterly* 25, no. 2, (Summer 2013): 335.

69. Zitkála-Šá, "VII: Big Red Apples," *American Indian Stories* (Washington, DC: Hayworth Publishing House, 1921), accessed online at University of Pennsylvania Digital Library.
70. Zitkála-Šá, "I: The Land of Red Apples," *American Indian Stories.*
71. Charles A. Eastman, *From Deep Woods to Civilization* (New York: Little Brown and Company, 1916), 5.
72. "Sioux Indians Die in the Railroad Wreck," *Omaha World Herald*, April 8, 1904, The William F. Cody Archive: Documenting the Life and Times of Buffalo Bill.
73. David R. M. Beck, "Developing a Voice: The Evolution of Self-Determination in an Urban Indian Community," *Wicazo Sa Review* 17, no. 2 (Autumn 2002): 123–125.
74. *Report of the Executive Council*, 45, 50. For more on Laura Cornelius Kellogg, see Catherine D. Cahill, *Recasting the Vote: How Women of Color Transformed the Suffrage Movement* (Chapel Hill: University of North Carolina Press, 2020).
75. Ibid., 45.
76. Ibid., 50.
77. *Report of the Executive Council*, 50.
78. Ibid. 54.
79. Laura Cornelius Kellogg, *Our Democracy and the American Indian: A Comprehensive Presentation of the Indian Situation as It Is Today* (Kansas City, MO: Burton Publishing Company, 1920), 62.
80. Ibid., 41.
81. Ibid., 41.
82. Kellogg, *Our Democracy and the American Indian*, 79–80.
83. *Report of the Executive Council*, 70.
84. Ibid., 70–71.
85. Ibid., 72–73.
86. Ibid., 76.
87. Ibid., 121.
88. Ibid., 119, 114.
89. Ibid., 115.
90. Arthur C. Parker to Alice Denomie, March 26, 1913, SAI Papers.
91. Quote in Parker to Public Library, Decatur, Illinois, April 29, 1915, SAI Papers. Parker to Public Library, Detroit, Michigan, April 29, 1915, SAI Papers.
92. Arthur C. Parker to J. B. Hewitt, August 30, 1913, SAI Papers.
93. On Zitkála-Šá, see Tadeusz Lewandowski, *Red Bird, Red Power: The Life and Legacy of Zitkala-Sa* (Norman: University of Oklahoma Press, 2016). On Montezuma, see Julianne Newmark, "A Prescription for Freedom: Carlos Montezuma, *Wassaja*, and the Society of American Indians," *American Indian Quarterly* 37, no. 3 (Summer 2013): 139–158; and Peter Iverson, *Carlos Montezuma and the Changing World of American Indians* (Albuquerque: University of New Mexico Press, 1982). Charles A. Eastman, *From Deep Woods and Indian Boyhood* (Garden City, NY: Dover Publications, 1971); Zitkala-Sa, *American Indian Stories and Old Indian Legends* (Garden City, NY: Dover Publications, 2014), and *Dreams and Thunder: Stories, Poems, and the Sun Dance Opera* (New York: Bison Books, 2005); and Arthur C. Parker, *The Indian How Book* (Dover Publications, orig. 1927, repr. 1975), *Seneca Myths and Folk Tales* (Lincoln: University of Nebraska Press, orig. 1923, repr. 1989), *Iroquois Uses of Maize and Other Food Plants* (Albany: University of the State of New York, 1910), and *Skunny Wundy: Seneca Indian Tales* (Syracuse, NY: Syracuse University Press, repr. 1925).
94. Richard A. Harper for Elmer Wilson to Arthur C. Parker, April 11, 1914, SAI Papers.
95. Ibid.
96. C. P. Hauke to Arthur C. Parker, October 27, 1913, SAI Papers.
97. Arthur C. Parker to Cato Sells, December 19, 1913, SAI Papers.
98. For a sampling of such correspondence, see Arthur C. Parker to Howell Hoof-on-Forehead, February 25, 1915; Parker to Abraham S. Horn, November 26, 1913; Parker to Jerry Holliquilla, February 9, 1915; Hauke to Parker, November 5, 1914; Hauke to Parker November 6, 1914; and Parker to Goes-to-War, February 21, 1914, SAI Papers.
99. Parker to Goes-to-War, February 21, 1914, SAI Papers.
100. Parker to Hewitt, August 30, 1913, SAI Papers.
101. Thomas L. Sloan, "The Indian's Protection and His Place as an American," *The Red Man* 4 (1911/1912): 399.

102. "Granting Indians the Right to Select Agents," March 9, 1916, 64th Cong., 1st sess., 39.
103. "Army Reorganization, Hearing Before the Committee on Military Affairs on H.R. 8287," 66th Congress, 1st and 2nd Congress, v. 2, 2224–2226.
104. Hoxie, *This Indian Country*, 261; Leicester Knickerbacker Davis, "Thomas L. Sloan, American Indian," *American Indian Magazine* 7, no. 4 (August 1920): 40.
105. Arthur C. Parker to George P. Deckler, August 12, 1913, SAI Papers.
106. For Coolidge, see *Proceedings*, 127–128; "Sherman Coolidge Will Visit Des Moines," *The Des Moines Register*, February 10, 1910, 45; "Pleads for the Uplift of the Indian, *The Inter-Mountain Republican*, January 28, 1907; "Interior," March 8, 1914, *Washington Post*, 10; "Annual Convocation of Episcopal Church," *Nevada State Journal*, June 16, 1918, 6; "The Rev. Mr. Coolidge to Talk," *Star Tribune* (Minneapolis, Minn.), March 10, 1915, 5.
107. Arthur C. Parker to S. B. Davis, June 12, 1913, SAI Papers.
108. J. B. Triest to Arthur C. Parker, September 15, 1913, SAI Papers. J. Francis to Arthur C. Parker, August 25, 1913; Francis to Parker, December 1913; Francis to McCauley December 1, 1914; S. B. Hege to Parker, August 1, 1913; and Francis to McCauley, November 1, 1915, SAI Papers.
109. For more on the Hayden Bill, see Maroukis, *The Peyote Road*, 53–57.
110. *Peyote: Hearings Before a Subcommittee of the Committee on Indian Affairs of the House of Representatives on H.R 2614* (Washington, GPO, 1918), 6.
111. Ibid., 6–7.
112. *United States v. Nice*, 241 U.S. 591 (1916), p. 241.
113. *Peyote: Hearings Before a Subcommittee of the Committee on Indian Affairs of the House of Representatives on H.R 2614* (Washington, DC: GPO, 1918), 81.
114. Quoted in Stewart, *Peyote Religion*, 178–180.
115. *Peyote: Hearings Before a Subcommittee*, 126.
116. Two organizations filed in Oklahoma, two in Nebraska, one in North Dakota, Montana, Colorado, and Idaho, and five in South Dakota. Some articles specifically called out the use of peyote as a sacrificial object, others did not. All stressed Christian influence and church organization. Stewart, *Peyote Religion*, 223–238.
117. Maroukis, *The Peyote Road*, 210.
118. Arthur C. Parker, "Certain Important Elements of the Indian Problem," *Quarterly Journal* 3 (1915), quoted in Frederick E. Hoxie, *Talking Back to Civilization: Indian Voices from the Progressive Era* (New York: Bedford, 2001), 99–100.
119. Hoxie, *Talking Back to Civilization*, 22.

Railway Journeys: Kiowa Travels

1. Bill Kroger, "The Trial of Satanta and Big Tree," Texas Bar Journal 75 (March 2012): 200.
2. Ibid.; and New York Times, July 26, 1871, 1.
3. Colin Calloway, Pen and Ink Witchcraft: Treaties and Treaty Making in American Indian History (New York: Oxford University Press, 2013), 550; Clarence Wharton, Satanta: The Great Chief of the Kiowas and His People (Dallas: Upshaw and Co., 1935); and Charles M. Robinson, Satanta: The Life and Death of a War Chief (Kerryville, TX: State House Press, 1997), 158–169.
4. ARCIA, 1872, 131.
5. Calloway, Pen and Ink Witchcraft, 550.
6. Robinson, Satanta: The Life and Death of a War Chief.
7. Luther Standing Bear, My People the Sioux (independently published, 2017, org. 1929), 105.
8. Nannie Chalanon to Hilon A. Parker, May 6, 1899; and Frederick Kyonta [spelling uncertain] to Hilon A. Parker, May 5, 1899, Drawings and Letters by Kiowa and other Native American Children, vol. 1, Hilon A. Parker Family Papers, 1825–1953, William L. Clements Library, University of Michigan, Ann Arbor, Michigan [hereafter Parker Papers].
9. Helen Esrago to Hilon A. Parker, May 5, 1899, Parker Papers.
10. Alma Big Tree to Hilon A. Parker, May 6 1899, Parker Papers.
11. Helen Esrago to Hilon A. Parker, May 5, 1899, Parker Papers.
12. Barbara De Wolfe, "Expressions of Assimilation?" *The Quatro* 32 (Fall/Winter 2009): 9; and March 28, 1899, Hilon A. Parker Diary, box 25, Parker Papers.
13. N. Scott Momaday, *The Way to Rainy Mountain* (Albuquerque: University of New Mexico Press, 1969), 16.
14. Enos Spanmko [spelling unclear] to Hilon A. Parker, May 5, 1899, Parker Papers.

Conclusion

1. Scott Richard Lyons, *X-Marks: Native Signatures of Assent* (Minneapolis: University of Minnesota Press, 2010), 20.
2. Joseph Medicine Crow and Herman Viola, *Counting Coup: Becoming a Crow Chief on the Reservation and Beyond* (Washington, DC: National Geographic Children's Books, 2006), 112–119.
3. Pendleton Woolen Mills was incorporated in 1895, financed by eastern and European capital, and powered by the Umatilla River. Theron Fell, founder, realized quickly that the nearby Umatilla Reservation and other reservations would provide markets for blankets. He created tribe-specific blankets. Robert W. Kapoun and Charles J. Lohrmann, *Language of the Robe: American Indian Trade Blankets* (Salt Lake City, UT: Gibbs Smith, 2005), 121–123.
4. Julie Tharp, "'Fire Ponies': Cars in American Indian Film and Literature," *American Indian Culture and Research Journal* 24, no. 3, (2000): 77–91.
5. Federal Highway Administration, "History of Modern Road Building in Indian Country," College of Engineering and Mines, University of Alaska-Fairbanks, pdf, http://cem.uaf.edu/media/188378/ncai-intro-tran-101-draft2.pdf. For more on the impact of car culture in the United States, see Virginia Scharff, *Twenty Thousand Roads: Women, Movement, and the West* (Berkeley: University of California Press, 2002); and Paul S. Sutter, *Driven Wild: How the Fight Against Automobiles Launched the Modern Wilderness Movement* (Seattle: University of Washington Press, 2005).
6. Deloria, Philip J., *Indians in Unexpected Places*, (Lawrence: University Press of Kansas, 2004), 144–180.
7. Peter A. Leavitt, Rebecca Covarrubias, Yvonne A. Perez, and Stephanie A. Fryberg, "'Frozen in Time': The Impact of Media Representations on Identity and Self-Understanding," *Journal of Social Issues* 71, no. 1 (2015): 39–53. See also Eric Stegman and Victoria Phillips, "Missing the Point: The Real Impact of Native Mascots and Team Names on American Indian and Alaska Native Youth," Center for American Progress, July 2014.
8. See Kent Blansett, Cathleen D. Cahill, and Andrew Needham, eds., *Indian Cities: Histories of Indigenous Urbanization* (Norman: University of Oklahoma Press, 2022); Coll Thrush, *Native Seattle: Histories of the Crossing-Over Place* (Seattle: University of Washington Press, 2008) and *Indigenous London: Native Travelers at the Heart of Empire* (New Haven, CT: Yale University Press, 2016); Myla Vicenti Carpio, *Indigenous Albuquerque* (Lubbock: Texas Tech University Press, 2011); Kyle T. Mays, "Indigenous Detroit: Indigeneity, Modernity, and Racial and Gender formation in an American City, 1871–2000," (PhD diss., University of Illinois Urbana-Champagne, 2015); and Rosalyn R. LaPier and David R. M. Back, *City Indian: Native American Activism in Chicago* (Lincoln: University of Nebraska Press, 2015).
9. "Canada: Thousands of Travelers Affected as Indigenous-Led Rail Blockage Continues," *The Guardian*, February 12, 2020; and Jourdan Bennet-Begaye, "Idle No More Was the Start . . . Rail Blockade Is the Next Chapter," *Indian Country Today*, February 17, 2020.
10. "'Washington Redhawks' Organizers Claim Success, Say Articles Were Satire, Not Fake News," *Washington Post*, December 14, 2017.
11. Patty Loew, "We Are the Seventh Generation: A Conversation with Winona LaDuke," *Edge Effects*, November 14, 2017. For more on Honor the Earth, visit honortheearth.com. See also "The Manifesto," *Idle No More*, at idlenomore.ca.
12. Monkman's alter-ego, Miss Chief Eagle Testickle, writes of the calamities that railroads brought. See Kent Monkman and Gisèle Gordon, *The Memoirs of Chief Eagle Testickle: A True and Exact Accounting of the History of Turtle Island*, vol. 2 (Toronto: McClelland & Stewart, 2023), 24, 37, 41.
13. "Kent Monkman's Subversive Art Creates a Counter-Narrative of Indigenous Experience," *CBC Radio*, June 30, 2022.

Bibliography

Archives and Manuscript Collections

Beinecke Rare Book and Manuscript Library, Yale University, New Haven, Connecticut
Yale Collection of Western Americana

Center for Southwest Research and Special Collections, University of New Mexico, Albuquerque, New Mexico
New Mexico Indian Affairs Historical Documents, 1689–1963
American Indian Oral History Collection, 1967–1972

Jesuit Archives and Research Center, St. Louis, Missouri
Missouri Province Archive

Oklahoma Historical Society, Oklahoma City, Oklahoma
Clippings File, Railroads
Quapaw Agency Records
Choctaw Nation Agency Records
Choctaw Nation File
Cherokee Nation Agency Records
Cheyenne and Arapaho Agency Records
Indian-Pioneer History Oral History Collection
Splitlog, Oklahoma History Center Vertical File
Amiel Weeks Whipple Collection

Minnesota History Center, St. Paul, Minnesota
Northern Pacific Railway Company, Northern Pacific Railway Corporate Records, 1861–1970
Great Northern Railway Company Records, 1854–1970
The Papers of the Society of the American Indians, 1911–1923. Personal Collection of John Lemer
Series I: Correspondence, 1911–1923

The Huntington Library, San Marino, California
Papers of Lauren Winfield Aldrich, 1868–1938
Papers of Edward G. Beckwith and John Laurence Fox, 1818–1881
Papers of John Stephen Casement, 1861–1869, 1939
Papers of Thomas Lord Kimball, 1859–1901
Papers of Montgomery Meigs, 1847–1931
Papers of Walter Scribner Schuyler, 1850–1932
Samuel Benedict Reed Letters, 1864–1870
Etha Mayo Woodruff Memorial Collection of Family Papers

The Helmerich Center for American Research at Thomas Gilcrease Museum, Tulsa, Oklahoma
Lester Hargrett Indian Pamphlet Collection
Grant Foreman Papers

The Newberry Library, Chicago, Illinois
Everett D. Graff Collection of Western Americana
Edward E. Ayer Collection

University of Colorado Boulder Archives and Special Collections, Boulder, Colorado
Omer C. Stewart Collection

William L. Clements Library, University of Michigan, Ann Arbor, Michigan
Hilon A. Parker Family Papers

Government Material

Board of Indian Commissioners. *Annual Report*, 1869–1933. Washington, DC: Government Printing Office.

Commissioner of Indian Affairs. *Annual Report*, 1862–1933. Washington, DC: Government Printing Office.

Congressional Globe and Record. 1850–1907.
Peyote: Hearings before a subcommittee of the Committee on Indian Affairs of the House of Representatives on H.R. 2614 to amend... Washington, DC: Government Printing Office, 1918.

Reports of Explorations and Surveys to Ascertain the Most Practicable and Economic Route for a Railroad from the Mississippi River to the Pacific Ocean... Washington, DC: William A. Harris, 1859.

Special Commission Appointed to Investigate the Affairs of the Red Cloud Indian Agency. *Report.* 1975. Washington, DC: Government Printing Office.

U.S. Senate, Committee on the Pacific Railroad. *Report on the Pacific Railroad.* Report No. 219. 40th Cong., 3d. sess, (1869).

Secretary of War. *Annual Report.* 1869. Washington, DC: Government Printing Office.
National Archives and Records Center, Denver, Colorado

Crow Agency Records. 1872–1992. Record Group 75. Records of the Bureau of Indian Affairs.

National Archives and Records Center, Kansas City, Missouri
Records of the Pine Ridge Indian Agency, 1867–1967. Record Group 75. Records of the Bureau of Indian Affairs.
Records of the Standing Rock Indian Agency, 1864–1974. Record Group 75. Records of the Bureau of Indian Affairs.

National Archives and Records Center, Riverside, California
Central Classified Files, 1897–1951. Record Group 75. Records of the Bureau of Indian Affairs.
Moqui Indian Agency. Bureau of Indian Employment. Moqui Agency Subject Files, 1907–1920.
Navajo Agency. Subject Files, 1900–1935. Record Group 75. Records of the Bureau of Indian Affairs.
Records of Eastern Navajo Agency, 1904–1944. General Correspondence. Record Group 75. Records of the Bureau of Indian Affairs.
Records of the Colorado River Agency, 1879–1975. Record Group 75. Records of the Bureau of Indian Affairs.

National Archives and Records Center, Washington, DC
Central Classified Files, 1907–1939. Record Group 75. Records of the Bureau of Indian Affairs.
Special Case Files, Records of the Bureau of Indian Affairs. Record Group 75. Records of the Bureau of Indian Affairs.

Newspapers and Magazines

American Indian Magazine
Bismarck (N.D.) Daily Tribune
Cherokee Advocate

Cherokee Editor
Cleveland (OH) Daily Leader
The Des Moines (Iowa) Register
Evening Star (Washington, DC)
Feast Magazine
Frank Leslie's Illustrated Newspaper
Harper's Weekly
Indian Chieftain
Indian Country Today
Indian Journal
Milwaukee (WI) Sentinel
Nevada State Journal
New York Sun
New York Times
New York Monthly Magazine
North American Review
Oklahoma Star
Omaha (Neb.) World Herald
Putnam's Monthly Magazine
San Bernardino (Calif.) Country Sun
Star Tribune
The Arizona Republican
The Coconino (Az.) Sun
The Daily Cleveland (Ohio) Herald
The Evening Times
The Guardian
The Inter-Mountain Republican
The New York Herald
The Ocala (FL) Daily Star
The Red Man
The Times Dispatch
The Tulsa (OK) Daily World
The Union Pacific Magazine
The Washington Times
The Wilmington (NC) Dispatch
Washington Post

Published Works

Abbot, Henry. *Memoir of Montgomery Meigs, 1816–1892.* National Academy of Sciences. Biographical Memoirs. Vol. 3. Washington, DC: National Academy of Sciences, 1895.

Adair, John. *The Navajo and Pueblo Silversmiths.* Norman: University of Oklahoma Press, 1944.

Adams, David W. *Education for Extinction: American Indians and the Boarding School Experience, 1975–1925.* Lawrence: University Press of Kansas, 1995.

Aguiar, Marian. *Tracking Modernity: India's Railway and the Culture of Mobility.* Minneapolis: University of Minnesota Press, 2011.

Akins, Damon B., and William J. Bauer. *We Are the Land: A History of Native California.* Berkeley: University of California Press, 2022.

Allen, Chadwick and Beth H. Piatote, The Society of American Indians and Its Legacies, a Special Combined Issue of *SAIL* and *AIQ*." *Studies in American Indian Literatures* 25, no. 2 (Summer 2013).

Andrews, Tarren. "Indigenous Futures and Medieval Pasts." *English Language Notes* 58, no. 2 (October 2020): 1–16.

Archambeau, Ernest A., ed. "Lieutenant A. W. Whipple's Transcontinental Railroad Survey Across the Panhandle of Texas." *Panhandle Plains Historical Review* 44 (1971): 37.

Arenson, Adam, and Andrew R. Graybill. *Civil War Wests: Testing the Limits of the United States.* Oakland: University of California Press, 2015.

Arnesen, Eric. *Brotherhoods of Color: Black Railroad Workers and the Struggle for Equality.* Cambridge, MA: Harvard University Press, 2001.

Bachmann, Frederick W., and William Swilling Wallace, eds. *The Land Between: Dr. James Schiel's Account of the Gunnison-Beckwith Expedition into the West, 1853–1854.* Los Angeles: Westernlore Press, 1975.

Bagley, Will. *Blood of Prophets: Brigham Young and the Massacre at Mountain Meadows.* Norman: University of Oklahoma Press, 2004.

Bailey, Minnie T. *Reconstruction in Indian Territory: A Story of Avarice, Discrimination, and Opportunism.* Port Washington, NY: Kennikat Press, 1972.

Bailey, William Francis. *The Story of the First Trans-continental Railroad and its Projectors, Construction, and History....* Fair Oaks, CA: W. F. Bailey, 1906.

Baker, Lee D. *Anthropology and the Racial Politics of Culture.* Durham, NC: Duke University Press, 2010.

Bartlett, Richard A. *Great Surveys of the American West.* Norman: University of Oklahoma Press, 1980.

Basso, Keith H. *Wisdom Sits in Places: Landscape and Language Among the Western Apache.* Albuquerque: University of New Mexico Press, 1996.

Beck, David R. M. "Developing a Voice: The Evolution of Self-Determination in an Urban Indian Community." *Wicazo Sa Review* 17, no. 2 (Autumn 2002): 123–125.

Belin, Esther G. *Of Cartography.* Tucson: University of Arizona Press, 2017.

Bent, George, and George E. Hyde. *Life of George Bent Written from his Letters.* Norman: University of Oklahoma Press, 1968.

Bernstein, David. *How the West Was Drawn: Mapping, Indians, and the Construction of the Trans-Mississippi West.* Lincoln: University of Nebraska Press, 2019.

Blakeslee, Donald J. "The Calumet Ceremony and the Origin of Fur Trade Rituals." *Western Canadian Journal of Anthropology* 7 (1977): 78–88.

Blakeslee, Donald J.. "The Origin and Spread of the Calumet Ceremony." *American Antiquity* 46 (October 1981): 759–768.

Blansett, Kent, Cathleen D. Cahill, and Andrew Needham, eds. *Indian Cities: Histories of Indigenous Urbanization.* Norman: University of Oklahoma Press, 2022.

Blee, Lisa. "The 1925 Fort Union Indian Congress: Divergent Narratives, One Event." *American Indian Quarterly* 31, no. 4 (Fall 2007): 582–612.

Bloom, Khaled J. "An American Tragedy of the Commons: Land and Labor in the Cherokee Nation, 1870–1900." *Agricultural History* 76, no. 3 (Summer 2002): 497–523.

Boudinot, Elias. *Cherokee Editor: The Writings of Elias Boudinot.* Ed. Theda Perdue. Knoxville: University Press of Tennessee, 1983.

Boudinot, Elias. *The Memorial of Elias C. Boudinot to the Congress of the United States.* Washington, DC.

Boudinot, Elias. *Speech of Elias C. Boudinot, a Cherokee Indian, Delivered Before the House Committee on Territories, Feb. 7, 1872 in Behalf of a Territorial Government for Indian Territory, in reply to Wm. P. Ross....* Washington, DC: McGill and Witherow, 1872.

Bowes, John T. *Land Too Good for Indians: Northern Indian Removal.* Norman: University of Oklahoma Press, 2016.

Bowman, J. N. "Driving the Last Spike at Promontory, 1869." *California Historical Society Quarterly* 36, no. 2 (June 1957): 96–106; and 36, no. 3 (September 1957): 263–274.

Brown, Dee. *Hear That Lonesome Whistle Blow: Railroads in the West.* New York: Holt Rinehart, and Winston, 1977.

Bryant, Keith. *History of the Atchison, Topeka, and Santa Fe.* Lincoln: University of Nebraska Press, 1992.

Bsumek, Erika Marie. *Indian-Made: Navajo Culture in the Marketplace, 1868–1940*. CultureAmerica. Lawrence: University Press of Kansas, 2008.

Byrd, Jodi. *The Transit of Empire: Indigenous Critiques of Colonialism*. Minneapolis: University of Minnesota Press, 2011.

Byrd, Jodi, Alyohsa Goldstein, Jodi Melamed, and Chandan Reddy. "Predatory Value: Economies of Dispossession and Disturbed Relationalities." *Social Text* 36, no. 2 (June 2018): 1–18.

Cahill, Cathleen D. *Federal Fathers and Mothers: A Social History of the United States Indian Service, 1869–1933*. Chapel Hill: University of North Carolina Press, 2011.

Cahill, Catherine D. *Recasting the Vote: How Women of Color Transformed the Suffrage Movement*. Chapel Hill: University of North Carolina Press, 2020.

Calloway, Colin. *Pen and Ink Witchcraft: Treaties and Treaty Making in American Indian History*. New York: Oxford University Press, 2013.

Carpenter, Cari M., and Carolyn Soriso, eds. *The Newspaper Warrior: Sara Winnemucca Hopkins's Campaign for American Indian Rights, 1864–1891*. Lincoln: University of Nebraska Press, 2015.

Carpio, Myla V. *Indigenous Albuquerque*. Lubbock: Texas Tech University Press, 2011.

Case, Theresa Ann. *The Great Southwest Railroad Strike and Free Labor*. 1st ed. Red River Valley Books no. 3. College Station: Texas A&M University Press, 2010.

Chandler, Alfred D. *The Visible Hand: The Managerial Revolution in American Business*. Cambridge, MA: Harvard University Press, 1977.

Chang, David A. *The Color of the Land: Race, Nation, and the Politics of Landownership in Oklahoma, 1832–1929*. Chapel Hill: University of North Carolina Press, 2010.

Child, Brenda, J. *Boarding School Sessions: American Indian Families, 1900–1940*. Lincoln: University of Nebraska Press, 2000.

Christiansen, James R. "A Study of Osage History Prior to 1876." PhD diss., Brigham Young University, 1962.

Cohen, Paul E. *Mapping the West: America's Westward Movement, 1524–1890*. New York: Rizzoli, 2002.

Connolly, Emilie. "Fiduciary Colonialism: Annuities and Native Dispossession in the Early United States." *American Historical Review* 127, no. 1 (March 2022): 223–253.

Cothran, Boyd. *Remembering the Modoc War: Redemptive Violence and the Making of American Innocence*. Chapel Hill: University of North Carolina Press, 2017.

Cowdry, Mike. "A Winter Count of the Wajaje Lakota 1758–59 to 1885–86." *Tribal Art Magazine* 77 (Autumn 2015): 128–133.

Cronon, William. *Changes in the Land: Indians, Colonists, and the Ecology of New England*. New York: Hill and Wang, 1983.

Cronon, William. *Nature's Metropolis: Chicago and the Great West*. New York: W. W. Norton, 1991.

Cronon, William, ed. *Uncommon Ground: Rethinking the Human Place in Nature*. New York: W.W. Norton and Co., 1995.

Curtis, Edward S. *The North American Indian: Tribes of Oklahoma, the Wichita, Southern Cheyenne, Oto, and Comanche*. Norwood, MA: Plimpton Press, 1930, vol. 19.

Cushman, H. B. *History of the Choctaw, Chikasaw, and Natchez Indians*. Greenville, TX: Headlight Printing House, 1899.

Davis, Clarence B., Ronald B. Robinson, and Kenneth Wilburn, eds. *Railway Imperialism*. Westport, CT: Praeger, 1991.

Davis, Colin J. *Power at Odds: The 1922 National Railroad Shopmen's Strike*. Chicago: University of Illinois Press, 1997.

Davis, Leicester K. "Thomas L. Sloan, American Indian." *American Indian Magazine* 7, no. 4 (August 1920): 40.

Dawson, Alexander S. *The Peyote Effect: From the Inquisition to the War on Drugs*. Los Angeles: University of California Press, 2018.

Deloria, Philp J. *Indians in Unexpected Places.* Lawrence: University Press of Kansas, 2004.

Deloria, Philp J. *Playing Indian.* New Haven, CT: Yale University Press, 1999.

Deloria, Vine, and Raymond J. DeMallie. *Documents of American Indian Diplomacy.* Norman: University of Oklahoma Press, 1999.

Demerits, N. J., Peter Dobbin Hall, Terry Schmidt, and Rhys H. Williams, eds. *Sacred Companies: Organizational Aspects of Religion and Religious Aspects of Organizations.* New York: Oxford University Press, 1998.

Deverell, William. *Railroad Crossing: Californians and the Railroad, 1850–1910.* Berkeley: University of California Press, 1994.

Dillon, Grace, ed. *Walking the Clouds: An Anthology of Indigenous Science Fiction.* Tucson: University of Arizona Press, 2012.

Dilworth, Leah. *Imagining Indians in the Southwest: Persistent Visions of a Primitive Past.* Washington, D.C.: Smithsonian, 1997.

Dodge, Grenville Melen. *How We Built the Union Pacific Railway, and Other Papers and Addresses.* Council Bluffs, IA: Monarch Printing Co., 1910.

Duarte, Marisa Elena. *Network Sovereignty: Building the Internet Across Indian Country.* Seattle: University of Washington Press, 2017.

Dubois, Cora. *The 1870 Ghost Dance.* Lincoln: University of Nebraska Press, 2007.

Dunlay, Thomas W. *Wolves for the Blue Soldiers: Indian Scouts and Auxiliaries with the United States Army, 1860–90.* Lincoln: University of Nebraska Press, 1982.

Eastman, Charles A. *From Deep Woods to Civilization.* New York: Little Brown and Company, 1916.

Eastman, Charles A. *From Deep Woods and Indian Boyhood.* Garden City, NY: Dover Publications, 1971.

Edwards, Paul N. "Infrastructure and Modernity: Force, Time, and Social Organization in the History of Sociotechnical Systems." In *Technology and Modernity: The Empirical Turn.* Cambridge, MA: MIT Press, 2002, 185–225.

Egan, Timothy. *Short Nights of the Shadow Catcher: The Epic Life and Immortal Photographs of Edward Curtis.* New York: Houghton Mifflin, 2012.

Eggert, Gerald. *Railroad Labor Disputes: The Beginnings of Federal Strike Policy.* Detroit: University of Michigan Press, 2016.

Ellis, Clyde. "'We Don't Want Your Rations, We Want This Dance': The Changing Use of Song and Dance on the Southern Plains." *Western Historical Quarterly* 30, no. 2 (Summer 1999): 133–154.

Ewers, John C. *Indian Life on the Upper Missouri.* Norman: University of Oklahoma Press, 1968: 61–63.

Fenn, Elizabeth A. *Encounters at the Heart of the World: A History of the Mandan People.* New York: Hill and Wang, 2015.

Fielding, Kent R., and Dorothy S. Fielding. *The Journal of Lt. Edward G. Beckwith Compared to the Final Report of the Gunnison Expedition in Utah Territory Including Trail and Campsite Descriptions.* Higganum, CT: Gunnison Memorial Associates, 2003.

Flinn, John Joseph. *Official Guide to the World's Columbian Exposition.* Chicago: Columbian Guide Co., 1893.

Fowler, Loretta. *Wives and Husbands: Gender and Age in Southern Arapaho History.* Norman: University of Oklahoma Press, 2010.

Fraga, Sean. "'An Outlet to the Western Sea': Puget Sound, Terraqueous Mobility, and the Northern Pacific Railroad's Pursuit of Trade with Asia, 1864–1892." *Western Historical Quarterly* 51, no. 4 (Winter 2020): 439–458.

Fricke, Suzanne Newman. "Indigenous Futurisms in the Hyperpresent Now." *World Art* 9, no. 2 (2019): 107–121.

Fried, Stephen. *Appetite for America: Fred Harvey and the Business of Civilizing the Wild West—One Meal at a Time.* New York: Bantam, 2011.

Frost, Richard H. *The Railroad and the Pueblo Indians: The Impact of the Atchison, Topeka, and Santa Fe on the Pueblos of the Rio Grande, 1880–1930.* Salt Lake City: University of Utah Press, 2016.

Gabriel, Ralph Henry. *Elias Boudinot, Cherokee, & His America.* Civilization of the American Indian Series vol. 20. Norman: University of Oklahoma Press, 1941.

Gage, Justin. *We Do Not Want the Gates Closed Between Us: Native Networks and the Ghost Dance.* Norman: University of Oklahoma Press, 2020.

Gage, Justin. "Intertribal Communication, Literacy, and the Spread of the Ghost Dance." PhD diss., University of Arkansas, 2015.

Garcílazo, Jeffrey M. *Traqueros: Mexican Railroad Workers in the United States, 1870–1930.* Denton: University of North Texas Press, 2012.

Gates, Paul W. *Fifty Million Acres: Conflicts over Kansas Land Policy, 1854–1890.* Norman: University of Oklahoma Press, 1997.

Gates, Paul W. *History of Public Land Law Development.* Washington, DC: Government Printing Office, 1968.

Genetin-Pilawa, C. J. *Crooked Paths to Allotment: The Fight over Federal Indian Policy after the Civil War.* Chapel Hill: University of North Carolina Press, 2012.

Gibson, Arrell M. *Oklahoma: A History in Five Centuries.* Norman: University of Oklahoma Press, 1981.

Goetzmann, William H. *Army Exploration in the American West, 1803–1863.* Austin: Texas State Historical Association, 1991.

Goetzmann, William H. *Exploration and Empire: The Explorers and the Scientists in the Winning of the American West.* New York: Alfred A. Knopf, 1966.

Gordon, Mary McDougall, ed. *Through Indian Country to California: John P. Sherburne's Diary of the Whipple Expedition.* Stanford, CA: Stanford University Press, 1988.

Gordon, Sarah H. *Passage to Union: How the Railroads Transformed American Life, 1829–1929.* Chicago: Ivan R. Dee, 1998.

Hall, Ryan. *Beneath the Backbone of the World: Blackfoot People and the North American Borderlands, 1720–1877.* Chapel Hill: University of North Carolina Press, 2020.

Hamill, James. "Being Indian in Northeast Oklahoma." *Plains Anthropologist* 45, no. 173 (August 2000): 291–303.

Harmon, Alexandra. *Rich Indians: Native People and the Problem of Wealth in American History.* Chapel Hill: University of North Carolina Press, 2010.

Harmon, Alexandra, Colleen O'Neill, and Paul C. Rosier. "Interwoven Economic Histories: American Indians in Capitalist America." *The Journal of American History* 98, no. 3 (December 2011): 698–722.

Harris, Douglas C. *Fish, Law, and Colonialism: The Legal Capture of Salmon in British Columbia.* Toronto: University of Toronto Press, 2005.

Harris, Douglas C. *Landing Native Fisheries: Indian Reserves and Fishing Rights in British Columbia, 1849–1925.* Vancouver: University of British Columbia Press, 2008.

Headrick, Daniel. *Power over Peoples: Technology, Environments, and Western Imperialism 1400 to the present.* Princeton, NJ: Princeton University Press, 2012.

Heath Justice, Daniel, and Jean M. O'Brien. *Allotment Stories: Indigenous Land Relations Under Settler Siege.* Minneapolis: University of Minnesota Press, 2021.

Hebard, Grace Raymond. *Washakie: An Account of Indian Resistance of the Covered Wagon and Union Pacific Railroad Invasions of Their Territory.* Cleveland, OH: Arthur H. Clark Company, 1930.

Heitala, Thomas R. *Manifest Design: American Exceptionalism and Empire.* Ithaca, NY: Cornell University Press, 1985.

Hertzberg, Hazel. *The Search for American Identity: Modern Pan-Indian Movements.* Syracuse, NY: Syracuse University Press, 1971.

Higgins, Hannah B. *The Grid Book.* Cambridge, MA: MIT Press, 2009.

Hopkins, Sara Winnemucca. *Life Among the Piutes: Their Wrongs and Claims.* Lincoln: University of Nebraska Press, 1883, repr. 1994.

Hosmer, Brian. *American Indians in the Marketplace: Persistence and Innovation Among the Menominees and Metlakatlans, 1870–1920.* Lawrence: University Press of Kansas, 1999.

Hosmer, Brian, Colleen O'Neill, and Donald J. Fixico, eds. *Native Pathways: American Indian Culture and Economic Development in the Twentieth Century.* Boulder: University Press of Colorado, 2004.

Howard, James H. "Cultural Persistence and Cultural Change as Reflected in Oklahoma Seneca-Cayuga Ceremonialism." *Plains Anthropologist* 6, no. 11 (February 1961): 21.

Howard, Oliver Otis. *My Life and Experiences Among Our Hostile Indians.* Hartford, CT: A. D. Worthington and Company, 1907.

Hoxie, Frederick E. *Parading Through History: The Making of the Crow Nation in American, 1805–1935.* New York: Cambridge University Press, 1997.

Hoxie, Frederick E., ed. *Talking Back to Civilization: Indian Voices in the Progressive Era.* Boston: Bedford/St. Martin's, 2001.

Hoxie, Frederick E. *This Indian Country: American Indian Activists and the Place They Made.* New York: Penguin, 2012.

Hubbard, Bill. *American Boundaries: The Nation, the States, the Rectangular Survey.* Chicago: University of Chicago Press, 2009.

Hudson, Angela Pulley. *Creek Paths and Federal Roads Indians, Settlers, and Slaves and the Making of the American South.* Chapel Hill: University of North Carolina Press, 2010.

Huffard, R. Scott, Jr. *Engines of Redemption: Railroads and the Reconstruction of Capitalism in the New South.* Chapel Hill: University of North Carolina Press, 2019.

Hundley, Norris, Jr. *Dividing the Waters: A Century of Controversy Between the United States and Mexico.* Berkeley: University of California Press, 1966.

Hundley, Norris, Jr. *The Great Thirst: The Californians and Water—A History.* Berkeley: University of California Press, 2001.

Hundley, Norris, Jr. *Water and the West: The Colorado River Compact and the Politics of Water in the American West.* 2nd ed. Berkeley: University of California Press, 2009.

Hyde, Anne. *Empires, Nations, and Families: A New History of the American West, 1800–1860.* Omaha: University of Nebraska Press, 2011.

Hyde, George E. *Spotted Tail's Folk: A History of the Brule Sioux.* Norman: University of Oklahoma Press, 1976.

Iverson, Peter. *Carlos Montezuma and the Changing World of American Indians.* Albuquerque: University of New Mexico Press, 1982.

Jackson, Clyde L., and Grace Jackson. *Quanah Parker Last Chief of the Comanches: A Study in Southwestern Frontier.* New York: Exposition Press, 1963.

Jacobs, Margaret. *White Mother to a Dark Race: Settler Colonialism, Maternalism, and the Removal of Indigenous Children in the American West and Australia.* Lincoln: University of Nebraska Press, 2009.

Jenish, D'Arcy. *Indian Fall: The Last Great Days of the Blackfoot Confederacy.* New York: Viking Press, 1999.

Kapoun, Robert W., and Charles J. Lohrmann. *Language of the Robe: American Indian Trade Blankets.* Salt Lake City: Gibbs Smith, 2005.

Kappler, Charles J. *Indian Affairs: Laws and Treaties.* Washington, DC: Government Printing Office, 1904.

Karson, Jennifer. *Wyáxayt, As Days Go By, Wiyáakaa'awn: Our History, Our Land, and Our People, the Cayuse, Umatilla, and Walla Walla.* Portland: Tamástslikt Cultural Institute and Oregon Historical Society, 2006.

Karuka, Manu. *Empire's Tracks: Indigenous Nations, Chinese Workers, and the Transcontinental Railroad.* Berkeley: University of California Press, 2019.

Kellogg, Laura Cornelius. *Our Democracy and the American Indian: A Comprehensive Presentation of the Indian Situation as It Is Today.* Kansas City, MO: Burton Publishing Co., 1920.

Kelman, Ari. *A Misplaced Massacre: Struggling over the Memory of Sand Creek.* Cambridge, MA: Harvard University Press, 2013.

Kidwell, Clara Sue. *The Choctaws in Oklahoma: From Tribe to Nation, 1855–1970.* Norman: University of Oklahoma Press, 2007.

King, Thomas. *The Truth About Stories: A Native Narrative.* Minneapolis: University of Minnesota Press, 2008.

Klein, Maury. *Union Pacific, Volume 1: 1862–1893.* Minneapolis: University of Minnesota Press, 2006.

Knight, Rolf. *Indians at Work: An Informal History of Native Labour in British Columbia, 1858–1930.* Vancouver, BC: Newstar Books, 1996.

Kovach, Margaret. *Indigenous Methodologies: Characteristics, Conversations and Contexts.* Toronto: University of Toronto Press, 2021.

Krech, Shepard, III. *The Ecological Indian: Myth and History.* New York: W. W. Norton, 2000.

La Barre, Weston. *The Peyote Cult.* Norman: University of Oklahoma Press, 1976.

LaPier, Rosalyn R., and David R. M. Back. *City Indian: Native American Activism in Chicago.* Lincoln: University of Nebraska Press, 2015.

La Vere, David. *Contrary Neighbors: Southern Plains and Removed Indians in Indian Territory.* Norman: University of Oklahoma Press, 2000.

Leavitt, Peter A., Rebecca Covarrubias, Yvonne A. Perez, and Stephanie A. Fryberg. "'Frozen in Time': The Impact of Media Representations on Identity and Self-Understanding." *Journal of Social Issues* 71, no. 1 (2015): 39–53.

Lee, Julia H. *The Racial Railroad.* New York: New York University Press, 2022.

Lee, Robert. "Accounting for Conquest: The Prise for the Louisiana Purchase of Indian Country." *Journal of American History* 103, no. 4 (March 2017): 921–942.

Leeds, Stacy, "By Eminent Domain or Some Other Name: A Tribal Perspective on Taking Land," *Tulsa Law Review* 41 (Fall 2005): 51–77.

Lempart, William. "Indigenous Media Futures: An Introduction." *Cultural Anthropology* 33, no. 2 (2018): 173–179.

Levine, R. R. "Indian Fighters and Indian Reformers: Grant's Indian Peace Policy and the Conservative Consensus." *Civil War History* 31, no. 4 (December 1985): 329–352.

Lewandowski, Tadeusz. *Red Bird, Red Power: The Life and Legacy of Zitkala-Sa.* Norman: University of Oklahoma Press, 2016.

Lewis, G. Malcolm. *Cartographic Encounters: Perspectives on Native American Mapmaking and Map Use.* Chicago: University of Chicago Press, 1998.

Lim, Julian. *Porous Borders: Multiracial Migrations and the Law in the U.S. Mexico Borderlands.* Chapel Hill: University of North Carolina Press, 2018.

Linsenmayer, Penny T. "Kansas Settlers on the Osage Diminished Reserve: A Study of Laura Ingalls Wilder's Little House on the Prairie." *Kansas History* 24, no. 2 (Autumn 2001): 171.

Littlefield, Alice, and Martha C. Knack. *Native Americans and Wage Labor: Ethnohistorical Perspectives.* Norman: University of Oklahoma Press, 1996.

Loew, Patty. "We Are the Seventh Generation: A Conversation with Winona LaDuke." *Edge Effects* (November 2017).

Lomawaima, K. T. "The Mutuality of Citizenship and Sovereignty." *American Indian Quarterly* 25, no. 2 (Summer 2013): 355.

Lomawaima, K. T., and Teresa L. McCarty. *"To Remain an Indian": Lessons in Democracy from a Century of Native American Education.* New York: Teacher's College Press, 2006.

Lyons, Scott Richard. *X-Marks: Native Signatures of Assent.* Minneapolis: University of Minnesota Press, 2010.

Macedo, Marta, and Jaume Valentines-Alvarez. "Technology and Nation: Learning from the Periphery." *Technology and Culture* 57, no. 4 (October 2016): 989–997.

Mapp, Paul. *The Elusive West and the Contest for Empire, 1713–1763.* Chapel Hill: University of North Carolina Press, 2011.

Marmon, Lee, and Tom Corbett. *Laguna Pueblo: A Photographic History.* Albuquerque: University of New Mexico Press, 2015.

Maroukis, Thomas C. *The Peyote Road: Religious Freedom in the Native American Church.* Norman: University of Oklahoma Press, 2010.

Martin, Jill E. "'The Greatest Evil': Interpretations of Indian Prohibition Laws, 1832–1953." *Great Plains Quarterly* 23 (Winter 2013): 37.

Marx, Leo. *The Machine in the Garden: Technology and the Pastoral Ideal in America.* Oxford: Oxford University Press, 2000.

Matthews, John Joseph. *The Osages, Children of the Middle Waters.* Norman: University of Oklahoma Press, 1981.

Mays, Kyle T. "Indigenous Detroit: Indigeneity, Modernity, and Racial and Gender formation in an American City, 1871–2000." PhD diss., University of Illinois, Urbana-Champagne, 2015.

McAdam, Rezin W. "An Indian Commonwealth." *Harper's Monthly* 87, no. 522 (November 1893): 895.

McDonald, Kate. "Asymmetrical Integration: Lessons from a Railway Empire." *Technology and Culture* 56, no. 1 (January 2015): 115–149.

McGraw, Thomas. *Prophets of Innovation: Joseph Schumpeter and Creative Destruction.* Cambridge, MA: Harvard University Press, 2007.

McLoughlin, William G. *After the Trail of Tears: The Cherokee's Struggle for Sovereignty, 1839–1880.* Chapel Hill: University of North Carolina Press, 1994.

McLuhan, T. C. *Dream Tracks: The Railroad and the American Indian, 1890–1930.* New York Random House, 1987.

Meacham, A. B. *Wi-ne-ma (the Woman Chief) and Her People.* Chicago: American Publishing Co, 1875.

Medak-Saltzman, Danika. "Coming to You from the Indigenous Future: Native Women, Speculative Film Shorts, and the Art of the Possible." *Studies in American Indian Literatures* 29, no. 1 (Spring 2017): 139–171.

Medak-Saltzman, Danika. "Transnational Indigenous Exchange: Rethinking Global Interactions of Indigenous Peoples at the 1904 St. Louis Exposition." *American Quarterly* 62, no. 3 (September 2010): 591–615.

Medicine Crow, Joseph. *From the Heart of Crow Country: The Crow Indians' Own Stories.* Lincoln: University of Nebraska Press, 1992.

Medicine Crow, Joseph, and Herman Viola. *Counting Coup: Becoming a Crow Chief on the Reservation and Beyond.* Washington, DC: National Geographic Children's Books, 2006.

Meeks, Eric. *Border Citizens: The Making of Indians, Mexicans, and Anglos in Arizona.* Austin: University of Texas Press, 2007.

Meriam, Lewis, et al. *The Problem of Indian Administration Report of a Survey Made at the Request of the Honorable Hubert Work, Secretary of the Interior, and submitted to him February 21, 1928.* Baltimore, MD: Johns Hopkins University Press, 1928.

Meserve, John B. "Chief Coleman Cole." *Chronicles of Oklahoma* 14, no. 1 (March 1936): 15–16.

Miner, H. Craig. *The Corporation and the Indian: Tribal Sovereignty and Industrial Civilization in Indian Territory, 1865–1907.* Columbia: University of Missouri Press, 1976.

Miner, H. Craig. *The St. Louis–San Francisco Transcontinental Railroad.* Lawrence: University Press of Kansas, 1972.

Minor, Nancy M. *The Light Grey People: An Ethno-History of the Lipan Apaches of Texas and Northern Mexico.* Lanham, MD: University Press of America, 2009.

Mitchell, Audra, and Aadita Chaudbury. "Worlding Beyond 'the End the World': White Apocalyptic Visions and BIPOC Futurisms." *International Relations* 34, no. 3 (2020): 32.

Möllhausen, Balduin. *Diary of a Journey from the Mississippi to the Coasts of the Pacific....* London: Longman, Brown, Green, Longmans, and Roberts, 1858.

Momaday, N. Scott. *The Way to Rainy Mountain.* Albuquerque: University of New Mexico Press, 1969.

Mooney, James. *The Ghost Dance Religion and the Sioux Outbreak of 1890.* Lincoln: University of Nebraska Press, 1991.

Moreton-Robinson, Aileen. *The White Possessive: Property, Power, and Indigenous Sovereignty*. Minneapolis: University of Minnesota Press, 2015.

Morgan, George Robert. "Man, Plant, and Religion: Peyote Trade on the Mustang Plains of Texas." PhD diss., University of Colorado at Boulder, 1976.

Morrison, James D. "The Union Pacific Southern branch." *Chronicles of Oklahoma* 14, no. 1 (March 1936): 181. Oklahoma Historical Society.

Morrison, Michael A. *Slavery and the American West: The Eclipse of Manifest Destiny*. Chapel Hill: University of North Carolina, 1997.

Nabokov, Peter. *Where the Lightning Strikes: The Lives of American Indian Sacred Places*. New York: Penguin, 2010.

Newmark, Julianne. "A Prescription for Freedom: Carlos Montezuma, *Wassaja*, and the Society of American Indians." *American Indian Quarterly* 37, no. 3 (Summer 2013): 139–158.

Nichols, Robert. *Theft Is Property: Dispossession and Critical Theory*. Durham, NC: Duke University Press, 2020.

O'Brien, Jean M. *Firsting and Lasting: Writing Indians Out of Existence in New England*. Minneapolis: University of Minnesota Press, 2010.

Oklahoma Historical Society. "American Indians." *The Encyclopedia of Oklahoma History*. https://www.okhistory.org/publications/encyclopediaonline

O'Neill, Colleen. *Working the Navajo Way: Labor and Culture in the Twentieth Century*. Lawrence: University Press of Kansas, 2005.

Orsi, Richard J. *Sunset Limited: The Southern Pacific Railroad and the Development of the American West, 1850–1930*. Berkeley: University of California Press, 2005.

Ostler, Jeffrey. "'The Last Buffalo Hunt' and Beyond: Plains Sioux Economic Strategies in the Early Reservation Period." *Great Plains Quarterly* 21, no. 2 (Spring 2001): 199.

Painter, Neil Irvin. *Exodusters: Black Migration to Kansas after the Civil War*. New York: W. W. Norton, 1992.

Parker, Arthur C. *The Indian How Book*. Garden City, NY: Dover Publications, reproduced 1975.

Parker, Arthur C. *Iroquois Uses of Maize and Other Food Plants*. Albany: University of the State of New York, 1910.

Parker, Arthur C. *Seneca Myths and Folk Tales*. Lincoln: University of Nebraska Press, reproduced 1989.

Parker, Arthur C. *Skunny Wundy: Seneca Indian Tales*. Syracuse, NY: Syracuse University Press, reproduced 1925.

Parnaby, Andrew. *Citizen Docker: Making a New Deal on the Vancouver Waterfront, 1919–1939*. Toronto: University of Toronto Press, 2008.

Parry, Henry C. Letters from the Frontier: 1867. *The General Magazine and Historical Chronicle* LX, no. II (April 1858): 1–15. Philadelphia: University of Pennsylvania.

Parsons, David. "The Removal of the Osages from Kansas." PhD diss., University of Oklahoma, 1940.

Paulin, Charles O. *Atlas of the Historical Geography of the United States*. Digitized at the Digitial Scholarship Lab, University of Richmond. https://dsl.richmond.edu/historicalatlas/.

Pearce, Margaret Wickens, and Renee Pualani Louis. "Mapping Indigenous Depth of Place." *American Indian Research and Culture Journal* 32, no. 3 (2008): 107–126.

Pearson, J. Diane. "Developing Reservation Economies: Native American Teamsters, 1857–1921." *Journal of Small Business and Entrepreneurship* 18, no. 2 (2005) 153–170.

Pego, Christina M., Robert F. Hill, Glenn W. Solomon, Robert M. Chisholm, and Suzanne F. Ivey. "Tobacco, Culture, and Health Among American Indians: A Historical Review." *American Indian Culture and Research Journal* 19, no. 2 (January 1995): 143–164.

Peters, Kurt M. "Continuing Identity: Laguna Pueblo Railroaders in Richmond, California." *American Indian Culture and Research Journal* 22, no. 4 (1998): 187–198.

Peyer, Bernd C. *American Indian Nonfiction: An Anthology of Writings, 1760s–1930s.* Norman: University of Oklahoma, 2007.

Philips, Katrina. *Stating Indigeneity: Salvage Tourism and National Identity, 1880–1940.* Chapel Hill: University of North Carolina Press, 2021.

Pierce, Roy Harvey. *Savagism and Civilization: The Study of the Indians and the American Mind.* Baltimore, MD: Johns Hopkins University Press, 1953.

Pisani, Donald. *Water, Land, and Law in the West: The Limits of Public Policy, 1850–1920.* Lawrence: University of Kansas Press, 1996.

Pisani, Donald. *To Reclaim a Divided West: Water, Law, and Public Policy, 1848–1902.* Albuquerque: University of New Mexico Press, 1992.

Prucha, Frances P. *American Indian Treaties: The History of a Political Anomaly.* Los Angeles: University of California Press, 1997.

Prucha, Frances P. *The Great Father.* Lincoln: University of Nebraska Press, 1986.

Pyne, Steven J. *Fire: A Brief History.* Seattle: University of Washington Press, 2001.

Quastler, I. E. "Charting a Course: Lawrence, Kansas, and Its Railroad Strategy." *Kansas History* 18, no. 1 (Spring 1995): 27–28.

Radin, Paul. *The Winnebago Tribe.* Lincoln: University of Nebraska Press, 1970.

Raibmon, Paige. *Authentic Indians: Episodes of Encounter from the Late-Nineteenth-Century Northwest Coast.* Durham, NC: Duke University Press, 2005.

Raibmon, Paige. "Theatres of Contact: The Kwakwa̱ka̱'wakw Meet Colonialism in British Columbia and at the Chicago's World Fair." *The Canadian Historical Review* 81, no. 2 (2000): 157–190.

Red Star, Wendy, and Shannon Vittoria, "Apsáalooke Bacheeítuuk in Washington DC: A Case Study in Re-Reading Nineteenth-Century Delegation Photography." *Panorama: Journal of the Association of Historians of American Art* 6, no. 2 (Fall 2020): 10.

Reed, Julie L. *Serving the Nation: Cherokee Sovereignty and Social Welfare, 1800–1907.* Norman: University of Oklahoma Press, 2016.

Report of the Executive Council on the Proceedings of the First Annual Conference of the Society of American Indians. Washington, DC, 1912.

Rhodes, Lynn, and Kenneth E. Vose Mayer. *Makin' Tracks: The Story of the Transcontinental Railroads in the Pictures and Words of the Men Who Were There.* Santa Barbara, CA: Praeger, 1975.

"A Rich Redskin, and Indian Who Is Building a Railroad Out West." *The Londonderry (Vt.) Sifter* 55, no. 3 (September 1887).

Richards, Kent D. *Isaac I. Stevens: A Young Man in a Hurry.* Provo, UT: Brigham Young University Press, 1979.

Richter, Amy G. *Home on the Rails: Women, the Railroad, and the Rise of Public Domesticity.* Gender & American Culture. Chapel Hill: University of North Carolina Press, 2005.

Roberts, Darwin P. "The Legal History of Federally Granted Railroad Rights-of-Way and the Myth of Congress's '1871 Shift.'" *Colorado Law Review* 82 (2011): 131–134.

Robinson, Charles M. *Satanta: The Life and Death of a War Chief.* Kerryville, TX: State House Press, 1997.

Robinson, Sherry. *I Fought a Good Fight: A History of the Lipan Apaches.* Denton: University of North Texas Press, 2013.

Rothman, Hal. *Devil's Bargains: Tourism in the Twentieth-Century American West.* Lawrence: University Press of Kansas, 2000.

Runte, Alfred. *Allies of the Earth: Railroads and the Soul of Preservation.* Kirksville, MI: Truman State University Press, 2006.

Rzeczkowski, Frank R. *Uniting the Tribes: The Rise and Fall of Pan-Indian Community on the Crow Reservation.* Lawrence: University Press of Kansas, 2012.

Samek, Hana. *The Blackfoot Confederacy, 1880–1920: A Comparative Study of Canadian and U.S. Indian Policy.* Albuquerque: University of New Mexico Press, 2011.

Scharff, Virginia, ed. *Empire and Liberty: The Civil War and the West.* Oakland: University of California Press, 2015.

Schivelbusch, Wolfgang. *The Railway Journey: The Industrialization and Perception of Time and Space.* Berkeley, CA: University of California Press, 1987.

Schulten, Susan. *Mapping the Nation: History and Cartography in Nineteenth-Century America.* Chicago: University of Chicago Press, 2012.

Schwantes, Carlos A., and James P. Ronda. *The West the Railroads Made.* Seattle: University of Washington Press, 2008.

Schwantes, Carlos D., ed. *Encounters with a Distant Land: Exploration and the Great Northwest* Moscow: University of Idaho Press, 1994.

Seymour, Silas. *A Reminiscence of the Union Pacific Railroad, Containing Some Account of the Discovery of the Eastern Base of the Rocky Mountains, and of the Great Indian Battle of July 11, 1867.* Quebec: A. Coté, 1873. Denver Public Library. Western History Collection. Denver.

Seymour, Silas. *Incidents of a Trip Through the Great Platte Valley, to the Rocky Mountains and Laramie Plains, in the Fall of 1866, with a Synoptical Statement of the Various Pacific Railroads, and an Account of the Union Pacific Railroad Excursion to the One Hundredth Meridian of Longitude.* New York: D. Van Nostrand, 1867.

Shaffer, Marguerite, and Marguerite S. Shaffer. *See America First: Tourism and National Identity, 1880–1940.* Washington, DC: Smithsonian Books, 2001.

Shepard, Jeffrey P. *We Are an Indian Nation: A History of the Hualapai People.* Tucson: University of Arizona Press, 2010.

Slotkin, James S. *The Peyote Religion: A Study in Indian White Relations.* Glencoe, IL: Free Press, 1956.

Slotkin, Richard. *Regeneration Through Violence: The Mythology of the American Frontier 1600–1860.* Norman: University of Oklahoma Press, 2000.

Sommer, Charles H. *Quanah Parker: Last Chief of the Comanches, a Brief Sketch.* St. Louis, MO: Buxton & Skinner, 1945.

Spence, Mark David. *Dispossessing the Wilderness: Indian Removal and the Making of the National Parks.* New York: Oxford University Press, 1999.

Standing Bear, Luther. *My People the Sioux.* 1928. New York: Bison Books, 2006.

Stands in Timber, John. *A Cheyenne Voice: The Complete John Stands in Timber Interviews.* The Civilization and the American Indian Series. Norman: University of Oklahoma Press, 2013.

Stanley, Henry Morton. *My Early Travels and Adventures in America and Asia.* New York: Charles Scribner's Sons, 1895.

Stegman, Eric, and Victoria Phillips. "Missing the Point: The Real Impact of Native Mascots and Team Names on American Indian and Alaska Native Youth." Center for American Progress. Uploaded July 2014. https://digitalcommons.wcl.american.edu/cgi/viewcontent.cgi?article=1003&context=fasch_rpt

Stegner, Wallace. *Beyond the Hundreth Meridian: John Wesley Powell and the Second Opening of the West.* New York: Penguin, repr. 1992.

Stevens, Hazard. *The Life of Isaac Ingalls Stevens*, 2 vols. Boston: Houghton and Mifflin, 1990.

Stewart, Omer C. *Forgotten Fires: Native Americans and the Transient Wilderness.* Norman: University of Oklahoma Press, 2002.

Stewart, Omer C. *Peyote Religion: A History.* Norman: University of Oklahoma Press, 1987.

St. John, Rachel. "Contingent Continent: Spatial and Geographic Arguments in the Shaping of the Nineteenth-Century United States." *Pacific Historical Review* 86, no. 1 (February 2017): 18–49.

Stockwell, Mary. *The Other Trail of Tears: The Removal of the Ohio Indians.* Yardley, PA: Westholme Press, 2016.

Stromquist, Shelton. *The Pattern of Railroad Labor Conflict in Nineteenth-Century America.* Chicago: University of Illinois Press, 1987.

Tharp, Julie. "'Fire Ponies': Cars in American Indian Film and Literature." *American Indian Culture and Research Journal* 24, no. 3 (2000): 77–91.

Thrush, Coll. *Indigenous London: Native Travelers at the Heart of Empire.* New Haven, CT: Yale University Press, 2011.

Thrush, Coll. *Native Seattle: Histories from the Crossing-Over Place.* Seattle: University of Washington Press, 2008.

Trachtenberg, Alan. *The Incorporation of America: Culture and Society in the Gilded Age.* New York: Hill and Wang, 2007.

Trafzer, Clifford E. *A Chemehuevi Song: The Resilience of a Southern Paiute Tribe.* Seattle: University of Washington Press, 2015.

Trask, David S. "Episcopal Missionaries on the Santee and Yankton Reservations: Cross Cultural Collaboration and President Grant's Peace Policy." *Great Plains Quarterly* 33, no. 2 (Spring 2013): 87–101.

Trennert, Robert A. "From Carlisle to Phoenix: The Rise and Fall of the Indian Outing System, 1878–1930." *Pacific Historical Review* 52, no. 3 (January 1983): 267–291.

Truman, Benjamin. *History of the World's Fair; Being a Complete Description of the World's Columbian Exposition from Its Inception.* Chicago: Mammoth Publishing Company, 1893.

Turnbull, David. "Maps, Narratives, and Trails: Performativity, Hodology, and Distributed Knowledges in Complex Adaptive Systems—An Approach to Emergent Mapping." *Geographical Research* 5, no. 2 (June 2007): 140–149.

Turner, Katherine. *Red Men Calling on the White Father.* Norman: University of Oklahoma, 1951.

Udall, Louise. *Me and Mine: The Life Story of Helen Sekaquaptewa.* Tucson: University of Arizona Press, 1969.

Utley, Robert, and Wilcomb E. Washburn. *Indian Wars.* New York: Mariner Books, 2002.

Van de Logt, Mark. *War Party in Blue: Pawnee Scouts in the U.S. Army.* Norman: University of Oklahoma Press, 2010.

Vetter, Jeremy. *Field Life: Science in the American West During the Railroad Era.* Pittsburgh, PA: University of Pittsburgh Press, 2016.

Viola, Herman. *Diplomats in Buckskin: A History of Indian Delegations in Washington City.* Washington, DC: Smithsonian Institution Press, 1981.

Vimalassery, Manu. "Skew Tracks: Racial Capitalism and the First Transcontinental Railroad." PhD diss., New York University, 2011.

Walker, David. *Railroading Religion: Mormons, Tourists, and the Corporate Spirit of the West.* Chapel Hill: University of North Carolina Press, 2019.

Wall, Leon, and William Morgan. *Navajo-English Dictionary.* Lawrence, KS: Haskell Indian Junior College, 1958.

Warhus, Mark. *Another America: Native American Maps and the History of Our Land.* New York: St. Martin's Press, 1997.

Warren, Louis S. *Buffalo Bill's America: William Cody and the Wild West Show.* New York: Knopf, 2005.

Warren, Louis S. *God's Red Son: The Ghost Dance Religion and the Making of Modern America.* New York: Basic Books, 2017.

Webb, Walter Prescott. *The Great Plains.* Lincoln: University of Nebraska Press, 1981.

Welke, Barbara Young. *Recasting American Liberty: Gender, Race, Law, and the Railroad Revolution, 1865–1920.* New York: Cambridge University Press, 2001.

West, Elliott. *The Contested Plains: Indians, Goldseekers, and the Rush to Colorado.* Lawrence: University Press of Kansas, 1998.

Whalen, Kevin. "Labored Learning: the Outing System at Sherman Institute, 1902–1930." *American Indian Culture and Research Journal* 36, no. 1 (January 2012): 151–176.

Wheat, Carl I. *Mapping the Trans-Mississippi West, 1540–1861.* San Francisco: Institute of Historical Cartography, 1957–1963.

White, Richard. *Railroaded: The Transcontinentals and the Making of Modern America.* New York City: W. W. Norton, 2012.

Whyte, Kyle. "Indigenous Science (Fiction) in the Anthropocene." *Environment and Planning E: Nature and Space* 1 (2018): 224–242.

Wiebe, Robert H. *The Search for Order, 1877–1920.* New York: Hill and Wang, 1966.

Wilkins, David E. *American Indian Sovereignty and the U.S. Supreme Court: The Masking of Justice.* Austin: University of Texas Press, 1997.

Wilkins, David, and K. Tsianina Lomawaima. *Uneven Ground: American Indian Sovereignty and Federal Law.* Norman: University of Oklahoma Press, 2001.

Wischman, Lesley. *Frontier Diplomats: Alexander Culbertson and Nayotist-Siksina Among the Blackfeet.* Norman: University of Oklahoma Press, 2004.

Wolf Woman, Mountain, and Nancy Oestreich Lurie, eds. *Mountain Wolf Woman: Sister of Crashing Thunder: The Autobiography of a Winnebago Indian.* Ann Arbor: University of Michigan Press, 1961.

Wolfe, Patrick. "Settler Colonialism and the Elimination of the Native." *Journal of Genocide Research* 8. no. 4 (2009): 387–409.

Worcester, David. *Rivers of Empire: Water, Aridity, and the Growth of the American West.* New York: Oxford University Press, 1992.

Wrobel, David. *Promised Lands: Promotion, Memory, and the Creation of the American West.* Lawrence: University Press of Kansas, 2002.

Young, Gloria A. "Powwow Power: Perspectives on Historic and Contemporary Intertribalism." PhD diss., Indiana University, 1981.

Youngdahl, Jay. *Working on the Railroad, Walking in Beauty: Navajos, Hózhý, and Track Work.* Logan: Utah State University Press, 2011.

Youst, Lionel, and William R. Seaburg. *Coquelle Thompson, Athabaskan Witness: A Cultural Biography.* Norman: University of Oklahoma Press, 2002.

Zitkala-Sa. *American Indian Stories.* Washington, DC: Hayworth Publishing House, 1921.

Zitkala-Sa. *Dreams and Thunder: Stories, Poems, and The Sun Dance Opera.* Ed. Jane Hafen. New York: Bison Books, 2005.

Index